PRAISE FOR WANDERLUST

"You've heard of going around the world in 80 days? You can do that in less time with Karen Gershowitz's new book, *Wanderlust*. From Marrakesh to Malaysia to Montana, Gershowitz mines her memories, notebooks, and photos to take you places you'll want to visit and introduce you to food you may or may not want to eat. Oh, and she'll explain why accepting a cup of tea from an Istanbul carpet salesman isn't always a good idea."

—Rudy Maxa, travel journalist & broadcaster

"For someone who's been stubbornly holding out for teleportation before undertaking any extensive travel (that would be me), *Wanderlust* is a Godsend. Karen Gershowitz offers what amounts to a virtual reality tour, including the smells, tastes, and personalities she's experienced on her many trips to the plethora of countries and cities she's visited over the years. Great book for the armchair traveler and by the time you're finished reading, I wouldn't be surprised if your first call (maybe even mine) isn't to your travel agent."

—Charles Salzberg, award-winning author of the Henry Swann series and *Second Story Man*

"With an eye for the unique and a penchant for trying everything, Gershowitz is the best kind of traveler. A master of sharing the essence of place, she makes us laugh, nod our heads, want to try new things. She inspires us to travel and learn about the world."

—Jessie Voigts, PhD, publisher at Wandering Educators

"Karen's globetrotting tale celebrates a truly inspiring lifetime worth of journey. Her voyage demonstrates that adventure and transformation begin with you – and how you can make it happen for yourself. An exhilarating story that is a must-read."

—Shebs Alom, travel professional, founder of Shebs The Wanderer & member of the British Guild of Travel Writers

"In *Wanderlust*, Karen Gershowitz once again transports us across the globe, and this time her whirlwind digest includes, well, digestion! From sipping lulada in Colombia to nibbling ugali in Tanzania, her tongue remains intrepid, her curiosity unquenchable, her storytelling delectable. "All artists are driven by a need to try something new, push the medium a bit further," she writes, and these pages prove that with a cherry on top. All puns aside, Gershowitz reminds us that travel's truest feast comes from the connections we make across the tablecloth, across perceived borders of state, and taste, and fear. This is a guidebook to breaking bread."

—Marc Nieson, author of *Schoolhouse: Lessons on Love & Landscape*

"As a fellow Travel Addict, I love to read stories about adventure travel, and *Wanderlust* didn't disappoint. Karen ventures to places where most humans would never consider. Just read about her camping escapades in Tanzania to admire her bravery, tolerance and quest to push the envelope of a quirky travel experience, including the consumption of scary looking food. *Wanderlust* is full of surprises and unforgettable experiences. Furthermore, Karen now has something that many of us do not: memories of a lifetime from her travels. Get the book everyone, and you never know, you might be adding some trips to your 'Bucket List.' Great stuff."

—Malcolm Teasdale, host of The Travel Addict Podcast

"Karen Gershowitz's second travel book, *Wanderlust,* is a tasting menu of travel. Vignettes from her decades of travel to dozens of countries are tempting morsels and a pleasurable read."

—Margo Weinstein, author of *Jalan-Jalan: A Journey of Wanderlust and Motherhood*

PRAISE FOR TRAVEL MANIA

"The book reflects the author's love of globe-trotting adventure and describes how she built her whole life around it by getting a job in which she effectively got paid to travel. Her recollections take readers to many places around the world, from Southeast Asia to the Galápagos Islands to the American West, as she trekked for business and pleasure. These stories are also, in some ways, about the passage of time, reflecting on how travel has changed, for better and worse, over the decades."

—*Kirkus Reviews*

"*Travel Mania* is a godsend. It's the perfect way to imagine I'm a seasoned traveler, without having to leave the comfort of my living room couch. Gershowitz who responds to the suggestion 'let's go' by packing her bags, hasn't quite turned me into a travel junkie, but she has hooked me on reading about a woman who just can't sit still."

—Charles Salzberg, two-time Shamus Award nominee and author of *Second Story Man*

"Prepare to be swept around the world in the capable and enthusiastic company of KG. You will climb Mt. Kilimanjaro, 'poli-poli', eat the famous-for-its-revolting-smell durian in Malaysia, trek through a scirocco in the Sahara, watch bribes being passed on Moscow sidewalks, ride a felucca on the Nile, and spend New Year's Eve in Saigon. Wherever she goes, Karen is an astute observer and willing experimenter. You are in for a treat."

—Christine Lehner, author of *What to Wear to See the Pope* and *Absent a Miracle*

"Alone or in the company of others, Gershowitz navigates the world with an open heart and a sense of adventure. This collection covers impressive ground, and whether she's rocking out with Moroccans to the Blind Boys of Alabama, struggling up the slopes of Kilimanjaro, or doing business in Asia, her sharp eye brings the wonders of the world in focus."

—Marilyn Johnson, author of *Lives in Ruins* and *This Book Is Overdue!*

"No 'guided' tour here. The only fitting description is: page-turner. Karen gives us wondrous—whether white-knuckled or resplendent—nuggets. Her own growth as a global citizen winds through the decades and essays and leaves me wishing I might have trailed along at least a few times. I'm already looking forward to dipping in repeatedly, and without booking a single flight."

—Carolyn Lieberg, author of *West with Hopeless*
and *Calling the Midwest Home*

"Karen Gershowitz suffers from the only traveler's disease that's fun to have and be around: the compulsion toward travel itself. This book is full of terrific stories, revealing with richness and particularity not just places and people, but the traveler herself—complicated and often conflicted, comforted by certain traveling companions and people met on the road, driven to distraction by others, but never daunted, never able to resist the pull of another journey. This book was a delight to me during these times of shutdown and is an inspiration for the times to come."

—Lon Otto, author of *A Nest of Hooks*, *Cover Me*, and *A Man in Trouble*

"A witty, insightful romp through a lifetime of travel that reads like a sit-down with a friend. You'll want to curl up and greedily gulp down *Travel Mania* in a single sitting—then read it again and feel like you are catching up with a dear old friend. If you like your wisdom laced with humor, look no further than this collection of tales from a traveler who has visited over ninety countries."

—Amanda Burgess, editor of *JourneyWoman Magazine*

"As a travel-industry professional, I've watched the world shrink as access has grown. Gershowitz's lovely travel memoir is a look back at a time when faraway places really were far away, distant cultures were very different, single women travelling alone were an unusual sight, and travelers with open hearts had extraordinary experiences. *Travel Mania* made me appreciate current travel opportunities even more."

—Sue Shapiro, former president of NY Skal, former president and
CEO of GIANTS consortium

"Buckle up! *Travel Mania* is pure adventure and passion, circling and crisscrossing our exotic globe, ever eager for the next horizon. From those pre safety-belt days in the back seat of a DeSoto to the uncertain risks of traveling during our present-day pandemic, each leg of Karen Gershowitz' life-long voyage is fueled with insights and intimacy, humor and poignancy. This is no mere itinerary or travelogue, but an inside passage."

—Marc Nieson, author of *Schoolhouse: Lessons on Love & Landscape*

"The author's depictions of exotic, international locations and experiences are spot-on! Reading *Travel Mania* really made me feel like I was right back in these destinations that I too have visited. It's a very fun read with a great message. Anyone reading will certainly get in touch with their adventurous side and be inspired to see the world for themselves!"

—Dr. Evan Antin, author of *World Wild Vet* and
host of Animal Planet's "Evan Goes Wild"

"Karen Gershowitz is to be applauded for her sheer verve, which is on delightful display in this rollicking travelogue: *Travel Mania*. From the beginning one senses that Gershowitz is experiencing a kind of undeniable, enthralling need—the near-manic need to go somewhere else then somewhere else again. We—as safer, armchair travelers—get the unexpected benefits of that addiction, learning so much more than if we had just stayed home."

—Tim Bascom, author of *Chameleon Days* and *Running to the Fire*

"I loved the vignettes of Gershowitz's life in far-flung places: Cairo, Singapore, a rodeo in Wyoming, climbing Kilimanjaro, on an elephant in Thailand. I was there with her, as she struggled with misadventures, found unexpected friends, or tested herself in places so utterly foreign that she needed to find something new within her to survive and thrive. That's what I valued most of all about this book: Gershowitz is a wonderful companion and excellent storyteller. *Travel Mania* will help you appreciate how traveling the world is one of the best ways to find out who you really are."

—Sergio Troncoso, author of *A Peculiar Kind of Immigrant's Son*

WANDERLUST

WANDERLUST

EXTRAORDINARY PEOPLE, QUIRKY PLACES, AND CURIOUS CUISINE

KAREN GERSHOWITZ

SHE WRITES PRESS

Published 2023
Printed in the United States of America
Print ISBN: 978-1-64742-557-9
E-ISBN: 978-1-64742-558-6
Library of Congress Control Number: 2023906797

For information, address:
She Writes Press
1569 Solano Ave #546
Berkeley, CA 94707

Interior design by Stacey Aaronson

She Writes Press is a division of SparkPoint Studio, LLC.

*To my many travel companions and the wonderful people
I've met in far-off corners of the globe*

"Traveling—it leaves you speechless,
then turns you into a storyteller."

—IBN BATTUTA

TABLE OF CONTENTS

FOREWORD

When my first book, *Travel Mania*, was released, I was writing my next book on an entirely different topic: entrepreneurship. Friends, members of my writing group, and readers all encouraged me to shelve the business book and again share stories of my myriad travels. I promised to consider it.

I thought about the number of people who told me *Travel Mania* had inspired them to get out of their comfort zone and explore. Some traveled solo for the first time. Others journeyed to places they'd always been curious about but hadn't been brave enough to visit. One friend was motivated by this thought: "If Karen can do it, so can I."

Perhaps a second book would inspire more people to see the world. I began a list of the unusual destinations, exotic food, and interesting individuals I encountered during my travels. It included an excursion to a remote Australian opal mining area, a trek through a jungle in Borneo, and an unexpected opportunity to see the world's largest potato chip in Blackfoot, Idaho.

Memories of meals I'd eaten, wonderful and horrible, bubbled up. I could almost taste the boozy fondue I ate in Zurich fifty years ago. After three pages of story ideas, it was clear I had more than enough material for another travel book.

My memory, aided by detailed journals and thousands of photos, holds a seemingly endless supply of travel experiences that have been intriguing, illuminating, and just plain fun. The exposure to new people, places, and food changed my understanding of the world and expanded my appreciation for both the similarities and differences between cultures. And it made for fantastic stories.

This book begins and ends in New York City. I was born in Manhattan, and New York has been my home off and on for most of my life.

My mother inspired curiosity about the world by exposing me to it while never leaving the city. We visited museums, ate at ethnic restaurants, and saw international performances. I often joke that I was one of the few American kids in the 1950s who loved sushi. Back then, eating raw fish was considered instant death—or, at a minimum, the source of severe stomach problems. My mother, unconcerned, insisted that if the Japanese safely ate it, so could we. Those early, positive introductions to cultures and cuisines far different from my own became central to my life. I was determined to see as much of the world as possible.

I retired in December 2019. My plan was to publish *Travel Mania* and resume traveling as much as possible. Then came Covid. Grounded in New York City, I explored the hidden corners of the city and surrounding areas. My goal was to see familiar places as if I were a tourist, with fresh eyes and an open mind.

Given the multiplicity of cultures and the vast number of creative people who reside here—alongside the natural and man-made beauty of the city—I was happily occupied for many months. I even developed a new passion, street art.

Once the world began to open up, and the threat of Covid had lessened, I started traveling where I'd left off. Things were different; I wore masks, always had hand sanitizer at the ready, and stayed away from crowds. Despite those inconveniences and the looming specter of Covid, the joy at being able to board a plane and fly to an unfamiliar place was undiminished.

My first overseas trip was to France, a country I've traveled in many times. But as with my explorations of New York, I experienced the country with a new perspective.

Since completing the writing of this book, I have returned to traveling often, filling my insatiable need for new experiences. As always, I'm creating and stockpiling the stories about my experiences.

My life, from my teens until now, has revolved around travel. It is my greatest passion, an itch that cannot be quelled. I'm now thinking about a third travel book. The entrepreneurship book will have to wait a bit longer.

TRAVELING THE WORLD WITHOUT LEAVING HOME: NEW YORK CITY, 1950s AND 1960s

My mother in 1958.

In 1961, I may have been one of the few ten-year-olds in New York City who was proficient with chopsticks and mad for tempura. Other kids loved burgers and fries, macaroni and cheese, and spaghetti with meatballs, but I craved tacos, gnocchi, samosas, and blini. I'd even tried, and almost liked, escargot and kimchi. My mother led the way on our culinary adventures; I was an eager companion.

Mom had always wanted to travel the world. When she was in her twenties, she dreamed of sailing across the Atlantic and exploring or even living overseas for a year or two. But the late 1930s weren't a time for a young woman to be frolicking in Europe, even an adventurous one and especially a Jew. Instead, she studied architecture at Cooper Union at a time when that was a profession all but closed to women. When she reached her twenty-fifth birthday and was still single, her parents feared she would become an old maid. So, she gave up her dreams, at least temporarily, caved into the familial mandate, and married.

After the war, she had babies to care for, and money was tight. Adventures would have to wait a little longer. Then, before I was born in 1951, she was diagnosed with type 1 diabetes. Her health became a further obstacle to travel. But none of that squelched her sense of adventure or desire to experience the world. If she couldn't go across the sea, at least New York was a large and diverse city. She'd poke around and see what she could find close to home.

After two boys, I was the daughter she'd always wanted. A girl, she thought, could be taught to like all the things she liked. She had, of course, tried to persuade my dad and brothers to explore with her, but that didn't work out very well. Meat and potatoes and the opera were what my father wanted. Mickey had been the brainy child, intense and focused. He was a whiz at baseball stats and fanatically followed the New York teams. If Mickey was given a choice between listening to a Brooklyn Dodgers game or seeing a Broadway show, theater didn't stand a chance. Roy was a picky eater. Our dad once offered to pay him a dollar to try a peach; Roy refused because he couldn't stand the fuzzy skin. There was no way he'd get excited about any food he hadn't eaten a hundred times before. I was her last chance.

Mom and I started to sample the cultural diversity of the city when I was so young that I can't remember a time when it wasn't an established routine. Once or twice each month, we'd dress up and take the subway from the far northern end of Manhattan down to Central Park, Times Square, Little Italy, or even Brooklyn.

Often our first stop was a museum. New York City is home to some of the finest art, history, and cultural museums in the world. We visited them all, but our favorite was the American Museum of Natural History. Other kids my age would go right for the dinosaurs. Not me. I always grabbed Mom's hand and headed for the African masks. The masks stirred strong feelings in me. I may have first loved them because my birthday is near Halloween, and I associated costumes with getting lots of gifts. But it quickly went beyond that. I would stare at the carved and painted ceremonial masks and know there was magic in them.

Mom would ask me to imagine the people who wore the masks. When I'd say something like, "They must have been really scary!" she'd challenge me to dig deeper.

"They probably were a little frightening. When do you think they wore the masks?"

"On holidays," I'd confidently reply, thinking of Halloween.

"Maybe, but maybe they also used them at ceremonies. They probably sang and danced, and everyone liked to watch them, like we do at the theater."

She often helped me see the parallels between the truly exotic and my own life. This brought the world at large closer. She also instilled deep within me a desire to see the places where these wonderful objects had come from. If the masks were great to see hanging on the wall, it would be even more fun to see them in action.

After getting my fill of Africa, I'd drag Mom to see the totem poles and masks in the hall of the Northwest Coast Indians or the dioramas of the Pacific Peoples. We'd be ready for a break after a couple of hours of walking around the exhibits. The cafeteria at the museum was an absolute last resort. We ate there only if it was drenching rain or freezing cold; Mom wanted lunch somewhere more in the spirit of what we'd just seen.

With its huge immigrant population, Manhattan was home to cuisines from around the world. Mom wanted to taste it all and, with only a little encouragement, so did I. We'd seek out inexpensive hole-in-the-wall eateries that served foods with names and flavors that were new to us. Compared to now, when there's a sushi place or two on many blocks in Manhattan and Thai is considered mundane, back then, our choices were limited. But we managed to find taquerias for spicy empanadas and cooling guacamole. We ate even spicier Indian food, learning to alternate bites of chili-laden curries with naan bread or creamy yogurt raita. Italian, French, and Greek foods became commonplace to us. By the time my age was in the double digits, I knew the difference between southern and northern Italian entrées.

On West 55th Street, across from the City Center theater, there was a Japanese restaurant that became one of our favorites. We loved going there for sukiyaki, teriyaki, and yakisoba noodles. Sushi may not have made it to New York yet, at least not to the places we frequented, but tempura had arrived, and I loved it.

Going to City Center was one of our favorite excursions, both because of the Japanese restaurant and the performances. In the '50s and '60s it was home to the New York City Ballet, hosted revivals of Broadway hits like *South Pacific*, and offered a variety of other performances. I loved the interior, which looked like it had been magically transported from tales of the *Arabian Nights*. I remember it as having bright, elaborately painted tiles decorating the lobby, dark red velvet seats, marble pillars, all manner of filigree carved into the walls, and, best of all, an enormous chandelier that glittered spectacularly in the domed ceiling. At some point, my mom told me it had been built as a meeting place for the Shriners. I had no idea who the Shriners were, but it made the theater seem especially mysterious. The theater was huge, with many tiers of seating. We usually climbed flight after flight to the topmost section, jokingly referred to as the nosebleed seats.

I would run ahead, impatient to get my first glimpse of the curtain and chandelier and the audience filing in. Mom would stop at each landing to catch her breath. When she finally caught up with me at the top, a white-gloved usher would look at our ticket stubs and lead us to our seats. I always held my breath until I saw our location. At that time, broad columns supported the tiers. If we were unlucky, we'd be seated in a place where they partially blocked our view, but that only happened once or twice. If we had a clear sightline, I didn't care that we were far from the stage. Looking through binoculars, the performers seemed close enough.

I loved hearing the orchestra tune up and watching everyone in their finery. In those days any theater outing required suits for men and dresses for women—even in the cheap seats. The real excitement began when the lights dimmed and the theater grew quiet with anticipation. When the curtain rose, I would be mesmerized, no matter what the performance. Perfect snapshots remain in my memory: the Christmas tree in *The Nutcracker*; the dancing cowboys in *Oklahoma* wearing boots, hats, and bandanas; Martha Graham with raised leg striking a pose; Marcel Marceau, in white face, silently miming his way out of a box.

We saw a lot of Broadway musicals. To this day I can remember the lyrics to my childhood favorites—*My Fair Lady*, *Brigadoon*, *The Music Man*, and *Camelot*. We alternated those mainstream productions with global dance and music. Sol Hurok, always referred to as "the impresario," brought performers from around the world to New York. My mother favored dance, though sometimes we'd go to a concert. I loved seeing Cossack dancers leap and kick in their flowing, brilliantly colored outfits. The gorgeous ballerinas of the Bolshoi Ballet Company, in their stiff pink tutus, made me swoon. I'd go home to demonstrate pirouettes for my father, usually ending up in a tangled heap on the floor. Grace and balance have never been my strong suits.

Though my introduction to New York's diverse culture was usually led by my mom, there were a few New York City neighborhoods that my entire family liked. The Lower East Side, home to waves of Eastern European immigrants, offered shopping at bargain-basement prices, which my father loved, and the kind of food he had grown up on. We often went to Katz's delicatessen for knishes and pastrami sandwiches, accompanied by sour kosher pickles and washed down by bottles of Dr. Brown's Cel-Ray soda. This was in my family's traditions. Compared to the bland food most Americans ate at the time, it was like a journey to the Old World.

More exotic was Chinatown, where we also frequently went as a family. It was the one foreign cuisine we all enjoyed. While my father and brothers ordered wonton soup, chop suey, lo mein, and egg foo yung, my mom would grab the waiter, point to the next table where a Chinese family was seated.

"What is that?" she'd ask, pointing to a glistening plate of food.

"For Chinese people. You use menu."

"But what is it?" she'd persist. "It looks delicious."

The waiter would continue to insist she should order from the menu, but Mom would finally wear him down. Then, listening carefully, she'd try to understand what was being described, then place the order. (However, even she would balk at some fare, such as chicken feet or hundred-year-old eggs.) Often the food was fabulous, with sauces and combinations of ingredients we'd never even imagined. Sometimes she didn't correctly translate the waiter's English and there'd be a disaster. I remember a plate of slimy goop that everyone except my mother refused to even consider trying. A woman at the next table told us they were sea cucumbers, and said, "They're delicious," smacking her lips. My mom valiantly tried a forkful, smiled at the woman who'd explained what they were, but didn't eat more than one bite.

At the restaurant we usually went to, one kind waiter taught me how to eat with chopsticks. I couldn't have been more than six or seven. When I could use them reasonably well, he brought over the other waiters to watch; I guess I was something of a novelty. That made me feel especially proud, and I insisted on eating with chopsticks whenever we were in Chinatown. I even brought a pair home and demonstrated to my friends how well I could pick up morsels of food and pop them into my mouth, rarely dropping a thing. My friends were duly impressed.

In the early 1960s, a Hunanese restaurant opened (until then, all the restaurants were Cantonese), and we were among the first non-Chinese to try it. I immediately fell in love with the fiery hot foods.

Outside of food, Mom tried to stretch the cultural boundaries at home. I owned a complete set of "Fairy Tales from around the World." Together we read tales from India about how the tiger got its stripes. In another volume were stories of fearsome Chinese

dragons and brave princesses. We'd pore over the illustrations, marveling at the fantastical landscapes and buildings and the unusual
clothing people wore.

She asked everyone we knew who traveled overseas to bring me
back a doll in native costume. Now I'd consider the small plastic
dolls cheesy, but then I loved the little wooden clogs on the doll
from Holland and the shamrock print dress on the teensy Irish girl.
Never mind that no one wore those kinds of clothes in the modern
world—to me, they were accurate representations of the people I'd
meet when I finally got to travel across the ocean.

As a kid I thought my childhood was pretty normal. Yes, I did
go to theater shows, dance performances, and museums more than
my friends, but it didn't strike me as anything exceptional. Other
families went camping or to football games or bicycle riding, things
we never did. As an adult looking back, I am amazed by how much
of the world I'd experienced as a child, without ever leaving New
York City.

I also realize that though she never said it to me directly, my
mom was grooming me for the life she envisioned for herself.
Through me, she would travel vicariously, have exciting adventures,
and sample all the world had to offer. I was happy to take on that
role.

THE GREAT AMERICAN DISASTER:
LONDON, 1970-1972

I lived in London for three years and never liked British cooking—either at home or in restaurants. When I ate out, it was always ethnic food, Indian or Italian. It was clear I'd never eat the kinds of food I ate in New York, but I longed for variety, colorful and appetizing meals.

B reakfast at the Princes Square Hotel, my first lodgings in London, was the same every morning. There was a choice of corn flakes or greasy fried eggs, bacon rashers—undercooked by American standards—broiled tomatoes, beans, and toast accompanied by tea or the worst coffee ever. I ate a lifetime's worth of cornflakes. In my room, I had an immersion heater and boiled water for instant coffee. Bad as that was, it was an improvement over what passed for coffee in the hotel.

A year later, I moved into a house I shared with four British medical students. The first morning there, one of them asked, "I'm making eggs, want some?"

"That would be great, thanks."

We chatted as he poured a half inch of vegetable oil into a pan. While it heated, he placed slices of white bread into an ancient toaster. When the oil started to bubble, he dropped in two eggs and spooned the hot oil over them until they were drenched. This was a new cooking technique to me, and I watched in horror. The toaster popped out the slices; he cut each in half and put them onto a rack to cool. By that point, the eggs looked like plastic, the whites and yolks glistening in their oily coat. With a deft turn of the spatula, he transferred the eggs to a plate, rivulets of oil dripping from them. Greasy eggs and cold toast yet again. Corn flakes at the Princes Square Hotel started to look pretty good. I never let anyone in the house cook for me again.

Lunch was often at the Polytechnic Institute, where I was enrolled in a fine arts program. The first time in the canteen (cafeteria) confirmed the generally held belief among Americans that British food was bland and heavy on carbs. There were never raw fruits or vegetables. A typical meal was beans on toast accompanied by chips (French fries) or mashed potatoes. Bangers and mash were another favorite. Bangers were overcooked sausages, which came with a side of mashed peas, with no seasoning of any kind. Sandwiches were two slices of white bread covered with a smear of butter about the depth of a sheet of plastic wrap, with cucumber rounds or one thin slice of ham. On rare occasions, there were colorful foods, like carrots or broccoli, that were boiled until mushy. The only fruit I ever saw there were tinned pineapples or peaches drowning in sweet syrup. Mystery meat at my college in New York seemed pretty good compared to what they offered in the Polytechnic's canteen. Still, it was cheap and convenient.

Dinner varied. I was on a tight budget, so I couldn't afford to eat out often. For the year I lived in the hotel, there were no cooking facilities. Prepared foods from Sainsbury's or Tesco, the local super-markets, were edible if not tasty. But their selection of English cheese, crackers, and fruit was great. I tried every cheese they offered, buying the smallest quantity possible since I had nowhere to keep it cool. Stilton, cheddar, Cheshire, Wensleydale, and Cornish blue became favorites, quite a change from the Swiss and Muenster at home. My palette for cheese improved, even as it longed for a decent salad, sandwich, or home-cooked meal.

Chip shops, serving fish and chips wrapped in day-old newspaper, were a treat. The fish was fresh, the batter tasty, and the chips crispy. Friends taught me to liberally pour malt vinegar into the packet. To this day, I like a lot of malt vinegar when I eat fish and chips. But even in my youth, I wasn't overly fond of fried food. Or, to be more accurate, it wasn't fond of me. I took a dose of Pepto-Bismol prior to tucking in and didn't indulge very often.

A friend once took me to a Chinese takeaway that offered fish accompanied by a bowl of chips and rice drowning in sweet and sour sauce. I took one look at the "half and half" and insisted we go to a traditional "chippy."

Pizza and pasta places were everywhere. I never ate a decent meal at one of them. Then again, I was eating at the cheapest of the cheap restaurants. The strange thing was that there seemed to be authentic Italians working at restaurants that served totally inauthentic Italian foods. How did they manage not to snicker as they served pasta cooked so long it congealed? Or pizza with sauce so sweet it made my teeth ache? I thought that if I snuck into the staff room in the back, there would be luscious eggplant parmigiana or perfectly cooked spaghetti aglio e olio.

On one memorable long weekend, I took a cheap student flight to Rome. I'm sure I saw the Colosseum, Vatican, and Trevi Fountain, but what I remember most vividly and fondly were the mouthwatering scents wafting from pizza places. The temptation was so strong I bought a slice a couple of times each day. I licked gelato while walking through the streets. At dinner I savored al dente pasta with pesto, Bolognese, funghi (mushroom), and a slew of other sauces. With each bite I tried to memorize the taste so I could conjure it up when I returned to London.

Flying Alitalia from Rome to Frankfurt, the flight attendant set the tray with a red and white checkered place mat. Lunch included a fresh salad, antipasto, and well-prepared pasta, accompanied by a glass of wine. On the connecting flight from Frankfurt to London on BOAC, I was handed a white cardboard box containing a cold pork pie and a plastic knife and fork. As I sliced through the doughy crust, there was a thick layer of what appeared to be lard. I closed the box. Then closed my eyes and tried to imagine myself back in Rome.

Indian was the one uniformly tasty cuisine in every corner of London. The range of Indian dining establishments went from hole-in-the-wall eateries offering curries and kabobs to elegant high-end restaurants. Usually, I got takeaway. As I waited for my curry, I studied the other customers. How was it that the British, with their bland, colorless meals, had fallen in love with fiery foods? Yes, India was part of the Empire, but so were Australia, Canada, and Ireland—countries with foods more similar to the British palette. I never could reconcile the love of the two cuisines. No matter the reason, I was grateful for inexpensive food that had some zip to it.

Back in New York, I had often eaten burgers and fries. Living in London, I longed for a thick, juicy medium-rare burger on a toasted bun, with onions, lettuce, and ketchup with a sour pickle on the side. I scoured London for something that would approximate my ideal burger.

On every shopping street, there was at least one Wimpy burger outlet. It was the original fast food in London, long before McDonald's arrived. Their burgers were fast and cheap. They were also nearly inedible. The buns were soggy, almost gluey. The burgers were small, gray, and overcooked to the point where they were stiff as cardboard. They reminded me of the Charlie Chaplin scene in *The Gold Rush*, where he is so hungry he eats his shoe.

I was about to declare defeat in my quest for a decent burger when The Great American Disaster opened. I stood in a queue breathing in a scent that made me salivate and my brain go to a place of pure joy.

The restaurant was small, the walls covered in photos of American disasters like the Great Chicago Fire, the explosion of the Hindenburg dirigible, and the San Francisco earthquake. Chuck Berry singing "Johnny B. Goode" blasted from speakers.

"Medium-rare burger, fries, and a chocolate shake," I said to the waiter.

"You're American," he stated as he jotted my order on a small pad.

"So are you," I returned.

"I knew there were a lot of Americans in London, but until I started working here, I had no idea how many." He shook his head. "It amazes me."

"Hey, you're probably serving every American in London. We're all desperate for a decent burger."

"Where you from?" he asked me.

"New York."

"The city?"

"Yep. You must also be from the East Coast." I was loving his accent and talkative, brash manner. I had two American friends in London, but neither had this guy's particular energy. It felt familiar and made me homesick.

"I'm from Jersey."

"I knew it."

With that, he turned and headed for the kitchen.

The burger was the best I'd had in London, but far from the best I'd had in New York. The fries weren't even close. I didn't care. This felt like a piece of home. It became a regular haunt where I brought British and continental friends. They liked the food and atmosphere. To them, this was an exotic foreign experience.

Perhaps restaurants weren't the best gauge of British food. It delighted me when a friend invited me to his parents' home in the Midlands. His family was friendly and gracious, with none of the stiff reserve often attributed to Brits. Their Sunday dinner, however, only deepened my longing for a decent meal. Because this was a festive meal, there was an appetizer of tomato aspic with a few corn niblets (from a can) floating in the blood-red gelatin. For the main course, each plate had two thin slices from the roast, boiled potatoes without salt, pepper, or butter, and watery Brussels sprouts. For dessert, there was a special treat—ice cream. His mother doled out generous portions into fancy crystal bowls. One spoonful, and I'd eaten enough. The ice cream was so chemical-laden, that's all I could taste. So much for home cooking.

Years later, when I returned to London for business and to visit friends, I still ate a lot of Indian food. But I wasn't going to the local curry house. I ate at extravagantly decorated restaurants with extensive menus.

Britain had elevated its status in the culinary world, and London was awash in terrific ethnic restaurants. And, I was traveling for business on an expense account, which meant that I ate in high-end restaurants. That changed my perception of British food. With clients, I dined on classic meals in club-like surroundings with polished wood walls and leather club chairs. We ate Dover sole, chops, or shepherd's pie. With fresh trifle, sticky toffee pudding, or strawberry fool for dessert.

Still, the memory of three years of awful meals stayed with me. I remember reading and enthusiastically agreeing with an article about food in 1970s Britain. The author described it as "the decade that good food forgot."

FONDUE, FOLLY, AND FEMINISM:
SWITZERLAND, 1971

> While living in London, I was determined to see as
> much of Europe as possible, although my finances
> were limited. Whenever I saw an inexpensive flight or
> rail deal, I jumped on it. When an ad for a cheap
> student airfare got my attention, I left London for a
> weekend in Zurich, my first time in Switzerland.

My student ID allowed me to book a bargain flight and my Youth Hostel Card got me into affordable center-city lodging. As in most youth hostels, the clientele was young, international travelers more interested in seeing the world and partying than in ambience. The sterile looking room was dormitory-style, lined with bunk beds and a shared bathroom down the hall. Separate dorms for women and men.

While checking in late morning, I met a group of five Swedish students, three women and two men, also in town for the weekend. Tall, blond, blue-eyed, and athletic looking, they were Nordic archetypes. We chatted briefly, and they took me in as part of their group. After securing our things in the dorms, we left to explore. All of them spoke fluent English and were willing to abandon their native language to accommodate me.

We walked for miles and many hours in Old Town and on Bahnhofstrasse, the main commercial thoroughfare. The streets were a mix of quaint and ultra-modern. There were high-end luxury retailers where we window shopped, looking at clothing, shoes, jewelry, and other goods with prices far exceeding anything any of us could afford. In the few shops we entered, the automatic, self-opening doors impressed me; it was the first time I'd experienced them.

At a park fronting Lake Zurich, we ate a picnic lunch we'd purchased at a grocery store. An adventurous group, we'd chosen a selection of unfamiliar (to them or me) cheeses, breads, and crackers. I'd expected we'd find the "Swiss" cheese I'd eaten in New York, but none of the cheese had holes. The names were unfamiliar; Sbrinz, Gruyère, Vacherin Fribourgeois, Tête de Moine, Schabziger. We passed around and ripped off hunks from brown bread and knotted loaves and took handfuls of seeded crackers.

The cheeses were flavorful and made me think about the pallid varieties we ate in the States. While my mother never, ever bought Wonder bread, a staple in the homes of all of my childhood friends, she purchased Velveeta, individually wrapped slices of American cheese and mild cheddar. Most cheese we ate at home more closely resembled plastic than food. These Swiss cheeses were pungent, each with a unique taste—buttery, tangy, salty, laced with herbs, and as far from American cheese as freshly squeezed orange juice is from Tang.

While we ate, I learned more about my new Swedish companions. They'd been classmates and friends for years and had started taking weekend jaunts together whenever they had time and money. Their goal was to visit every European country, then explore Asia.

When we'd had our fill, our group left together to explore the far reaches of Zurich.

"There's a tram. Let's catch it," said one of my new Swedish friends.

"Where's it headed?" I asked.

"No idea."

"But don't you want to know?" I was puzzled. Why would anyone board a tram randomly?

"That's part of the fun." Her bright blue eyes shone with delight. "It will be an adventure."

Another of my new Swedish friends explained that, when traveling, they made it a practice to visit the outer reaches of a city, never knowing what they might discover. It allowed them to see how ordinary people lived.

We all scrambled onto the tram.

One of our group called out, "Sit at a window. Yell if you see something interesting."

Glued to the passing view, when anything caught someone's eye, they'd call out, "Here!" and we'd scurry off to our next adventure.

Usually what attracted us was an interesting-looking café or bar. We began some serious midafternoon drinking. Wine, beer, brandy—we wanted to try it all. I couldn't tell you specifically what we drank, only that we drank a lot of it. I also don't remember how we found our way back to Old Town, an area with restaurants and bars on almost every block.

We agreed that fondue was a must for dinner. It was the one Swiss food with which I was familiar. In the 1960s, fondue pots and parties were popular. Restaurants specializing in fondue had opened in New York City. Here, in Zurich, I'd get to eat an authentic version.

As with our earlier tram ride, we selected a restaurant in an arbitrary way. A cheery young woman in a bright blue and white dirndl, the traditional Swiss dress with a full skirt and laced bodice, led us to a round table. The room was designed to look like a Tyrolean hut, with wooden tables, small-paned windows, checkerboard tablecloths, and paintings of the Alps.

The Swedes not only spoke Swedish and English, but they were also fluent in French and German. I left the ordering to them.

First to appear was a pair of raised gas heaters to keep the fondue chafing dishes warm. Next came two bottles of wine, two pots of bubbling cheese, a basket of warm chunks of bread, and long, slender forks for skewering the bread to dip it into the melted cheese. There was a lot of laughter as bread fell irretrievably into the pot. Next, the server brought another bottle of wine and a plate of raclette (a melted cheese dish). After that, the meal is a blur. I'd guess we had chocolate fondue for dessert. Considering the quantity of alcohol I'd consumed, it's a wonder I didn't fall headfirst into the fondue pot. I know we were there for hours because there was a sudden screech from one of the Swedish men: "We have to get back. NOW!"

The youth hostel had strict hours. If we returned late, the doors would be locked. In our inebriated state, we tried to figure out how to get back.

The man who'd alerted us to the nearing deadline held his liquor better than the rest of us. He took it upon himself to pay the bill, then hustle us out onto the street and into a taxi. We made it back with ten minutes to spare.

In the dorm room, I stood on the ladder to the top bunk and spread my nylon sheet sleeping sack onto the mattress. The sack, a kind of sleeping bag liner, was a required item since hostels didn't supply sheets or pillowcases. I tucked the pillow under the top of the sack and flung a heavy, scratchy blanket on top. Then, too drunk to get into pajamas, I climbed the ladder fully dressed and wriggled my way into the sack. My new friends did the same, all of us trying to be as quiet as possible since others were asleep in the room. We didn't do well at that, whispering and giggling. I fell asleep to Swedish chatter.

"AARGHHH!"

"*Vada är det där?*" I vaguely heard a disembodied voice.

"AARGHHH!"

"What's the matter?" came another voice.

The scream was coming from me.

The light flicked on.

"Oh my God!"

I heard scrambling, but in my stupor had no idea what was going on. Then several pairs of hands were on me, shoving me back into the bunk. I'd impaled myself on the ladder and was dangling over the edge of the bunk bed. The ladder had stopped me from dropping about six feet to the floor. I rubbed my side, which felt as though someone had skewered me.

"Are you okay?"

"I think so. What? What happened?"

"You slid partway out of bed."

"Oh."

With that, I fell back to sleep.

In the morning, through a crushing hangover and a very sore side, I got the full story. There are bands on the sheet sleeping sack that are supposed to be tied to the bed to keep it in place. I hadn't bothered to do that. Tossing and turning in my sleep, the slippery nylon sack had caused me to slide over the edge of the bunk.

I thanked my rescuers, who'd probably saved me from serious injury.

That day I went off on my own and kept my drinking to a minimum. I spent my time touring and tasting. Breakfast was Bircher muesli and hot chocolate. I'd tasted both at home, but they'd been pale imitations. The Swiss hot chocolate was creamy, with an intense chocolate flavor that lingered long after I'd drained the mug. No marshmallows needed. The muesli was crunchy and earthy with a hint of sweetness. The yogurt served was plain, thick, and slightly sour and, when mixed with the muesli, balanced it perfectly.

I walked, took trams, visited museums, and mentally drooled at confectionary shop windows. It seemed as though every third shop had an elegant, extravagant, and tempting display of chocolates. I resisted, deciding I'd buy some right before I returned to London.

While I sat at a café sipping a coffee, resting, and people watching, a smartly dressed woman a bit older than me approached my table.

"May I join you?" she asked in English, waving her hands to indicate that all the tables were occupied.

"Of course." I was delighted to have company.

"You are American, yes?"

"I am." I thought it must be my jeans and sneakers. I'd noticed Americans stood out from Europeans by the way we dressed. My tablemate wore a suit, pearls, and heels. "Are you from Zurich?"

"I live here now, originally from Geneva."

We chatted for a while, sipping coffee and nibbling on pastries. It was all inconsequential small talk. Then she told me something that both astounded and stayed with me.

"Women just got the right to vote earlier this year."

"This year?" I was incredulous. "Really?"

"Yes, this year. A few months ago. We've been fighting for it for a long time."

That news saddened and angered me. How could a well-educated populace allow this to happen? I'd assumed this was a progressive country, far ahead of the U.S. in many ways. But voting was a right I took for granted, as did my mother and grandmother. My grandmother Bella, an immigrant, was very proud of her citizenship, American passport, and ability to vote. As soon as I'd become eligible, I'd registered.

"How do you feel about that?" I asked, expecting to hear anger, frustration, and something about how long it had taken.

"It's exciting. We've even got a woman running for office!"

Her enthusiasm was genuine, without a tinge of bitterness or regret. It appalled me. How could she take this so lightly?

With that, my new acquaintance excused herself and left. I sat there thinking about women's rights. The growing women's liberation movement in the States was fighting hard for equality, though I hadn't actively participated in it. I knew we had a very long way to go, but compared to the Swiss, we were light-years ahead.

I wanted to speak with other Swiss women to get their take on voting rights. Perhaps the woman I'd spoken with had been an exception. I swiveled in my chair, hoping to see a woman sitting by herself. No luck.

That evening I met up with my Swedish friends for dinner. Different restaurant, different food, but once again a lot of wine. I told them what I'd learned about Swiss women and voting. They were aware of it and expressed the sadness and bitterness I'd expected. Swedish women had acquired voting rights in the early 1920s, at about the same time as American women. I couldn't get over the fact that it took an additional fifty years for the Swiss to do so.

We shared a feast of rosti, which I thought of as a Swiss latke (potato pancake), sausages with onion gravy, mushroom ragout, and carrots. It was a rich, heavy meal, which, combined with alcohol, and the weighty discussion, made me a bit woozy.

This time, we all kept an eye on the clock and left the restaurant early enough to walk to the hostel with time to spare. I'd traded bunks and slept on the bottom. I also securely tied the bands to the bed. Though I wasn't nearly as drunk, I didn't want any risk of repeating the previous night's excitement. My side still hurt. I vowed to never sleep on a top bunk again. To this day, I've kept that vow.

The practice of exploring far corners of cities on public transport became my second vow. To this day, I do it whenever possible.

I'd traveled to Switzerland on a whim. That short stay left me with a revised impression; the Zurich I saw wasn't the land of Heidi. It also wasn't the sophisticated, enlightened society I'd anticipated. As I'd expected, Zurich was efficient, clean, and expensive. The food was better than I'd imagined. But learning about Swiss women just getting the vote left me with a simmering anger. While I hadn't given it much thought, my actions, even traveling to Switzerland by myself, made me a feminist.

Though I didn't consciously think about it at the time, that trip awakened my self-perception as a feminist. My third vow from this excursion was to do whatever I could to help advance women's equality. While I never joined a women's group, throughout my career I have tried to mentor and advance other women. I try to set an example by demanding equality in my work and personal life.

TONY HILLERMAN'S SOUTHWEST: NEW MEXICO, AND ARIZONA, 1979

As great fans of the mystery novels of Tony Hillerman, my boyfriend Marty and I set out to visit as many places as possible mentioned in his books. Over multiple trips, we saw large swathes of the Native American Southwest, guided by fictional Navajo Tribal Police detectives Jim Chee, Joe Leaphorn, and Bernadette Manuelito.

Our first trip, a large circle through New Mexico and a slice of Arizona, began in Albuquerque. I'd never spent time in the Southwest or in any desert environment. Everything seemed as different from New York as it could be. Buildings were low, and instead of steel and glass, many were constructed in adobe or wood. Cacti, not begonias or geraniums, decorated yards and front porches. In the distance, the Sandia Mountains were brownish-gray and parched-looking, unlike the lush green of the Northeast.

An unfamiliar smoky scent permeated the mid-September air. I quickly learned it was from roasting chiles. Every few streets, there was a three- or four-foot-long cylindrical wire mesh drum lying on its side, rotated by a handheld crank. Below was a propane flame heating the green chiles within. The sound effects were as distinctive as the smell—the propane whooshed, the peppers popped and crackled. Smoke streamed from the cage as the chiles' skin blistered. It's a scent I always associate with New Mexico, even though I've been there other times of the year when the only chiles to be found are hanging strings of them drying outside homes.

We rode the Sandia Peak tramway up into the nearby mountains. The ride gave me a bird's-eye view of the landscape. It was a clear day, and the city shrank as the enormity of land grew, making Albuquerque appear to be as small as a child's toy village. After a day hiking in the Sandia foothills, we headed west into Navajo country. It's an immense expanse of land, over twenty-seven thousand square miles spanning New Mexico, Utah, and Arizona. I'd never seen so much undeveloped land. Other friends who've traveled there describe the land as bleak. I found the emptiness peaceful and beautiful.

We drove on county roads and meandered down back lanes to see what we might find. There were few services available. My city upbringing hadn't prepared me to think about the inability to get gas, water, or food for long distances. I made a mental note to fill the tank whenever there was a gas station and to bring along supplies.

While few vehicles were on the road, periodically we had to slow down or stop as livestock or horses ambled across. We saw dirt roads that seemed to veer off into nothingness. I knew from reading Hillerman's books that these tracks eventually led to a family's hogan (home).

Our first stop was in Gallup, at the western edge of New Mexico. It isn't on the Navajo reservation but borders it and is the business center for a vast area. It started as a frontier mining town, and remnants of its rough beginnings still existed. The guidebook, as well as passages in Hillerman's books, warned that excessive drinking was a serious problem in Gallup and on the reservation. With a casual stroll on the streets, the reason for the warning became obvious. Men swigging from brown-bagged bottles were sprawled on benches or shakingly walked around town.

Every other store seemed to be a pawnshop or bar. I'd never set foot in a pawnshop before and was reluctant to enter one. In New York, pawnshops have a reputation for being sleazy. Marty assured me it would be fascinating. He was correct.

The first pawnshop we walked into was large and busy with people bringing in items to pawn, redeeming them, and buying. Their clientele was a mix of Native Americans, white locals, and tourists. It resembled a gift shop: neat, cheerful, and well lit. Hanging on the walls were handwoven rugs and baskets with handsome geometric patterns. Glass cases displayed silver and turquoise necklaces, earrings, bracelets, and rings. The intricacy of the designs and skilled craftsmanship made them showpieces. The prices reflected the value of the materials, artists' talent, and hours of work needed to create them. Other cases contained guns—also new for me. I'd seen them on TV or holstered on a police officer, but never up close. Some guns on display had ornate grips and looked more for show than use. Most, however, looked all business and lethal.

After examining the goods in the first shop, I was eager to see more. I wondered if we'd found an unusual one and if others would be more in line with my preconceptions. All the pawnshops we spent time in were equally attractive and businesslike. I couldn't resist buying something. To this day, I own a string of turquoise nuggets, one of the least expensive items on display. My ideas about pawnshops changed. I now thought of them as lending institutions for people with valuable goods and a need for immediate cash. It also seemed likely that the locals trusted these shops more than banks.

We got a room at El Rancho, a historic hotel. Who could resist a place that had been the temporary home for stars acting in westerns? Humphrey Bogart, James Cagney, Jane Fonda, and dozens of others filmed in and around Gallup. Outside, the hotel looked a bit tacky, neon lights blazing. But once inside, I gaped as I did a slow, full turn, taking in the ambience. The massive stone fireplace could have swallowed a car. The wooden furniture and beams looked as though they'd been designed for a giant. Native American woven rugs and antlers decorated the walls. The light from wagon wheel chandeliers bathed the lobby in an amber hue. This sounds tawdry, but it wasn't. The decor was extraordinary.

The receptionist at the front desk recommended a local restaurant. When we pulled up, I thought, *Here?* It looked tiny and seedy. But she'd sworn it was her favorite and had the best New Mexican food in Gallup. By this time, I was learning to throw away my assumptions, realizing they were prejudices based on urban experiences.

While I knew enchiladas, tacos, and burritos, many of the items on the menu were new to me. I decided to eat a meal of only unfamiliar foods.

"Okay, you need to explain some of this to me," I said to Marty, who'd spent a great deal of time in the Southwest. "I don't know what a lot of this is, and the menu doesn't describe them. I guess the regulars don't need to ask." I glanced back at the menu. "What's posole?"

"It's great. It's kind of a hominy stew. Sometimes it has meat, sometimes vegetarian. We'll have to ask what they have."

"*Carrizozo? Choriqueso?*" I glanced at the menu. "*Carne Adovada?*"

"Haven't a clue," Marty said.

I was glad he didn't know. It made me feel like less of a green-horn. "All right, how about *sopapilla?*"

"That I know, but I always thought of it as dessert, and it's listed as a main."

"Okay, what is it as a dessert?" I asked.

"It's a puffy fried bread drizzled with honey. Kind of like zeppole at the street fairs in Little Italy." Marty paused. "But it's a thicker dough. You'll get to taste fry bread at some point. It's a Navajo staple."

The waiter came over to the table, bringing a basket of tortilla chips and cups of red and green hot sauce.

Marty dug in almost before the server placed them on the table. "We'll need more hot sauce," he said as he finished a mouthful. "This is great."

The waiter chuckled as he looked Marty up and down. Marty is 6'6" and an eating machine. "I'll bring more chips too." He laughed. "What can I get you?"

"I have a couple of questions," I said. "What's Carrizozo?" I read from the menu. "Choriqueso?"

"Carrizozo are our special enchiladas. Think of them as the kitchen sink of enchiladas. Choriqueso is a cheese and cilantro dip with chorizo sausages. It comes with tortillas."

Marty and I conferred and ordered a slew of dishes. It was way more than I could possibly eat, but we wanted to try almost everything. And the prices were ridiculously low—especially compared to New York restaurants. I knew anything I couldn't eat, Marty would finish.

When all the dishes had been brought out, they filled the table. The posole stew tasted like the smokiness from the roasting chiles I'd smelled in Albuquerque, mixed with sweet corn and spicy pork. Marty and I almost fought over it. Choriqueso was like fondue with a southwestern twist. We dipped tortillas into the thick, saucy cheese laced with spicy sausage bits. I tasted and Marty finished plates of tacos and enchiladas, served with towering piles of rice and beans. No one ever left this restaurant hungry.

The next morning, Marty was looking forward to huevos rancheros. I was on a food hangover and only wanted coffee and dry toast. When our breakfast was on the table, I almost couldn't look at his overflowing plate of food. But as I bit into a slice of toast, I couldn't resist stealing a bite of his eggs. I needed some protein, after all. They were light, spicy, and delicious. *Tomorrow morning*, I thought.

Back on the road, we headed to Window Rock on the New Mexico/Arizona border. In both fact and fiction, Window Rock is home to the tribal council of the Navajo Nation and the main tribal police department. It's also where the fictional Joe Leaphorn works. The town was named for a rock formation that looks like a circular window. Looking through the "window," the sky was intense blue against the red rock.

We stopped in at the Navajo Nation Museum. The exhibits, through artifacts, photos, and detailed signage, reinforced what I'd learned from Hillerman about the Dineh (Navajo) way of life. I wondered how much about their society wasn't told, since I knew that the Navajo don't discuss their culture, history, taboos, and, most critically, their religion with outsiders.

The exhibits emphasized the Navajo belief in living in harmony with the earth. That is far more complex than it sounds. There are specific rules to maintain one's spiritual and physical health and preserve family connections. In the Joe Leaphorn mysteries, the importance of family is stressed, and knowing one's clan and heritage is integral to that. According to Hillerman, most Dineh know their lineage through many generations, often going back hundreds of years. In my family, I can only go as far back as my grandparents, who immigrated to the United States in the early 1900s. That's true for many Americans.

At a local ice cream parlor, we took a break and people watched for a while. Four Mennonite young women in cotton dresses and hair coverings ate ice cream cones at a table next to a Navajo family. The kids squirmed while the parents tried to get them to behave. Across from them was a young Native American couple on what appeared to be a date. He in a clean, pressed T-shirt and jeans, she in jeans and a sequined blouse. An elderly couple emerged from an RV, came in, and ordered shakes, followed by a couple of guys looking as if they'd come from a day on a ranch. It was good to be reminded that even in remote areas, the U.S. is a diverse country with a population that usually is amazingly tolerant.

We headed north to Canyon de Chelly, a sacred site for Native Americans and the setting for several Hillerman books. It's an area that was inhabited by the Anasazi, ancestors of the Hopi, stretching as far back as 1500 BC. From the rim of the canyon, which goes for miles, we could see ancient cliff dwellings carved into the steep sandstone walls. I couldn't tear myself away from the view. This put ancient cathedrals in Europe into perspective. Civilizations thrived before any of the history they taught me in school.

I wanted to go to the canyon floor for a closer look, but the only way there was to hike in. Down would have been doable. But it was a hot afternoon, and it looked to be a long distance on a zigzag path. The return trip would have been brutal. I contented myself, and drove Marty crazy, by insisting we stop at every lookout. Each viewpoint gave a unique perspective, and the changing sun lit up different features. Far in the distance, I could see horses, homes, and what I assumed were people. At one viewpoint, we looked down at Spider Rock, a tall, narrow spire that rises from the canyon floor. It looked as though it had been constructed, rather than sculpted by time, the elements, and Mother Nature. I caught sight of a river snaking through the canyon, rimmed with trees.

We delayed departing in the hopes we'd see the sun set over the canyon. It was worth the wait. The sky flamed red, made vivid by blowing sand. For a few minutes, the entire canyon seemed on fire. Then, as the sun moved west, darkness closed in. There were no lights, and it was as if a magician had swept the canyon floor away. The moon was a thin crescent. When the stars emerged, a whole new show started. Away from light pollution, the constellations were clear against the black sky. I could imagine someone a thousand years ago looking at the identical view.

By that time, it was getting late. We headed toward Chinle and the Thunderbird Lodge, the only tourist accommodation in the area. Fortunately, we'd had the forethought to reserve a room. The Navajo call this area Ch'ini'li, which translates as "where the water flows out." In September, there wasn't all that much water flowing from Canyon de Chelly, but I could imagine raging springtime waters.

Apart from its proximity to the canyon, we'd wanted to stay in Chinle because much of Hillerman's *The Blessing Way* takes place in and around that area. It's also mentioned in several of his other mysteries. But, apart from being close to Canyon de Chelly, it had little to offer tourists.

We left early the next morning, driving north and then east to Shiprock in New Mexico. As we drove, the sky grew dark. I expected that, at any moment, we'd hear thunder, see lightning, and sheets of rain—maybe even hail—would come crashing down. None of that happened. The intense dry desert air sucked up all the moisture before it ever neared the surface. I later learned this phenomenon is called virga.

Shiprock is a massive natural formation. Looked at from the right angle, it resembles a clipper ship sailing through the desert. Like The Devil's Tower in Wyoming, best known from the movie *Close Encounters of the Third Kind*, the surrounding land is almost completely flat. Shiprock is visible for many miles. We saw it long before we got anywhere near it. That was good because indigenous people consider it sacred and don't appreciate tourists.

Though I was becoming accustomed to the enormity of the land, the size of Shiprock was striking. I wished I knew about the geologic forces that created it. But alas, the only information in the guidebook said it was the remains of a volcano.

We spent the next couple of days in and around Farmington. This area introduced me to more landscapes unique to the Southwest. The city is the meeting place of three rivers—the San Juan, Animas, and La Plata. On a trail bordering the Animas, we saw cottonwood trees stretching their branches far over the water. Hiking in the Bisti Badlands, I felt as though I'd become a Lilliputian in *Gulliver's Travels*. The area's weathered sandstone and shale are some of the strangest natural formations anywhere. Marty taught me the term *hoodoo* to describe the spires that have been formed by thousands of years of erosion. Many hoodoos are topped with protruding caps that make them look like gigantic mushrooms.

Marty told me that on a previous trip to the area, he'd found fossils while hiking. That wasn't too surprising. The area was so unusual that I could imagine tripping on a petrified bone. Plus, we'd seen loads of roadside stands selling rocks and fossils. We didn't find any fossils, mostly because I was so entranced by the views it seemed criminal to look down. But it convinced me we had to stop at a roadside stand.

We pulled off the road at the first large stand we saw after leaving Bisti. Sheets of plywood propped on sawhorses held hundreds of specimens. I was surprised the wood wasn't bowed from the weight. While I recognized agates, turquoise, and a few other minerals, most of what was on display was unfamiliar.

"Hi there." An older man with a well-worn slouch hat perched on his head approached us from a parked trailer. "Anything special you're looking for?"

"No, just looking. You've got some amazing things here," I said. "Are they all local?"

"I'm a rock hound, and a lot of them are. But not everything." He pointed to a chunk of stone striated with yellow and black. "That's tiger's eye jasper. It's from New Mexico, but not around here."

It was so large I could barely pick it up. "What's this?" I put my hand on an almost translucent pale blue rock.

"Ah, that's a beauty. It's chalcedony. That one's local. I found it in Bisti."

"How often do you go rockhounding?" Marty asked.

"Whenever I can convince my wife or son to mind the shop." He chuckled. "That's about once a week. Not as much as I like, but . . ." With that, he picked up another rock and explained what it was and where he'd found it. "Where you folks from?" he asked. When he heard New York City, he seemed surprised. "Don't get too many East Coasters out here. Too remote for them."

"It's my first time here," I said. "I absolutely love it and am sure I'll be back soon."

"Yep. This area can really grab you. It did me." With a wide grin, he continued, "Came here fifty years ago from outside Pittsburgh. It was supposed to be for two weeks, and here I still am."

We spent about an hour chatting and looking at his amazing collection. Marty and I each walked away with several souvenirs.

The next morning, we headed east toward Taos. We were going from Hillerman country and entering into what I thought of as Georgia O'Keeffe territory. Along the way, we stopped at several Anasazi ruins. I was glad the tank was full when we left Farmington. There were stretches of fifty miles or more with no gas stations.

In Chama, we stopped for lunch. I knew nothing about the town but got a quick education from the paper place mat. It described the town as having "a rowdy and exciting history." It went on to say it had become prosperous because of the railroad, mining, and lumber. There were lots of saloons, gambling dens, and prostitution to entertain the workers. Because there was money in town, it also attracted outlaws. Sounded pretty exciting to me. When we visited, it was a lot sleepier.

As an admirer of O'Keeffe, I knew it was a trip to Taos that made her fall in love with New Mexico and the desert. I could understand why. What I hadn't expected, though I should have, was the proliferation of art in town. The Harwood Museum exhibited local artists. Every other shop around the main square seemed to be an art gallery or craft shop. After a while, the turquoise, silver, rugs, and baskets all ran together. I was glad I'd purchased my souvenirs early in the trip. I was on art overload.

To get away from the art, something I never imagined I would even think of doing, we headed to Taos Pueblo. The pueblo, at first glance, appeared to be a high-rise cluster of adobe buildings. The red earth buildings, with doors and window frames painted a vivid turquoise and backed up by a low range of hills, were a hive of activity. Rounded ovens in front of some homes were being used to bake bread. I will always associate the scent of yeasty bread, mixed with sage, lavender, juniper, and dust, with the pueblo.

As we walked toward the buildings, a young woman, her shiny black hair in braids, greeted us with an unfamiliar-sounding word. She explained that *yá'át'ééh* means "it is good," and is used to say hello.

"Would you like a tour of the pueblo?" she asked.

"Absolutely," Marty and I said in unison.

For the next half hour, she led us through the pueblo, explaining village life. She told us she was a student and worked for the tribal council who preferred to have visitors walk with a guide rather than wander alone. We learned the main part of the buildings had been constructed about five hundred years before. It astounded me that adobe, earth mixed with water and straw, could last that long. Then I remembered ceramics that had survived from ancient Egypt, Greece, and China, and thought, *I guess it could*. She explained local customs and told us most people living in the pueblo were practicing Catholics. Again, that came as a surprise. I realized there were sizable gaps in what I knew about this way of life, even with everything I'd learned from Hillerman.

She pointed out homes where the owners sold crafts they made and said we could visit them after the tour. We, of course, did that, buying small baskets and bowls.

Our final destination before returning to Albuquerque was Santa Fe. After all the wide-open space and small towns, Santa Fe felt like a big city. The outskirts of town where we stayed was a jumble of strip malls, fast-food chain restaurants, and motels. After the unspoiled land we'd traveled through, *unattractive* barely describes my reaction to this. I know people need to shop and eat and get cars repaired, but couldn't it have been designed more tastefully?

Center city was more appealing. Shops selling everything from shlock to Native American jewelry at Tiffany prices surrounded the main plaza. On one side, shaded by an arcade, Native Americans displayed handcrafted jewelry, baskets, and rugs. I spent a long time looking at their wares, chatting with them and buying a pair of turquoise earrings to match the necklace I'd bought earlier on the trip. Canyon Road, leading up to a cluster of museums, was a half-mile-long art lover's dream. Galleries exhibited the work of well-known and rising artists at prices far out of my range. At the top of the road was the International Folk Art Museum. That became my favorite place in the city and one that I've returned to many times.

The city also offered a plethora of dining choices. We searched for ones with local cuisine and ended up at Tomasita's, a haven for locals and tourists. By this point, I didn't need help understanding the menu, but I could have used help in deciding what to order. The waiter told us the restaurant was known for chile, so we ordered bowls of red and green chile. They were thick with beans, posole, beef, and Lord only knows what else. A small bowl would have been enough, but Marty also ordered flautas. They came with guacamole, pico de gallo, salsa, sour cream, and, of course, the ubiquitous rice and beans. While the food was delicious, after eating fried and rich foods, I was ready for a simple salad. It was time to head home.

HYENAS' LAUGHTER:
TANZANIA, 1983

When we'd first thought about a trip to Africa, my friend Diane and I pored over travel brochures. Close-ups of lions, elephants, zebras, and cheetahs urged us on, but the prices held us back. After months of looking, we found a company that had recently begun offering tours to Tanzania, a country known for being unspoiled and having a vast number of animals.

For the bargain price they were asking, we didn't mind camping, though it was clear it wouldn't be of the luxury variety touted by most outfitters. The upscale camping catalogs showed picture after picture of smiling tourists—leaning out of sparkling Land Rovers to get a closer look at a lion; lounging in comfortable chairs, drinks in hand, with the vast Serengeti plains as a backdrop; or eating lavish dinners on tables laid with linens and china. The pamphlet for our trip focused exclusively on the animals, one beat-up Rover in the background.

I t was after we'd paid our nonrefundable deposit that the equipment list arrived. Most of the gear, the sleeping bags, flashlights, insect repellent, toilet paper, hats, and such, seemed quite reasonable. It was the requested food items that gave us pause. Why exactly did they ask us to bring cans of tuna, whole salamis, jars of jam and peanut butter, condensed milk, and other nonperishable foods?

While I knew it wouldn't be gourmet, weren't they planning to provide any food? I took it as a warning and packed a large supply of granola bars.

On the day of our arrival in the country, Lauren, one of our guides, asked the eight tour members to give her the food we'd brought. Diane and I held back some granola bars but dutifully handed over the rest of our supplies.

Then, as a group, we went to the market. The women at the stalls wore colorful outfits in eye-popping prints. They laughed and flashed us broad smiles. Despite not understanding a word of Swahili, we could tell that the women knew Ian, our other guide, well and felt comfortable teasing him as he bargained for goods. We could see for ourselves that there was little variety. Though the market was small and relatively sparse, we managed to fill one of the Rovers with carrots and potatoes, some local fruits, beans, rice, pasta, eggs, and flour, as well as ancient tins of fruit salad, sardines, and a few other nonperishable items. We almost cleaned out their collective stock. Ian mentioned that this was one of the few markets we'd see over the next two weeks and definitely the one most geared toward foreigners. Curiosity piqued, we asked what the local population ate.

"Depends on where you are. Traditional Masai in the bush eat fermented milk, as well as animal blood, and some vegetables. Here in Kigali, people make a sort of stew out of boiled cassava and vegetables that's eaten with *ugali*."

"What's ugali?"

"Cassava root is plentiful here. Locals grind it and then make a paste from the flour. They eat it with every meal." That didn't sound so bad.

"We'll make some so you can taste it."

I was looking forward to that. I always like to sample the local cuisine.

That evening Ian brought out a large bowl of what looked like a thick, beige gruel. He took a spoonful, rolled it around in the palm of his hand, flattened it out, and dipped it into our communal bowl of stew.

"This is a staple that's eaten at every meal. For breakfast and lunch, the ugali is thinned out, so it resembles porridge and is drizzled with a vegetable sauce." He continued, "There isn't much variety in their diet."

After we'd tasted it, the request for Western foodstuffs made more sense. To our palates, ugali was tasteless and, to me, closely resembled wallpaper paste. Even though part of the appeal of this trip was to experience the culture, eating mush for two weeks would have been too much of a local encounter, even for the most intrepid of us.

Ian and Lauren were a British couple who'd been living in Africa for two decades and liked to think of themselves as more African than European. Between them, the drivers, mechanic, cook, and general helpers, our convoy of ancient Land Rovers held more locals than tourists. We met few other foreigners, both because we were camping and could stay in areas far off the usual tourist routes, and because most people wanting to see wildlife went to Kenya. At that time, Tanzania and Kenya were having border disputes, and Tanzania was considered unsafe.

Over the next week, we saw more animals than I'd fantasized about. These weren't animals seen through a pair of high-powered binoculars; our Rovers got right up to them—they were often a few feet away. Late one night, a lion padded by our tent. Diane swore she heard it breathing. Monkeys jumped onto our vehicles and clung to the sides, banging on the windows and hooting. Packs of elephants, hippos, water buffalo, and zebras surrounded us. In the distance, we saw leopards. Brilliantly colorful birds, lilac-breasted rollers, perched on tree branches. Thousands of shockingly pink flamingos danced in Lake Manyara. We woke to blazing-white sunrises. Blood-red sunsets marked cocktail hour—along with bottles of lukewarm Safari Lager. In campsites hundreds of miles from the nearest town, I saw the stars as I never had before. Who cared about food?

By the time we'd arrived at the Ngorongoro Crater, a national park known for having one of the densest populations of animals, we'd been camping for just over a week.

Our first excursion was late afternoon. We'd seen more than a dozen lions, packs of zebras, wildebeests, and water buffalo. There were too many elands, dik-diks, and other deer to count. But on our way back to camp, we couldn't stop talking about the pack of mangy hyenas we'd seen. Five of them had crouched shoulder to shoulder at the shoreline of a small lake. The size of large German shepherds, with jagged teeth and intense, glittering eyes, they were menacing looking. Their howling, like Dracula laughing maniacally, made them terrifying. First one, then another, of us would try to imitate the sound, our lips twisted into a vicious snarl. We created some horrible noises, but none approached the shrill, evil tones that chilled me and made my arm hairs stand at attention.

Our hyena imitations stopped when we returned to camp. The sky was darkening. With only candles and a few flashlights for illumination, we scurried about organizing ourselves for the night before the sun set. From around the camp came sounds of water splashing, shuffling, and the clink of cutlery and plates as our dinner table was laid out. Then, a yelp, a shriek. A very loud one. One that had overtones of shock and frustration. A noise that would have startled the hyenas, had they heard it. We all, tourists and staff, rushed to find out what was happening.

"It's nothing, really," Ian said. "Sorry I screamed. Dinner will be ready in a few minutes. I'll call you." He repeated this in Swahili for the staff. Reluctantly we all returned to what we'd been doing, anxious to know what had provoked his almost inhuman cry.

When the dinner bell rang, the eight of us converged on the table in record time. Unsuccessfully struggling to hide his emotions, Ian announced, "There's been a slight problem with dinner. But I know you're all adventurous. Think of this as another adventure." We kept silent, waiting to see what this "slight problem" was. Ian beckoned over the chef's assistant. He came bearing a large plastic bowl and placed it in the center of the table, then quickly backed away.

"The cook misunderstood my instructions," Ian said. We peered into the bowl. There was a collective groan. He went on, "We were supposed to have dessert tonight as a special treat."

"Is there anything else we can eat?" asked one of our fellow travelers.

"No, not really."

"But the peanut butter? The salami I brought? Where are they?"

"Not here. They're back in Kigali. And if we ask the cook to make something else, it will be hours, and anyway, we won't have enough food for the rest of the trip."

"Shit."

"Yeah, that's pretty much what it looks like."

The bowl contained a goopy mix of boiled vegetables, rice, Vienna sausages, and crushed saltines. On top of that, several tins of fruit salad and sweetened condensed milk had been poured. The final topping was an artful arrangement of sardines, the oil they'd been packed in drizzled over the whole mess.

Ian had asked the cook to prepare three dishes. The cook, not understanding the concept of appetizer, entrée, and dessert, had combined them into a single dish.

One couple who had squirreled away a significant stash of food opted out of dinner. I thought about all the food the group had brought and handed over to Ian and Lauren; now would have been a good time for it to magically reappear. But it didn't then, or ever. I suspected, but couldn't confirm, that they'd requested foods they couldn't get in Tanzania and wanted for their own use.

It was the worst meal I've ever been served. But with no other food available, I stared into the bowl, then reached in and picked out a Vienna sausage. Following my example, everyone in the group joined in, scavenging for anything that looked edible. As I wiped the sausage off on a napkin, a small, uncontrollable burbling of laughter erupted. With the first bite, my laughter multiplied. Soon we were all holding our sides, gasping for breath, coughing up food, further eating impossible. One member of our group began hyena howling. The rest of our pack joined in.

I wondered, what would the hyenas have made of our howling? I couldn't imagine and howled, and laughed, even louder.

WAY DOWN BELOW:
AUSTRALIA, 1985

My first trip to Australia was in 1985. My boyfriend Marty and I were determined to see as much as we could, especially the sites and wildlife unique to the continent. We explored cities and the ribbon of fertile land at the continent's edge.

Kangaroos, koalas, wallabies, echidnas, and fabulous birds entranced us. We took a four-night cruise on The Great Barrier Reef and snorkeled, marveling at the giant clams, abundance of coral, and vast variety of colorful fish. Then we headed for the "empty" interior.

When I'd been planning our trip, I wanted to see less touristy areas of the outback in addition to the renowned Ayers Rock, Alice Springs, and the Olgas. When I came upon a tour company that flew visitors to small opal mining towns, I signed us up for it.

The trip's itinerary was for six tourists to fly on a prop plane from Adelaide to Andamooka, where we'd spend the night, then fly to Coober Pedy to explore the town and return to Adelaide the next day. When we arrived at the designated meeting point, a lanky man who introduced himself as Noah met us. "Well now, you must be Karen and Marty."

"We are."

"Well, you're very lucky. The other group canceled at the last minute, so you'll be having a personal tour."

That sounded good until he walked us across the tarmac to a somewhat battered-looking four-seater plane. I'd never been in such a small aircraft before. With deeply tanned, wiry arms, Noah grabbed our bags and heaved them aboard. Then he prepped the plane, removing chocks from in front of the wheels, releasing the tethers, securing the wings, and doing a walk-around to make sure everything looked in order.

"Climb aboard."

I looked hesitantly at the plane, then at him, and back at the plane. "How do I do that?"

"Step up on the wing." He glanced at me as if saying, how else would you get into it? Then he said, "Oops," and produced a plastic box for me to use as a step.

I got on without embarrassing myself too badly. Marty, at 6'6", had no trouble stepping onto the wing, though he banged his head with a loud thump as he ducked through the doorframe.

With the doors closed and propellers whirring, I tried to breathe steadily to keep my mounting anxiety in check. I cinched my seat belt a bit tighter. Daylight creeping through the door seams and a crack in the windshield ratcheted my fear up.

Noah, speaking to the tower, said, "Roger that." He turned to Marty, sitting beside him up front. "Here we go. Ready?"

"Oh yeah."

We taxied over to the runway, and with a surprisingly smooth takeoff, we were aloft.

"We won't be flying very high, so you should have a clear view."

I peered out the window, watching the city recede and empty land with sparse vegetation appear. From this vantage point, kangaroos looked like cartoon characters as they hopped across the landscape. Then, there was only dirt, rocks, and scrubby shrubs. What occasionally appeared to be water were mirages. When I questioned him about them, Noah told me they were dried-up riverbeds and lakes.

"How do you know where we are?" Marty asked.

Noah rifled through a stack of papers, finally pulling out a road map. He unfolded it, then pointed to a thin line. "See that road?" He moved his finger along the line and then pointed down to the landscape below.

I looked to the ground, squinted, and detected only the slightest of dirt tracks.

"That's what I'm following."

All I could think of was, *Yikes.* I wondered what happened when there was a dust storm and all those faint traces were obliterated.

I could feel the plane descending but saw nothing that resembled a runway, much less an airport. "Where are we landing?" Marty asked.

Noah pointed straight ahead. In the distance, I could see a limp windsock surrounded by a lot of nothing. The plane continued down, and soon we were bumping over a rocky red earth surface. There were no buildings in sight. In fact, there wasn't much of anything other than a strip of land outlined by tires—"the runway."

We disembarked by jumping off the wing. Noah secured the plane, tossed us our bags, and handed Marty a large, heavy box. "Supplies for Marge," he told us. Still, there was nothing around us except a lot of empty space.

"No worries, she'll get here soon. Sometimes Marge gets forgetful. But I spoke with her this morning, and she knows to expect us."

With that, a beat-up station wagon careened toward us, kicking up a cloud of dust. I coughed. Marty coughed. The car lurched to a stop. A plump older woman with a leathery face emerged. "Sorry, sorry. There was something in the oven I had to take out." Almost breathlessly, she added, "Welcome to Andamooka."

"Where exactly is Andamooka?" I asked.

"Not too far. About a mile that way." She pointed vaguely ahead of us. "Can't have the runway any closer because of the mines. You'll see."

Minutes later, after a ride worthy of an amusement park, Noah, Marty, and I arrived at Marge's home, a small cottage amidst a cluster of small, dusty, ramshackle-looking buildings.

Inside, her home could have been in a small British countryside town. There were comfy chairs, flowery curtains, knickknacks, and photos. But a glance out the window and it was anything but a typical countryside town. The earth was red and baked, while dust motes turned the air pinkish. There wasn't a hint of anything green.

"Come, let me give you a tour of the house. Then, make yourselves at home." With that, Marge led us through the living room to the bedroom where we'd be sleeping, then showed us the bathroom, kitchen, and a small parlor. It all looked cozy and tidy. I wondered how she kept the dust at bay, remembering stories of the dustbowl in the U.S. and how the wind and dust drove people crazy.

She lifted a hatch on the floor and led us down a flight of stairs carved into stone. "This is where I live during the hot season. It can stay at one hundred degrees for weeks on end. But down here, it's a constant, cool seventy degrees." The room was as large and comfortable as upstairs, but even with the lights on, dark. The walls were polished stone.

"Nearly every house here has at least one room like this. Actually, most folk have lots of rooms like this. What you see above ground is like the tip of an iceberg." She walked through the room into another equally large area with rough stone walls and no furniture. "This is going to be my summer parlor." She laughed. "I'll let you in on a little secret." She beckoned us in close, though we were alone. "People dig new rooms hoping to find opals." She whispered, "I found a great vein when we were digging in this area."

"Why is this a secret?" Marty asked.

"You're supposed to have a permit to dig for a new mine. But, of course, no one gets one. We're so remote, the government mostly leaves us alone. But if they do come, they can't enter our homes."

"What do you do with the rock you dig out?"

"When you go out and take a walk, you'll see. Piles of slag everywhere. If you want to know which houses are the largest underground, look at how much rock surrounds their home."

We returned to the light upstairs. Marge set the table while we settled in. After a lunch we might have been eating in Gloucestershire—shepherd's pie, chips, and a slice of tomato—Noah said, "Let's go for a walk. I'll show you town and introduce you to Bill."

The light was searing, despite sunglasses and a hat. Though not the peak of summer (in March we were at the beginning of autumn), it was hot and dry. I could almost feel my skin beginning to shrivel. Every step kicked up dust, and Marty and I coughed frequently.

DANGER, DEEP SHAFTS, read signs dotting the landscape. The signs showed a person falling into a hole. "Pay attention to those signs," Noah said. "Those shafts go way down." Tall piles of slag lined the road and stretched far into the distance.

"It seems like it must be a honeycomb beneath the surface. Is it safe to walk off the road?" I asked.

"That rock is plenty solid. No worries. But the signs are accurate—watch out for shafts." He added, "Some of the best opals in the country come from the mines here. They're very high quality, with brilliant colors. Marge will show and sell you some later." He chuckled. "Marge may seem like a sweet old woman, but she's a shark when it comes to opals. Make sure you haggle with her. You'll get a fair price, far below what you would pay in Sydney, but it takes a bit of negotiating."

I was looking forward to seeing the opals. I'd been restraining myself from buying any until we got here.

By the time we arrived at Bill's home, a coating of reddish dust was clinging to every bit of my skin and clothes.

Sitting in a rocking chair on the sagging porch of a shack, Bill had deep wrinkles chiseled into his face. He could have been forty or eighty—it was impossible to know. A broad-brimmed hat partially shaded his face, leaving only his Cheshire-cat smile totally visible.

Noah introduced him as Bill McDougall, "town historian, chief raconteur, and one of the wisest, wittiest men I know."

Bill tipped his head, acknowledging the compliment. Then he started talking, and we barely got a word in. He told us about how he'd come to Andamooka in a long, rambling recitation. There were frequent detours into stories about the town and people who'd come and gone. I never did figure out exactly why or how he got there. He spoke about his quest to get money for the flying ambulance service. "It's really critical. We don't have a doctor or nurse," he explained. "I can do some basic first aid, but not much more than that." With lightning speed, he switched topics. "I have these lovely tea towels. Buy a few as souvenirs. I guarantee none of your friends have anything like it. And all the money will go to the ambulance corps." He went on at such length it was clear we'd have to buy some, and he was certainly correct that no one I knew had a tea towel from Andamooka. He offered us a drink, which I gratefully accepted, thinking it would be water. It wasn't. The clear liquid was more like fire water, easily 120-proof.

Through our alcohol-induced haze, we learned about the Andamooka opal, the largest one found in the area. He told us it was presented to Queen Elizabeth II on her first visit to Australia in 1954 and is a point of pride among residents.

"I have a mug that shows that opal being given to the queen," he added. "That money also goes to the ambulance corps." When we protested that we'd be traveling for a couple more weeks and would certainly break it, he offered us more tea towels. "Or use the tea towels to wrap the mugs." By the time we took our leave, my head was spinning from the stories, alcohol, and heat.

The sun was setting, and the sky was a uniform, deep rosy pink, caused by light refracting against the dust. In this unearthly light, the town, such as it was, looked almost beautiful.

After dinner, Marty and I went out to stargaze, thinking the lack of ambient light would allow for fabulous viewing. But with a slight breeze kicking up dust, the sky didn't have the clarity we'd hoped for.

Before we left the following morning, Marge took us to a back "showroom." She brought out box after box of opals, explaining the differences in quality. "You need to look at color, pattern, and clarity. And I'm sure you already know about solids, doublets, and triplets." We assured her we had been told about the practice of layering slices of opals. Doublets and triplets are thin slices of opal layered with glass or plastic to protect the fragile stone. But, more commonly, it's done to lower the cost. "All these opals are solid and the highest quality."

I didn't know how I could possibly choose. There were so many, all beautiful, and the differences so subtle that before I'd even gone through the first box, they all began to appear similar. I eventually picked out a few, and as Noah had said, the prices were far below what we'd seen in Sydney. Still, we haggled a bit, and I came away with three lovely stones. Marge wrapped them for me and gave me a receipt way below what I'd paid. "For customs," she said.

We again boarded the tiny plane, and after a short flight across more of the unpopulated red center, we touched down in Coober Pedy. Bumping onto the concrete runway felt as if we were returning to civilization. But if we'd traveled there first, I'd have thought we were on the set of the movie *The Back of Beyond*.

In 1985, Coober Pedy had a population of roughly three thousand people, or about twenty times that of Andamooka. There was a church, hotel, several restaurants, and what seemed to be a dozen shops selling opals. I wondered how the shops survived. This seemed a very remote place for hordes of tourists. Noah told us these weren't aimed at tourists. Rather, they were for wholesale buyers, most of whom came from Asia. The town supplies most of the world's gem-quality opal; at the time, it was the largest opal mining area in the world.

As in Andamooka, the heat can be extreme, and many people choose to live underground. "Down below" was also where the church, hotel, and some restaurants were located. Like Marge's home, the stairs and walls were polished stone and lacked any natural light. After visiting several below-the-surface establishments, I felt like a prairie dog, sticking my head up to peer around outside and then scurrying back to the cool below.

A few days later, we traveled to Alice Springs. For most tourists,

this is as much of the outback as they're likely to see. After Andamooka, it felt very civilized, with paved roads, clear signage, a
selection of restaurants, modern hotels, and gift shops galore—and
lots of tourists. Once we were in the area, we were never alone,
though we'd rented a car and drove to what we thought would be
pristine, uncrowded hiking areas. That, however, wasn't the case. I'd
been on less crowded trails back in New York.

Hiking around the Olgas was like walking on solid sand dunes,
rocks sculpted by millennia of strong winds. Along with crowds of
tourists we stood in perfect position to see Ayers Rock light up at
sunrise and sunset, going through a palette of colors from deepest
red to shimmering gold. While in town I bought several Aboriginal
paintings, each dot painting telling a story. Even with all of that, I
loved our time in Andamooka even more. I felt I'd had a tiny taste
of true Australian wilderness.

BARGAINING:
MOROCCO, 1988

At home, I'm not much of a shopper, but place me in a foreign market filled with handcrafted goods, and I become a fanatic. Morocco has a rich tradition of crafts, leather, metal, cloth, carpets, pottery, jewelry, and much more. On each

of my trips there, I spent a lot of time wandering through souks and medinas in search of craftspeople and their wares.

Early morning at the medina, the old central city of Fes, I passed through the ancient keyhole gates along with a dense throng of Moroccans and tourists. Inside the walls, there was little evidence of the 20th century. A world heritage site, this area of Fes is said to be the largest walled city on the globe and is car-free. Satellite dishes perched on the tops of the walls were the only things that appeared modern rather than at least a thousand years old. The narrow lanes create the largest maze imaginable. Without a guide, non-locals are certain to get lost.

In the cramped stone lanes, donkeys take precedence. "*Balek!*"

("watch out") shout the donkey tenders as they shove their way through the crowded alleyways. I learned to jump to the side the second I heard the unmistakable cry. If not, there was a high probability I'd get run over, or at least banged into by the donkey or his cargo. They stop for no one. The donkeys serve as the local Coca-Cola delivery vans, carry bales of wool, leather, and hay, rolls of copper, stacks of two-by-fours, wire mesh, cans of food, and boxes of unidentifiable goods. On my first trip to the old city, I didn't move away quickly enough and got my T-shirt streaked with red from a donkey laden with freshly dyed leather.

Later that day, on an official tour of the medina, with a guide and group, we were taken to fancy shops displaying carpets, jewelry, and leather, all at exorbitant prices.

"Best quality," repeated the guide over and over.

When no one seemed interested in buying anything, he changed his chant to "best price." No one believed him. All of us were convinced he'd get a sizable cut of any purchases. Though sometimes tempted by a handbag or a pair of earrings, I restrained myself, knowing I'd be in the city for a full week and could wander and bargain on my own.

The next morning, I decided to return alone and explore the medina. Within five minutes of entering the walls, I stopped at a jewelry shop. I'm fond of traditional handcrafted jewelry and own a large collection. That has never stopped me from acquiring more, often on the pretense of buying gifts. By American standards, the pieces were well priced, but knowing that all prices are negotiable, I only showed a smidgen of interest. I picked up a silver ring, tried it on, and put it back. I tried another ring with a lapis stone surrounded by elegant swirls, then repeated the try, put down, and move on with a couple of necklaces and pairs of earrings. The goal was not to appear serious about any single item, but to display an overall interest.

As I looked, the owner offered me mint tea. I accepted, and he sent out his young assistant to get a cup for me. We chatted as I sat, sipping the overly sweet tea.

"I like this ring," I said, pointing to one of the first I'd tried on. "How much is it?"

"Very good quality." He smiled. "You have good taste."

I knew that meant it would be expensive.

"Yes, it is beautiful. Also well made." I smiled back at him. This negotiation was going to be fun. "How much?"

"For you, good deal. One thousand dirhams."

I calculated the price in dollars, roughly $110. I pointed to another ring I'd been looking at. "And this one? How much?"

"Nice, but not so good quality."

"So, less expensive?"

"Nine hundred dirhams."

We played the game for about ten minutes, then I circled back to the lapis ring I really wanted. "Best price for this one?"

"Eight hundred."

"Too much. It's early morning, and there are lots of shops to look at." I started to get up and take my leave.

"None will have this ring, this good quality." He pulled out a calculator. "You pay me in dirhams or dollars?"

"Whichever you prefer."

"Fifty U.S. dollars."

"Forty and you have a sale." I shot him my broadest grin. "First sale of the day brings good luck, right?"

He nodded in agreement; we haggled a bit more and settled on $45. We were both happy. I slipped the ring onto my finger.

As I thanked him, delighted with my purchase, he asked, "Do you have a guide?"

When I told him no, he suggested that for ten dollars, his nephew and assistant, Said, could take me through the medina for the day. "Said speaks English well and can take you anywhere you want to see. Without him, you will get lost."

It turned out Said spoke English as well, if not better, than the official guides. He led me through the medina, venturing into tiny alleys and odd corners.

"How old are you, Said?"

"Fifteen."

"How did you learn to speak English so well?"

"In school. From my uncle. And movies. I love American movies."

"Oh, what are some of your favorites?"

"Any Schwarzenegger movie. And *Star Wars*." His smooth, boyish face, framed by a mane of lustrous black hair, blossomed into an enormous smile. "Action. Excitement. Fes is too old and sleepy."

When he learned I was from New York City, he became wistful. "Always I have wanted to visit that city. Many times, I have seen it in movies and TV. It is so exciting."

We stopped at a shop specializing in copper. Burnished tagine pots and kettles shimmered. Etched trays and bowls in sizes from miniature to large enough to cook an entire lamb were strewn on the ground in front of the shop. Mugs and pitchers dangled from an awning. I took dozens of photos, then entered the small shop. Said stood in a corner, ready to help with anything I needed. "What is this used for?" I asked him, pointing at a small deep pot with a long handle.

Said glanced up, as if trying to find the right word. He spoke in

Arabic with the owner for a minute. Then he said, "They are for boiling milk for coffee. We call them, how do you say, pixie pan?"

I had no idea what I'd do with a pixie pan, but they were irresistible. For almost nothing, I bought several.

"Let me carry." Said reached for the parcel. Then he turned the conversation back to New York City. "I have an uncle there. Someday I will visit him."

I hoped he would get the chance to see New York City. I could imagine him gazing at skyscrapers and wanting to see the sites he'd seen on-screen.

In another shop, I was drawn to a display case of intricate silver filigree jewelry. The shopkeeper, Ahmed, noticed my interest. He sat me on a tooled-leather hassock and signaled for his assistant to bring me mint tea. I suggested he also bring tea for Said. That surprised him, but he raised three fingers, indicating tea for all of us.

Then, one by one, he lifted necklaces out of the case and brought them over for me to inspect, all the while chatting me up.

Ahmed insisted I try on any necklace in which I showed even the slightest interest. When I had narrowed the choices to a couple, he commented, "That one—the color matches your eyes; it will attract every man you meet. And that one, it is very magnificent on you."

"Yes, they are very nice. How much are they?"

"Not so much. Not for someone from the United States."

"I wish I were, but I am not rich. How much?"

"You will wear it for the rest of your life!" Ahmed said emphatically.

We went on like this for several minutes before he finally named a price. I laughed, knowing that it was his starting offer, and that we had a long way to go before we settled on an amount agreeable to both of us.

"That is a beautiful blouse you are wearing."

So, we've moved on to flattery, I thought. The knit shirt was nothing special, ocean blue with a V-neck and a shirred waistband.

"Thank you," I said aloud.

"Really. It is lovely."

After another cup of mint tea, this time accompanied by sweet biscuits, a stroll to see what was in the other cases, and yet more flattery, we returned to negotiating.

"So, how much do you want to pay?"

When I gave my answer, it was Ahmed's turn to laugh.

An hour later, we had negotiated a price—a few dollars plus the blue knit shirt I was wearing. "My wife, she will love that shirt. She will treasure it, as you will treasure the necklace." As I had nothing else with me to wear, we arranged to meet later near my hotel.

After hours of walking, Said bid me goodbye at the keyhole gate. He said, "I enjoy this day. You are a good bargainer. And fun. And kind."

I returned the compliment. "You are an excellent guide." I wrote down my contact information. "I hope you will visit me. I'd like to show you my city."

His gorgeous smile returned. "One day, I will visit you in New York."

I doubted he would, but I would have loved to be a guide for him. I could imagine his excitement at seeing the city in person.

That evening, feeling as though I was a spy taking part in the exchange of state secrets, I met up with Ahmed, the jewelry store shopkeeper, outside my hotel. He led me a few blocks away to a small tea shop. Over still more mint tea, I slid the bag containing my blue shirt across to Ahmed. In return, he handed me a small, wrapped parcel. Neither of us said a word about the exchange, and neither of us opened the packages. We both knew the other would honor their part of the deal.

In Morocco and many other countries, bargaining is considered a social necessity, even a nicety. Americans, unused to this, are often daunted by this practice. Some believe it is rude to try to talk the seller's price down. Over many years, I have learned to bargain, making it a game where both the seller and I win. And the win is not only financial; it is one of learning about each other's culture and life. In bantering and bartering, our exchange enriches us.

INTO THE JUNGLE:
MALAYSIAN BORNEO, 1992

Borneo is an island shared by three countries, Indonesia, Malaysia, and the tiny sultanate of Brunei. On my fortieth birthday sabbatical, I spent two months in Indonesia, then headed to Borneo.

I'd been told Borneo was one of the most ecologically diverse

places on the planet, with thousands of plant species unique to the island. And, traveling into the jungle, I might get to see rare wildlife—proboscis monkeys, orangutans, macaques, and numerous bird species. It sounded wild, untamed, and untouristy. Exactly the kind of place I love.

I flew into Kuching in the Malaysian section of Borneo. Guidebooks indicated that the Malaysian part of the island was easier to get around than the Indonesian side, which remained wild with almost no hotels or other tourist facilities.

Exiting the plane, I walked into stupefying heat. I had sweat my way through Indonesia for two months, but that was nothing relative to the heat here. Borneo is mainly rugged, dense rain forest, much of it national parkland. Even when in the city, the humidity is high, converting the already-intense heat into a steam bath. While I was there, it rained for at least an hour every day, feeding the humidity.

While I generally prefer to stay at local hotels, the Hilton became my home base. My selection criteria were simple—pool, reliable air-conditioning, affordable.

The first afternoon I relaxed at the pool under the shade of an oversized umbrella, which protected me from direct rays of the blazing sun and periodic downpours. I occasionally slipped into the bathtub-warm pool. A waiter came by, offering a variety of drinks. All I wanted was water, lots of it.

I was surprised that almost everyone around me spoke German. Later, at dinner, the hotel menu listed typical international fare, plus some Chinese dishes and a couple of local specialties. But there was also a wide offering of wiener schnitzel, multiple varieties of sausages and sauerkraut, spaetzle, and other German foods. I hadn't met many Germans while traveling through neighboring Indonesia and wondered why this particular spot was such an attraction. I never did find out.

Early the next morning, a local guide met me for a tour of the city and a jungle walk. Yi-Ling was part of the Chinese diaspora that settled in Malaysia. She was a college student studying tourism, and her English was flawless. As we toured Kuching—including its vibrant Chinatown—and then drove to the rain forest, she told me about her personal history. Both sets of grandparents came in the early 20th century to farm, believing the prospects for advancement would be better in Malaysia than in China. They wanted their children to have more opportunities and made sure they got an education. Yi-Ling's father was an accountant, and her mother a secretary. The parallels between her history and my own surprised me, though it shouldn't have. Our geography and ethnicities were different, but our grandparents' motivations were the same, a better life for themselves and their children.

We stayed in the air-conditioned comfort of the car as we leisurely wended our way through the city. "Kuching," Yi-Ling told me, "is known as 'cat city.' That's a translation from Sarawak [one of the indigenous languages]. No one is quite sure what the connection of cats is to the city, but you'll see cat statues and tributes everywhere." She pointed out several as we drove past. The city was filled with mosques, Buddhist temples, and churches, displaying the diversity of the population. Markets were bustling in the early morning, the coolest part of the day. Each time I exited the car to take a photo or walk around, the heat was like a wet sheet dropped onto my body.

Leaving the city, we entered an intense green world. We pulled onto a small gravel patch bordering an area that looked identical to the landscape we'd been passing through. Nothing indicated it was a trailhead. Getting out of the car, my glasses fogged. After cleaning them, I peered and peered but couldn't see a break in the dense jungle.

"Where are we walking?" I asked.

Yi-Ling pulled out a short machete with a lethal-looking blade. She pointed the tip. "Right there. We must be the first ones here today. Overnight, the growth tends to camouflage the entrance to the path."

With that, she began to hack at the foliage. It didn't take much for a bright marker to appear. We were indeed at the trailhead. The forest floor had been covered with pebbles and mulch to try to inhibit plants from overtaking the trail. They weren't very effective. Yi-Ling frequently had to slash our way through the vegetation. I felt a bit like Hansel and Gretel following a narrow trail of pebbled breadcrumbs. The growth was so thick and so green that we couldn't have strayed off the trail even if we had wanted to.

As instructed, I wore a long-sleeve cotton shirt and long pants to protect me from sun and insects. Within ten minutes, there wasn't a dry patch on my body. My clothes clung to my sticky body and looked as though they'd come out of a washing machine.

We didn't speak. Yi-Ling led; I trailed behind. Despite the discomfort, I marveled at the impenetrable tunnel of green, the elephantine fronds, variety of plants, and rich earthy scent of growth and decay. We could hear the clack and buzz of insects and the occasional movement of animals. Yi-Ling said they were proboscis monkeys, but they were deep in the jungle, so we didn't see one clearly.

I've been in rain forests in Costa Rica, Australia, New Zealand, and Puerto Rico, but none of them compared to the lush, damp, overpowering presence of this jungle. I could easily imagine Tarzan, Jane, and Cheetah here, though we were on the wrong continent.

After about an hour, we arrived at a lake with a sandy beach encircled by the jungle. Following Yi-Ling's lead, I took off my shoes and jumped into the water with all my clothes on. By that point, they were so wet it didn't make any difference. The water was warm and clear and helped to bring down my feverish feeling. Our pace was slower on our return, as we slogged along.

"What happens if we meet people heading in?" I asked. There was only enough space for us to walk single file.

"I'll hack out a niche for us to stand in as they pass."

Back at the hotel, my face reflected in the mirror was flame red. I hadn't gotten sunburned—little direct light penetrated the forest canopy—but I was near heat exhaustion. I stood under a cold shower until my body cooled down. For the remainder of the day, I read and napped in my blissfully air-conditioned room.

Two days later, I departed for an overnight tour to a remote Dayak (a local ethnic group) village. I'm always curious about how people live, and this promised to be a unique experience. The trip brochure explained that as many as thirty families used to live together under the same longhouse roof. That's no longer the case— each family has its own home—but the longhouse is where the community gathers for ceremonies and celebrations. We'd get to spend time with the villagers, and we'd sleep in the longhouse.

A van picked me up at the hotel. Three other intrepid single travelers, all German, had signed up for the excursion. We drove through the city and onto newly paved roads leading into the countryside. On some roads, we could smell asphalt, an indication of the recency of construction. The signs of human habitation diminished with each passing mile, until we were into thickly forested areas and then jungle. The Germans occasionally made some remark I didn't understand, but mostly we were riveted by the scenery. After an hour or so, the driver pulled off into a small, paved parking area.

"Take everything with you," he said. He'd been silent throughout the drive, eyes intent on the road before us. When he spoke, I'd expected to hear German, given the other passengers and what I'd heard at the hotel. But no, he spoke in English. Everyone understood him.

He unlocked a waiting Land Rover, and we piled in. The roads on the next section were due to be paved and gave an indication of what had surely been the state of the roads we'd just driven on prior to their recent paving. We drove at a snail's pace, up and over rutted muddy trails onto which the jungle was encroaching. A couple of times, the driver stopped, got out, and whacked at branches impeding forward movement. After about an hour, we arrived at a small dock by the edge of a tributary of the Sarawak River. We hadn't covered much distance.

Until the new roads had been built, the drive from Kuching would have taken a full day, rather than a couple of hours. Without a motorized vehicle, this trip would have been nearly impossible. I began to think about isolated villages in Asia and Africa that had only been exposed to the world in the mid-1950s. What a shock that must have been for both explorers and villagers—meeting people in the 20th century who'd lived the same way for hundreds or thousands of years. While I would never have been brave enough to do it, I like to imagine traveling with Richard Burton (the explorer, not the actor) or David Livingstone.

We transferred from the Rover to a small single-engine motorboat at a dock. The driver introduced us to a man I guessed to be in his forties and a member of the community we were about to visit.

"This is Joe. He'll be taking care of you until I meet you back here tomorrow."

Joe, I thought. *I don't think so.* I recollected the many people I'd met around the world who'd simplified their names to make it easier for foreigners to remember. While I understood the logic, it seemed to take away their true identity. I was meeting Joe the tour guide, not the person he was around the village and with his family.

Joe was ruddy, barefoot, and bare-chested with a sarong-like cloth wrapped and tied at his waist. He wore a baseball cap, no doubt a gift from previous tourists.

"Let's get going," he said in English.

We puttered off in the boat with the swift current moving us quickly downstream. Mesmerized by the mountains in the distance, trees, grasses, occasional sandy beaches, and birds, we watched quietly, taking it in. One of the Germans pulled out a fancy-looking camera with a long telephoto lens. He clicked away with abandon at things I didn't see.

Joe pulled the motorboat over at a sandy beach, where two carved dugout canoes floated and another man awaited us.

"Last part of the trip. The rest of the way, we paddle."

The water ahead flowed quickly but was shallow; hence the dugouts. With a steadying hand from Joe to balance myself, I managed to safely sit down on the dugout's low bench. The current and a few deft strokes to steer us got us to the village within minutes.

While waiting for our backpacks to be taken from the boats, I looked around the village. A massive building on stilts dominated an area that had been cleared of vegetation. This was the village's longhouse. It was unadorned wood with a tin roof, unlike the ornately decorated buildings I'd seen in Indonesia. There were smaller buildings surrounding it where I assumed the villagers now lived. The avid photographer had slipped in a new roll of film and was furiously shooting as if he had to capture it before it disappeared.

"Are you a journalist?" I asked him.

"*Nein.*" He shook his head. "Sorry, no." He shot a few more pictures. "Photo crazy."

I gazed in the direction he'd been aiming his camera. Past the houses, I could see people working in fields. In the far distance was a wall of green. Remembering my experience in the jungle, I wondered how they managed to keep the vegetation from overtaking the cultivated land. It had to be a constant battle. It was interesting, but to my eye, not worth a roll of film.

Before I got to ask him anything else, a woman who looked to be about my age, with creamy brown skin, wearing a cotton shirt and skirt, beaded necklace, and armful of bracelets, walked in our direction. She carried a woven straw tray with steaming cups. In heavily accented English, she said, "Welcome," and offered us each a cup. The woman gestured for us to drink. A welcome drink is a tradition I've experienced in all corners of the world. I had no idea what was in the cup but knew I'd have to drink it, or it would be considered an offense. The floral taste was unfamiliar, slightly sweet but not from sugar or honey. I hoped I wouldn't get sick from drinking the liquid.

We stood around awkwardly smiling at her and each other waiting for our guide, Joe, to reappear.

"Come. Come. I will show you where you will sleep," Joe said as he led us to a series of rooms. They were clean and basic; each had a bed, chair, a nightstand with a lantern atop, a bug repellent coil, and a box of matches. He showed us Western-style bathrooms, including modern toilets and showers, which surprised me. Then again, whoever had helped them organize tours had probably told them it would be necessary. I wouldn't have cared. In fact, staying in what seemed like a youth hostel seemed a bit like cheating. This wouldn't exactly be an authentic experience. However, it was comfortable.

Once settled in, Joe took us for a tour of the village. Along the way, we stopped to see the fields where crops were growing that I couldn't identify and Joe couldn't translate. With the oppressive heat and humidity, plants surely thrived. I thought if I sat down for an hour and looked closely, it would be like time-lapse photography. I'd be able to see them grow an inch or two and sprout new leaves.

There were chicken and pig pens. Near the river, we were shown how a dugout canoe is made. The canoe was sculpted with a metal chisel, which made me suspect they did a fair bit of trading with city dwellers.

Then came the demonstration touted in the tour description as most representative of the Dayak, the use of a blowgun. Joe explained that these guns weren't often used now for hunting but that as part of a rite of passage, young men learned to use one. The blowgun was a narrow tube, about three feet long, made from wood. One end was carved to form a mouthpiece. When used for hunting, the darts, made from what looked like thick quills, were tipped with poison. Joe passed the blowgun around. It was difficult for me to fully comprehend how something so insubstantial looking could be lethal. It was as if a kid's slingshot could be used to bring down bears.

While Joe explained, a bare-chested young man with tattoos snaking up his back and around his muscled shoulders held another blowgun and demonstrated. He took a deep breath, then forcefully blew into the tube. The dart flew out and soared across the field.

"Do you want to try?" Joe asked the group.

One burly guy enthusiastically raised his hand. He confidently held the blowgun and tried to replicate what he'd seen. The dart fell to his feet. On his second attempt, it went only a smidge farther. What had appeared so simple when the Dayak youth had demonstrated it clearly required skill and a lot of practice. Even with several tries each, none of us was able to get the dart to fly more than a few feet.

We returned to our rooms to prepare for dinner. What that meant was changing to long-sleeved shirts, slacks, and dousing ourselves in bug spray. Bugs were fierce at sunset.

Dinner was filling, if mysterious. There was chicken in a stew made with vegetables I couldn't identify. What I noticed more than the taste was the texture. The stew had softened veggies, crunchy ones, and chewy ones. I think of stews as overcooked foods, so this amalgam of consistencies was a pleasant surprise. Accompanying the stew were fried vegetable patties that had an earthy taste, as if filled with mushrooms, though I didn't see any.

I asked my travel companions if they knew what any of the vegetables were. The three conferred in German.

One said to me, "Most we don't know. This one"—he pointed to a purplish medallion—"might be a type of a carrot."

I speared what he had pointed to and carefully bit into it. It wasn't like any carrot I'd ever eaten. "Maybe," I said. "In any event, it tastes good. I like the crunch."

"Crunch?" He looked at me quizzically.

"The texture. It kind of snaps when you bite into it."

"Oh, I see. Crunch. I didn't know that word. It's *knirschen*." He snapped his jaws a couple of times to demonstrate.

That little exchange led to an ongoing conversation over dinner. I asked why they'd come to Borneo.

"I got a good airfare," one said.

"Me too," said another.

"I'm traveling for several months in Asia, and I'd never been here, so . . ."

"Will you also go to Indonesia?" I asked.

All three said they'd only be traveling in Malaysia. Though I prodded more into their reasons, I never really understood the German influx in Malaysia and the dearth of German travelers in Indonesia.

After dinner, we were each handed a small cup with what I feared would be firewater.

"This is *tuak*," Joe told us. "It's made from rice."

I took a shallow sip. The drink was mild, slightly sweet, and seemed to have a low alcohol content.

"If you are brave"—Joe showed us another bottle—"try this." The green bottle had no markings on it, so this, too, was a home brew. "This is *langkau*. Much more alcohol." He poured a smidgen into each outstretched cup.

One sip caused nearly everyone to gasp or cough. I could feel the liquid burning its way through my system. I switched back to tuak.

After dinner, we were led to the main part of the longhouse. We sat in a row on straw mats. The waning sun filtered through open slits. Burning torches had been strategically placed to light the central area. The Dayak community filed in, about forty people, and sat opposite us. Directly across from our small group was an older couple adorned with tattoos of birds and leaves. They wore feathered headdresses. I wondered if they were community leaders or simply respected elders. The woman had a sweet smile and shyly waved at us. I waved back and wished I could speak with her. No doubt she'd seen her world change dramatically; it would have been wonderful to hear her speak about those changes. But without a common language, that wasn't possible. Joe wasn't nearby, or I would have engaged him to help translate.

Instead of intimate conversations, we saw a performance. There was dancing and music and a melodic recitation. The musicians and dancers showed a lot of skin, everyone inked with sprawling tattoos that wound around arms and necks. There were drums, bells, and a lute-like stringed instrument. I didn't know what to expect. Once they began playing, I found it soothing and almost trance-inducing.

Between the music and alcohol, I slept well that night, lulled by the sound of rustling leaves and flowing water from the nearby river.

Early the following morning, Joe led us on a walk into the jungle. This time I was prepared for the heat, the need for a machete to hack through the dense growth, and the constant chittering of bugs. We were looking for wildlife: orangutans, birds, frogs, lizards, and the area's rare pigs, leopards, and pygmy elephants. We heard birds but spotted nothing except lush foliage. Joe described some of the uses for the plants we saw, including medicine, food, and building materials. His explanations were long-winded.

I tuned out and turned my attention to the appearance of the vegetation. Ireland is known as the Emerald Isle, but in the Borneo jungle, there were many dozens of shades of green, from the palest mint to olive, hunter, lime, and more. I couldn't possibly have named them all. Similarly, the structure of the plants, shapes of the leaves and seeds, fruits, and flowers all seemed new.

Standing in the jungle, listening to unfamiliar bird calls, surrounded by little that looked familiar, I felt a thrill as if I were an explorer. This world seemed untamed, new, and full of possibilities. As a New York City native, this was an unaccustomed feeling. It was one I liked a lot.

Back in Kuching, I luxuriated in the swimming pool and air-conditioned hotel. The contrast between the "modern" world and the world of the Dayak was stark. I ruminated about how little of the world remained wild and untainted. Even our overnight stay at the village must have an impact, especially on the younger members of the tribe.

The road being paved to make the trip to the village faster would dramatically change their world. It would allow them access to medical care, schools, and material goods. How much of their traditional life could they hold onto? How much would they want to hold onto?

THE UNEXPECTED:
TASMANIA, AUSTRALIA, 1994

When I traveled internationally for business, I typically took a few extra days to explore. Sometimes I had specific destinations in mind. At other times, my travel plans were by whim or based on  recommendations from colleagues. Often, an administrative assistant arranged for my flights, rental car, and hotels.

In 1994, I flew to Australia three times. On my third visit to Melbourne for a large financial institution, I decided to explore Tasmania, known for being a mix of bucolic and wild environments.

For four days, I explored from my base in Hobart, Tasmania's capital and largest city, but in reality, more like a small town. It felt more British than anywhere else I'd been to in Australia. Teashops, cafés, and pubs were plentiful. Gardens filled with roses and other imported flowers had a distinctly English look. The port—the city's main economic driver—was busy with freighters as well as pleasure and fishing boats.

One morning I drove through apple orchards and farms that had more than a passing resemblance to the English countryside, to the original British penal colony, Port Arthur. Built during the 18th century, it was a grim, eerie place set amid a gorgeous landscape surrounded by water. Its history was brutal, with rampant starvation, cruel punishment, and little chance of prisoners ever seeing freedom. Learning that juvenile convicts, some as young as nine, lived in the same conditions and were used in hard labor nearly made me ill. I recalled hearing that Australia's independent spirit, machismo, and defiance of rules stemmed from the population's origins as convicts and rule breakers. Understanding Port Arthur's history, this made sense to me.

I'd hoped to see a Tasmanian devil, which I'd been introduced to as a *Looney Tunes* cartoon character. A pair at the Sydney Zoo had fascinated me. About the size of a cocker spaniel, they are the largest carnivorous marsupial. They appeared cute when their mouths were closed, but could be menacing when their powerful jaws were open.

There are many natural areas near Hobart. The descriptions of the trails tempted me, though knowing about the ferocity of Tasmanian devils made me consider the wisdom of hiking solo. Then I remembered they are nocturnal.

My final day was spent hiking in a nearby park, dwarfed by towering, pungent eucalyptus trees and ancient conifers. While the dense vegetation blocked out most direct sunlight, in areas of sun there were native flowers completely unfamiliar to me. The walk was slow as I watched my footing, snapped photos, and appreciated the majestic scenery. Only a few other people were on the trail, which led to a waterfall. Looking at the thundering cascade, I slipped and became covered in a layer of mud.

I arrived at the airport hotel (I was flying out early the next morning), dirty and sweaty. When I told the desk clerk my name, he looked up my reservation. He looked at me, then looked again at the reservation.

"Are you sure you want this room?"

"Is there some reason I wouldn't want it?"

"It's quite expensive."

I looked at the reservation. The price seemed reasonable. "It's fine."

"Well, okay. Enjoy it." He said this with a hint of a giggle in his voice. I wondered what I was getting myself into.

When I unlocked the door and walked in, I knew why the clerk had been skeptical. The admin had booked the hotel's best suite— three bedrooms and bathrooms and an immense living room / dining room. The table held an enormous bowl of fruit and a bottle of wine.

Too bad I hadn't made a lot of friends while in Tasmania.

LIFE AFTER THE SOVIETS:
HUNGARY AND THE CZECH REPUBLIC, 1994

The Soviet Union collapsed in 1991. I was curious to see how member nations of the bloc were adapting to their new reality. My friend Linda and I decided to visit the Czech Republic and Hungary.

I imagined Hungary represented one place where the change was most welcome. It was one of the first countries to break away from the Soviet Union and had quickly and peacefully transitioned to a democratic government. Our experiences there confirmed that. People were friendly and optimistic about their personal prospects and the future of their country.

In 1993, Czechoslovakia split into two independent countries, the Czech Republic and Slovakia. The population was dealing with two major changes: the move from communism to capitalism and the split from Slovakia. I didn't know what we would find there.

In Budapest, musicians fiddled cheerful tunes in many restaurants and almost everywhere we walked. People were celebrating their newfound freedoms by starting small businesses. The bright colors of Easter decorations adorned the hotel, shop fronts, and outdoor vendors, who were doing a brisk business selling hand-painted eggs and plush bunnies. Frolicking dogs bounded joyfully through parks and accompanied their owners to restaurants and on trams. Linda, who owned a Dalmatian, was delighted to say hello to dozens of her dog's distant relatives.

When we arrived at the Gellert Baths, an ornate, tiled, must-see attraction, the woman at the front desk explained the procedure to us in a mixture of broken English and pantomime. Then she handed us each a locker key and a small square towel. I assumed the towel was for washing. But when we got into the locker room, other women were modestly holding the towel in front of their genitals or, if they didn't mind walking around nude, on their heads. It was, it seemed, the only towel we would have to dry ourselves off with. We followed their lead and wore it on our heads to keep it dry while freeing our hands to grasp the railing to enter the deep, hot pool. Once in the soothing bathwater, anyone who spoke a smidgen of English waded over to chat with us. They wanted to hear both about America and our impressions of their city. I couldn't miss the sense of glittery optimism that surrounded everything and everyone.

After visiting Hungary, we headed to Prague. From the moment we got there, the vibe was noticeably different. We'd reserved a couple of nights at a hotel the Russians had previously managed. It maintained a bleak grayness, and the staff displayed a total lack of interest in serving guests.

"We'd like to take a walking tour of the city," I said to the hotel's concierge. Without a word, he shoved a map across the desk. I showed him my guidebook, and he yanked the map back.

"Are there any organized walking tours?" He gave me a blank stare as if he didn't understand what I was saying or he'd never been asked such a strange question. I knew he spoke English as I'd heard him speak fluently with another guest.

"Would it be possible to hire a guide?" Another blank stare.

I turned to Linda. "Come on, let's go wander." At that, the corners of the concierge's mouth turned fractionally upward. He'd gotten rid of us without needing to say a word.

Baroque statues, red-tiled roofs, domes and ornate spires atop wedding cake buildings, and a castle looking as if it had come straight from *Cinderella* make Prague look like a fairy-tale city come to life. The Vltava River runs through the city center, crossed by a series of stone bridges. As we stood on the Charles Bridge, taking in the dazzling view, a middle-aged woman in a drab, shapeless mud-brown coat approached us.

"First time in Prague?" she asked in heavily accented English. Her voice was low and raspy.

"Yes."

"Would you like me to show you around? I am a professor of history at the university, and I have lived here my whole life."

Wow, I thought. A fabulous guide has magically materialized. I couldn't believe our luck. I looked over at Linda, but before we responded, she added, "I will show you all the sights and explain them to you. Twenty U.S. dollars." Her mouth drew into a tight smile as she waited expectantly.

That seemed reasonable to me. Linda and I agreed to have her take us around.

She took off at a brisk pace. "This bridge is one of the iconic sights in Prague. It was built in the 14th century. It took forty-five years to build and was the only bridge over the Vltava until the mid-1800s." Rattling off dates and people and places, she talked as she walked, never looking at either of us.

"What is your name?" I finally interjected.

"Vera." She didn't ask our names and continued with her lecture.

A few minutes later, I interrupted again. "Vera, I'd like to stop for a moment and take some photos."

"If you must."

After an hour of walking and recitation, my head was filled with information I knew I'd immediately forget. I never was much good with memorization and didn't really care about the historical details. I'm more of a headlines kind of person, and then I want to observe for myself. What I was curious about was how Vera was coping with the changes in her country. I tentatively asked, "How have things changed over the last few years? Prague has certainly been through a lot."

That ended the history lecture and set off a torrent of complaints. "This has been very bad for many, many people. We have become a country of paupers. Prices have gone up, and everything is too expensive." She scowled, then growled, "The government doesn't care about anyone on a fixed income. Prices keep going up. Everything is too expensive," she repeated. "As a university professor, I should be prosperous. I am not. Why else do you think I am doing this?" Her scowl deepened into an angry frown.

Linda asked, "So things were better for you before the country left the Soviet Union?" I could tell she was trying to be as neutral as possible.

"Yes," Vera replied emphatically. "Not great. But I understood how the system worked." With that, she turned, motioned for us to follow, and we were off to another site.

When we passed a shop filled with marionettes, I stopped to look more closely. Vera didn't even glance back to see if we were following, so I reluctantly tore myself away and trotted to catch up. Our next stop was the famed astronomical clock in the Old Town Hall square. Vera talked at great length about the beautiful, intricate work of art built in the 1300s. "But the clock is cursed," she said, "like all of Prague is now." She interwove the clock's macabre history with more complaints about everything she disliked about the new government. She finished with, "Watch carefully now. When the hour strikes, a skeleton will emerge to ring his own death knell."

Linda and I were both glad to end the tour and take off on our own. Vera's doom and gloom wasn't a tone we wanted to be around for very long.

Strolling through the old part of town, we admired the architecture. Hearing music, we entered a stunning Baroque church a few minutes before a free concert started. It was enthralling; superb musicians played a Mozart string quartet. Swept away by the music, I closed my eyes and imagined a well-dressed audience from the 1700s sitting around me. Afterward, we window-shopped displays of marionettes, fine crystal, and jewelry. I kept thinking about Vera and imagining her disapproval of our capitalist tendencies.

We'd only reserved two nights at the hotel. When we asked to stay for a couple more days, the price they quoted was almost twice what we had been paying. The next morning, we visited the tourist office to reserve new lodgings.

After waiting in line for a long time, while we watched lackadaisical clerks manage other tourists in slow motion, we finally stood in front of an older woman. She could have been Vera's sister; she had the same pasty complexion, shapeless clothes, and hangdog look.

"We need to find a room for a couple of nights."

"None are available."

"In all of Prague, there are no rooms?"

"Busy tourist season. No rooms." She started to shoo us away and was signaling for the next person to come over.

"Okay then. We want to get to Karlovy Vary. What is the best way to get there?"

"Take a tour." She reached down and slid a brochure across the counter.

"Thanks, but we've got a hotel reservation there on Wednesday. We just need transportation."

"Take a bus."

"Which one? Do you have a schedule?"

She took back the tour brochure and again reached beneath the counter. "This has schedule." With a sigh, she handed over a badly printed sheet of paper with information in Czech.

I glanced at it, and with some effort, saw a bus number and times. "Where do we catch it?" My patience was wearing thin.

This time, we received a map. "Here." She pointed.

I circled the spot with a pen. "How much is the fare and how do we pay for it?"

She rolled her eyes and sighed. It was clear we were making her do her job, and she didn't want to.

After extracting the information we needed, we left the counter. Instead of calling over the next person, she put up a sign in front of her station. I guessed she needed a break to rest after her exertions.

A man approached us as we exited the tourist office. "Do you need lodging?" he asked.

"Yes, we do," Linda and I said in unison.

"The tourist office is the wrong place to find a room." The man cracked the first genuine smile I'd seen on a Czech citizen since we arrived. "I can help you." And he did. We arranged for lodgings in a private home in center city at a reasonable price. We'd meet him the next morning in front of the tourist office with our luggage, and he'd take us there. I was a bit leery about this plan but couldn't think of what else to do.

That day, we heard two more concerts and strolled through the city. In the old Jewish quarter, we explored the Old New Synagogue, built in the 13th century. It was one of the few synagogues to survive the Nazis. The Gothic interior, with vaulted ceilings, tiled floors, and candelabra, was still being restored. After, as we sat at a café resting, I people watched. It was easy to tell tourists from natives. The tourists were far better dressed. But even more than that, locals' faces looked fatigued and drawn, as if life was an extreme burden. Were they disillusioned and negative about the political and economic transition like Vera? Were their lives truly worse now than before the revolution? What would it take for things to improve? I had no answers, only a lot of questions.

When we arrived at the tourist office the next morning, our smiling "arranger" was there to greet us. We walked down a few cobblestoned streets, our rolling bags thumping. Turning down a street of buildings with elaborate facades, we stopped in front of one.

"Here we are. Mrs. Horak lives on the third floor." He grabbed our bags and walked up the steps to the front door. "Sorry, there is no elevator."

Another Vera clone opened the apartment door, a glowering scowl on her face. She allowed us to enter, then carefully locked the door. A lengthy conversation, of which we didn't understand a word, followed.

"Mrs. Horak has a few rules she wants you to obey." With that, he launched into a lengthy list of what we could and could not do in the apartment. We'd be sleeping in two narrow beds shoved up against one wall of the already overfilled living room. Breakfast would be between seven and seven thirty. We must leave by ten in the morning on departure day. "Shower quickly. Water is very expensive."

After he had us repeat all the rules and Mrs. Horak nodded her grudging approval, he handed us a set of keys and took his leave, saying, "Have a pleasant stay." I somehow guessed we wouldn't.

The enormous living room was filled with elegant furniture. In one étagère, crystal glasses and decanters sparkled. Another had porcelain figurines. The paintings on the walls were framed in ornate gold. But the room was dark, lit only by bulbs that couldn't have been over forty watts. I guessed that Mrs. Horak had once been quite wealthy, but her circumstances had worsened. I understood why she wasn't happy about having two strangers camping out in her home.

We got out of there as quickly as possible, spending the day roaming around. We saw a matinee of a shortened *Marriage of Figaro* performed by marionettes. It was enchanting. After that, I had to buy a marionette as a souvenir. In pursuit of the perfect puppet, we spent hours in shops selling them. I finally decided on a smiling chef. He was cheerful, even if the shop proprietor wasn't.

After dinner, we returned to Mrs. Horak's apartment. At night, with the curtains drawn, the room was dark and gloomy, the dim bulbs providing barely enough light to prepare for bed. Linda and I spoke to each other in hushed tones, trying not to disturb our hostess. We went to sleep early, there being no possibility of reading.

We ate the breakfast Mrs. Horak served, then went out for a real breakfast. One slice of toast with a thin layer of jam and watery coffee for which she had no milk didn't cut it.

We still had one more day in Prague and another night in the bleak apartment. We were anxious to leave for the spa town of

Karlovy Vary. Our guidebook gushed about the town's beauty, the healing properties of the waters from over eighty springs, and the charming architecture.

Despite the horrible directions from the tourist office, we located the bus stop. The two-hour drive took us through small towns and winding hills adorned with trees in various stages of new foliage and budding spring flowers.

After dropping our bags at the hotel, another leftover from the Soviet era, we headed out. We quickly got our bearings; Karlovy Vary is shaped like a T, formed by the meeting of the Teplá and Ohře Rivers. Beautiful, narrow buildings lined the rivers, framed by hills in the background covered in pink and red trees. Other than the hills, it reminded me of Amsterdam. In areas of the river, the springs burst up, jets of water shooting high into the air, shrouding the riverbanks in steam.

The healing waters were free. You only needed to bring a container. Shops sold special "spa cups." Tourists walked through the streets clutching the porcelain cups designed with a handle and spout and stopped at each water source to imbibe small sips. It was like doing a walking water tasting.

Several fountains were highly embellished, others simple faucets. The only difference I could detect in the water was the temperature. People come to the town to treat gastrointestinal diseases, metabolic disorders, and periodontal problems. As I suffered from none of those, I had no idea if the water had any effect. Still, it was like going on a treasure hunt to find all the public water sources.

One thing I most wanted to do was to go for a soak in the waters, which the guidebook claimed was a noteworthy, relaxing experience. I recalled how much fun we'd had in the Gellert Baths in Budapest and looked forward to interacting with Czech locals.

However, the guidebook didn't provide information on where to do this.

At the front desk, I inquired about the baths. The clerk gave me a blank stare. "I've been told it is possible to soak in the waters," I repeated.

"You can drink water. Fountains are everywhere." His look conveyed, *You're an idiot. Anyone can find the mineral waters.*

Linda chimed in, "No, not to drink. We know about that. We want to go into a spa for the baths."

"No spas open."

"In Karlovy Vary, there are no spas? I thought that's what you're famous for."

"Yes, there are spas. But not open."

"None of them are open?" I asked, feeling as though we were edging into Kafka territory.

"Not for you."

"That seems odd," Linda said. She tried to butter up the glum man. "This is such a beautiful place and has such a great reputation. We'd hate to miss out on something so famous as the baths." She went on like that, explaining how lovely the setting was and how exciting it was to be in such a historic place.

"Maybe I can find one," he grudgingly admitted and wandered off to chat with a coworker.

When he returned, he handed Linda a slip of paper. "Go here." Then he turned and walked off before we could ask for directions.

We located the imposing building and headed in. At the reception area, we stood while a woman in uniform sat behind her desk reading. She didn't look up. We politely cleared our throats. We lightly knocked on the top of the desk. She studiously avoided us. After a minute or two of being ignored, I said, "Pardon me."

No response.

Linda looked in our phrase book and, reading the phonetics, said, "*Promiňte.*"

The woman looked up.

After many frustrating minutes of hunting for phrases, butchering them even with the phonetics, she scribbled a number on a small square pad. She ripped off the page, handed it to us, and went back to reading.

"*Děkuji vám.*" ("Thank you.")

A ghost of a smile flashed on her face.

"Okay, now we hunt for room 98."

The halls, set up in labyrinth fashion, were deserted. Each room had a number etched into a glass panel. The first floor went sequentially to thirty. The second and third floors had what appeared to be random numbers: 37 was next to 84, 102 next to 46. Hard as we tried, we couldn't find 98. We returned to the front desk.

The woman was still reading, and once again, it took effort to get her attention. More butchered phrases led to her snatching the paper, turning it over, and underlining the number so that it now read 86. She returned to her book.

After a half hour, we gave up. The spa town had no spa, at least not for unwanted tourists. I gained a new understanding and appreciation of Kafka's writings.

We spent the remainder of the day walking in a nearby park, happy to be in nature and away from a populace that seemed in need of therapy and antidepressants.

As we waited for the return bus to Prague, we stood next to an American couple. As chatty Americans always seem to do, we got into a conversation about our impressions and experiences traveling.

"The biggest disappointment," the woman said, "was that we couldn't find the baths."

"Neither did we," I said. "We had difficulty getting anyone to tell us where to look."

The couple smiled in recognition. "Did you go to that strange building with all the numbers?"

"Oh yeah, 98."

The man cut me off, "Then 86."

"Oh my God, they must do that to every tourist who enters the building."

"Or at least every American."

We all burst into such loud guffaws that people stared at us. Other tourists laughed or smiled, getting infected by our laughter. Czechs stared and glared at us.

THE RICHEST OF ALL:
VIENNA, 1994

Hungary and the Czech Republic had recently broken away from the Soviet Union. Our visit there demonstrated how differently those two countries were dealing with their newfound independence.

That hadn't been Austria's history. I assumed correctly that it would present a very different demeanor. My friend Linda and I arrived in Vienna via a ferry on the Danube. Looking from the boat, the city glittered, unlike Budapest and Prague, which were repainting and repairing after decades of neglect. I'd never seen so many golden roofs.

O n our first afternoon, we walked through the city. The imperial squares lived up to their majestic heritage. Large, highly embellished buildings dominated them, surrounded by pristine landscaping. Endless marble sculptures of heroic figures were a counterpoint to the golden roofs. Every government office, museum, and park was impeccably maintained. We entered several baroque churches and gaped at their ornate interiors. Paintings and stained-glass windows dominated, and between them, golden gewgaws covered every surface.

Men and women alike were well dressed. Most of the women

wore expensive-looking jewelry. Even their dogs, and there were many, looked perfectly groomed. Shop windows were showcases filled with appealing merchandise. After the paucity of goods in Prague, this was especially noticeable.

Despite the beauty, something set me on edge. Wearing jeans and a T-shirt, I could almost feel disapproving eyes on me. As I looked at the people passing by, I viewed anyone who appeared to be in their sixties or seventies with suspicion. I couldn't get it out of my head that they might have been Nazis or Nazi sympathizers. They all seemed to have self-satisfied looks and to be staring at me, aware that I am Jewish. The Austrians had welcomed the Nazis. Nearly every Jew in the country had been killed during World War II. I told myself not to be paranoid.

By late afternoon we were dragging and needed a pick-me-up. The guidebook directed us to Café Mozart, a renowned patisserie. The sun was setting as we arrived, lighting up the windows. Stepping through the door was like entering a different era. The elegance of the city was on steroids in Café Mozart. The wooden tables and counter gleamed with a patina of age and constant scrubbing. Gold chandeliers dangled from the ceiling. Mirrors reflected their light and the stream of sunlight through the front window, setting the shop aglow. Jewel-like pastries were displayed as if Tiffany's had arranged them.

As in the rest of the city, the clientele was well dressed and prosperous-looking. There was an overabundance of older couples. I wanted to back out, sure that my casual attire and Jewishness were unwelcome. But Linda forged ahead, drawn to the aroma of coffee and freshly baked pastries, and I followed her in.

We paused by the large glass display case. I wondered how anyone ever decided which one to choose. There were fruit tortes, cream and chocolate cakes, cookies, powdered sugar donuts, as well as a selection of chocolates. Each was tempting and looked to provide caloric overload. That said, I figured we'd walked enough so that I could afford to eat at least one of these rich treats.

As we stood gawping, a waiter came over and directed us to a table. A good-looking young man with blond hair and strong features, his name tag read Franz. I thought of Franz Kafka. Then I thought of Nazi youth. "I must get this out of my head," I repeated to myself. But stories I'd read about Holocaust atrocities in Austria kept intruding. The truth was the young waiter was charming and could speak a little English.

"You are American?" he asked.

"Yes," I stammered, willing myself to stop thinking about Nazis.

"Where in America?"

"I'm from New York City."

"Oh, how wonderful. It is a great city." His expression was one of genuine delight, and a trace of my anxiety melted away.

Linda took over the conversation. "I'm from Washington, D.C.," she said. "We just arrived and were told we had to visit Café Mozart."

He said, "A good choice. Our bakers are the best in Vienna." He handed us menus. "You must try the *apfelstrudel*. It is our specialty."

Apple strudel, I thought. *No.* Growing up, my grandmother baked something she called strudel. It was a horrible concoction of rubbery dough, with overly sweet jam that oozed out and was often burned. If it was more than a few hours out of the oven, it became brick hard. I'd sworn never to eat strudel again.

"That sounds great, Franz," Linda said. "Otherwise, I'll have to decide, and I don't think I can do that."

Despite my misgivings, I also ordered apple strudel and a coffee.

It had to be better than my grandmother's. Besides, when in Vienna, do as the Viennese do. As we waited, I glanced around at the people near us and what they were eating. I would have been happy with any of the rich-looking desserts. But as I glanced around, a woman noticed me looking. I twisted away. My paranoia convinced me this fashionable older woman wearing perfect makeup, a hat with netting, and white gloves disapproved of such uncouth customers as us. Next time, if there was one, I'd be sure to wear something a bit classier. But I doubted anything in my travel wardrobe would have met her standards.

Franz returned with a silver tray. He gently placed two porcelain cups and saucers, a creamer, and a sugar bowl on the table. With a flourish, he poured coffee from a silver pitcher.

"I will be back in a minute."

This time, he set two delicate plates in front of us. On them were pastries that were so far from my grandmother's "strudel" as to have originated on another planet. They looked airy, with bits of apple tucked between flaky layers of pastry. The top was dusted with a fine layer of powdered sugar and on the side was a puff of whipped cream. It could have come straight off the pages of *Gourmet* magazine, food that a stylist of the highest caliber had arranged.

"Enjoy," Franz said as he turned away.

The apfelstrudel looked almost too good to eat. I sat for a moment, fork hovering over the plate. Then, ever so slowly, I lifted a small piece and lowered it into my mouth. Sweet, but not overly so, slightly crunchy apples, delicate buttery dough, a hint of cinnamon and vanilla. This was revelatory.

"Oh my God." I turned to Linda, who'd already tucked into her slice and looked blissful. "This is unbelievably delicious."

I began to laugh, nearly uncontrollably. Franz rushed over.

"Is something wrong?" he asked, a concerned expression on his face.

I tried to stifle my laughter, both to answer him and so as not to attract more attention to myself. "Nothing's wrong. This is wonderful," I managed to say. "Best strudel I ever had." Images of burnt rubbery dough and this fabulous creation in front of me danced through my mind. With that, my giggles refused to be suppressed.

Out of the corner of my eye, I noticed the woman who I'd sworn had been giving me the evil eye. She smiled in my direction. Clearly, I'd been wrong about the strudel. No doubt I'd also been wrong about the people. In a flash, my entire attitude changed. I sat back, enjoyed the remainder of the strudel, the atmosphere, and looked forward to the rest of my stay in Vienna.

FOOD OF THE GODS:
CRETE, GREECE, 1996–2006

For six summers, over a ten-year period, I stayed with a group of friends in the small Greek village of Moxlos on Crete.

We chose Moxlos because my friend Maggie had lived for several years on Crete in the 1970s. When she  returned there twenty years later for a visit, she took a drive to the village and fell in love with it. She decided on the spot to return for a longer stay. As if preordained, Maggie met the owner of one of the few rental houses in the village. The rest, as they say, is history. While there, I learned to slow down and appreciate the fine details of weather, sunrises, and sunsets. I even came to appreciate minute details of the food.

There were four eating establishments in Moxlos, each with a distinct personality. Limineria quickly became our favorite. It was down the hill from where our rental home was perched. The owner, Manolis, spoke English well and loved to banter with us. His Swiss wife, Gaby, made sure the place was spotless and efficient, characteristics not typically Greek. When not serving other customers, he'd come over to our table and drink a glass of retsina with us.

The restaurant's printed menu had no relationship whatsoever to what could be ordered; that depended on what was fresh and available. The first summer, we learned not to even bother looking at it. Manolis determined what each of us liked and, when possible, had the ingredients on hand to prepare it. The menus also had no prices, and when Manolis brought out the food, we didn't know what our dinner would cost. But as the prices were always inexpensive, we didn't bother asking.

There was almost always Greek salad, tzatziki, spanakopita, and souvlaki. All simple, made with the freshest ingredients, and delicious. After that, one never knew. Moxlos is a fishing village, so fish, octopus, and squid were often available. Occasionally there would be pork or goat or lamb. If we were lucky, there was lobster. On request, Manolis would cook his specialty, fish soup, Cretan style. The fish comes out first on an enormous platter, followed by a large bowl of broth and potatoes. The broth was a creamy, almost velvety consistency, with a sharp taste of lemon and a hint of thyme. Gaby baked each day, and a slice of cake ended every meal.

On our third stay, we walked to their restaurant for dinner and a reunion.

"You're here!" Manolis greeted us. He gave each of us a bear hug. "Gaby," he yelled, "the Americans are here!"

Gaby flew from the kitchen, apron neatly tied around her trim figure, her chestnut hair in a ponytail. While she hugged and kissed us, Manolis disappeared briefly. He returned with a bottle of ouzo and glasses.

"To a happy stay in Moxlos!" Manolis toasted. We all tossed down the drink, and he refilled the glasses.

"To old friends," Maggie said.

"To sun, sea, and beach brain," Penny, another regular at these gatherings, saluted the group.

The toasts continued on and on, getting sillier with each drink. With ouzo in me, the sun setting over the harbor, the warm, honeyed air, and sounds of water lapping at the shore as a soundtrack to friends chatting and laughing, I had a sense of well-being down to the cellular level. Wars, poverty, hatred, and bigotry didn't seem possible in this world. We ended the evening staggering up the hill to our rental home, grateful we didn't need to drive.

"Delicious" is a word usually associated with food, and it certainly applies to the food in Moxlos. But there, the sensations of smell, sound, and touch can all be described as delicious. They are the sensory equivalent of a cool drink on a hot day, a warming mug of cocoa in the depths of winter, a crisp apple right off the tree, raspberries picked off the bush and popped into the mouth. It's the purity of the sensations, not the complexity, that makes them so noteworthy and delightful. In a world where things move faster and faster, where what's new today is passé tomorrow, where gimmickry and gadgetry, glamour and glitz, as well as plain goofiness, rule, it's a pleasure and relief to notice and appreciate simplicity.

Three more cafés rimmed the harbor's shoreline. One had a large, hand-painted sign in English out front. It included all the expected items: salad, ouzo, lamb, and fish. Sandwiched between beer and ice cream, some joker had written "Greek village" as an item to be ordered.

The favorite swimming spot of the town's children was directly in front of the café most often frequented by the old men of the village. They'd sit for hours, smoking, drinking, playing cards, and keeping a watchful eye on the kids. The one time we ate there, we felt like intruders. The men mostly ignored us, unless we became loud and animated. They'd cast looks of annoyance or amusement in our direction. A few gave us the evil eye.

The final restaurant had a specialty much beloved by Maggie but disliked by the rest of us—raw abalone eaten directly from the shell. Though the Greeks consider it a delicacy, I found raw abalone to be too chewy and salty. A liberal squeeze of lemon juice made it more palatable, but not enough to make me want to eat it often. We'd go there on occasion to humor Maggie, the rest of us struggling to order something we'd enjoy.

On another trip, I spent a few days visiting Chania, the largest city in western Crete. Chania is filled with eating establishments, variously labeled restaurant, taverna, cafeteria, café, pizza place, bar, fountain, and sweet shop. Before I went there, Manolis tried to explain the subtleties that differentiate one from another. According to his explanation, restaurants are the most formal and have the best chefs. Tavernas are relaxed, comfortable places to hang out in, with good, basic food. Pizza places are less formal yet, where people eat and go, but don't hang out. Bars serve only drinks and mezze (appetizers or bar food).

That may be the theory, but in practice, the designations meant nothing. Fountains and sweet shops are specialized for drinks and desserts, but the rest all have virtually the same menu. Restaurants have pizza, and pizza places serve fish and souvlaki. How a taverna differs is beyond my comprehension. There doesn't appear to be any difference in price or service level. Maybe it's got something to do with how comfortable the chairs are. That's how I selected places to eat, as I couldn't determine anything else that made any difference.

Seated in a restaurant near the market gave me a splendid view of tourists, locals, the intrigue between the elegant young shopkeeper across the way and her two competing suitors. I ate perfectly cooked squid I'm certain had been swimming that morning. It was tender, crispy at the edges, tasting of lemon, olive oil, and the sea. With it, I had a vegetable dish of a zucchini-like squash, potatoes, fresh oregano, crumbled feta, and olive oil, baked until the veggies softened and the feta browned. To prolong the meal and continue people watching, I ordered fig ice cream. The sweet bits of fig tasted of sunshine.

Every morning we ate breakfast on the back patio of our rented Moxlos home, the restaurants never opening before midday. We'd enjoy the gentle breeze, a cup of strong Greek coffee, and a bowl of thick, creamy yogurt laced with honey and fresh peaches. I'd savor each bite, trying to commit the taste to sensory memory.

A drive to Satia became a favorite excursion. It's the largest town on the eastern end of Crete and home to shops, restaurants, ice cream parlors (a real treat), banks, a movie theater, and a twice-weekly market. We'd go to the market as much for the ambience as for the food; the clientele were mostly locals, not tourists. It stretched down a narrow street, the only long, straight one in town. Umbrellas covered each vendor's goods for protection from the blazing sun. The sweet scent of fresh tomatoes and peaches filled the air. Dank, rich goat cheese was a contrasting undertone. Piles of jewel-toned peppers, cucumbers, cherries, beets, and lemons filled vendors' stands. The karpoozi (watermelon) truck would be stacked high with enormous green fruits, a few sliced open to reveal the succulent pink interior.

Boxes of horta, a leafy dark green vegetable loved by the locals, took up a lot of space. The first time I visited the market, I wondered about the volume of horta available. Then Maggie bought a shopping bag filled to the top with it. When we boiled it down, with garlic, lemon, and olive oil, there was barely enough for four people.

In an area past the produce sellers, dry goods sellers displayed heaps of jeans and T-shirts, polyester skirts, lace tablecloths, shoes, socks, and lingerie. Sprinkled throughout were hardware stands, pots and pans, salt and pepper shakers, cutlery, and dishes. There wasn't a single thing I needed or wanted, but the people watching made it worthwhile.

Nearly everyone had the wild dark hair and eyes that are so characteristically Greek. Some of the faces were smooth and young. Some were lined, weather-beaten, well-lived in for many years. Children tugged at mom's arm, hoping to wheedle a special treat, a toy, or ice cream. Babies, mostly asleep in their strollers in the heat of the day, made a peaceful counterpoint to the activity that swirled around them. The *yayas*, the grandmothers, swathed in black, elbowed their way through the crowd.

In Satia, I drank my first frappe, an iced coffee drink with an extra-heavy dose of caffeine. The caffeine revved up my brain circuits and heaved me full tilt into overdrive. Words flowed from me fast but not fluidly. My body buzzed. My brain raced. It reminded me that in my "real" world I often ran on artificial stimulants, rather than being driven by an inner force. Yet the frappe's cool sweetness felt like a real treat, and over the years, I drank many of them.

One summer, we arrived during an intense heat wave. The air was tinged with dust, the usual saltiness stifled by the baking temperatures. There was no breeze and so little motion that the sound of the sea disappeared. The water looked glassy. It even smelled hot, as if an oven had been left on for too long. Grays and browns predominated, not the blues of the sea and sky, nor the green of the olive trees and gardens. It was the kind of weather that seduced everyone into sleep. In New York, it would have meant cranking up the air conditioner, pulling down the shades, submerging into the cool cave, and not coming out until the temperature fell. In Moxlos, that wasn't possible. No air-conditioning existed anywhere in the town. Mornings and late afternoons, we floated in the bathtub-warm water of the sea; it was an activity that required almost no energy. In the middle of the day, we sought shade wherever we could find it, reading, napping, and drinking gallons of liquids.

Evenings, when the temperature dropped to tolerable, everyone moved to the harbor in the hope of a cooling breeze. You could have taken an accurate village census by counting noses at the restaurants, on stoops, in the streets. People ate sparingly, the heat sapping the desire to consume much of anything except cooling drinks. Several older women in the middle of dinner got up from their table, made their way across the rocks that separated the restaurant from the sea, and waded into the water. We followed them in. Children played in the streets, then as a pack made a run for the water, where they splashed about loudly. Menus became fans, the most use they'd had in ages.

Several days later, when the temperature dropped, the entire village seemed perkier, livelier, happier. I could almost hear a collective sigh of relief. There were also far fewer people in the restaurants, it being comfortable enough for the locals to tolerate being in the kitchen and away from the cooling breezes of the shore.

A friend once told me I needed to learn how to not do. That's a lesson I finally learned in Greece, where doing things is mostly beside the point. In the States, and especially in New York, there is status conferred from what you do, how many appointments are on your calendar, which new restaurants you've eaten at, plays you've seen, books you've read. In Moxlos, status is conferred based on who you are, and there is a premium for hospitality, gregariousness, and generosity. But it could be a small-town thing that I would find if I spent time in a village in America far from urban sensibilities and craziness.

One summer, I stayed on for a few days in Moxlos after all my friends had left. I wanted to have time by myself to write. I was heading out to go to my final dinner in town when Yurgo, our land-lord, stopped by and invited me to dinner with his wife, children, in-laws, and their children. He introduced me to his brother Theo and sister-in-law, Federa, and their four children: Maria, a girl of about twelve; Antonio, perhaps ten; Manolis, seven; and Anastasia, about five. The three little ones reminded me of my nephews and niece when they were about that age. They even looked a bit like them. Though they spoke no English, and my Greek is limited to tourist phrases, we got along fine, with hand signals, drawings, some sporadic translation by Yurgo, and a lot of laughter.

Watching their family interact reinforced the idea that there are some inherent human behaviors that cross national boundaries. Children are children. Anastasia alternately flirted and became shy. The two boys were rough and tumble. They were in constant mo-tion, as though the effort of sitting for more than three minutes was a strain. They made up games, sang songs, and pestered their much-adored uncle Yurgo. Maria acted as mother's helper, keeping her siblings in line, as well as bringing food to the table and clear-ing. The adults clearly adored and enjoyed the children. Kisses, hugs, and praise among family members were frequent.

They had prepared enough food, fried potatoes, salad, and grilled lamb for an army. They joked I couldn't leave Moxlos until it was all eaten. After they conceded that wasn't going to happen, they cleared the table. They replaced the remainders of dinner with a bowl of fruit and a jug of raki. After final farewells, I staggered the hundred yards from their house to mine.

Yurgo stopped by the next morning to say goodbye. He handed me a parting gift of oil made from the family's olives, grown in the orchard outside the house we rented. The oil was a pale green color from the first pressing, the type that costs a small fortune in gourmet shops. The only question was how to get it home. Yurgo had put the olive oil into a one-liter water bottle, screwed on the cap, and that was that. I had visions of the bottle opening and leaking onto everything in my suitcase. It came home with me foil-wrapped and swaddled in a half dozen plastic bags. It arrived safely, and for the next six months, I used it parsimoniously. Each teaspoonful transported me to warm summer days on Crete.

It's been more than fifteen years since I last visited Crete. During that time, I've tried to find meals that match my fond memories. I've eaten at expensive top-tier restaurants, diners, and dives. I've scoured Manhattan and searched through Astoria, a neighborhood with a large Greek population. While some meals have been wonderful, all have been pale replicas. It's hard to match sitting seaside in a small village surrounded by locals who have become friends.

SUCKERED IN:
ISTANBUL, TURKEY, 1997

Istanbul has often been described as the crossroads between Europe and Asia. It's where East meets West in location, culture, history, and food.

My friends Penny, Maggie, and I arrived in mid-April, a month when the weather is usually perfect. It wasn't. That should have been an omen of what was to come. When we'd left New York, the weather had been balmy, and the prediction for Istanbul was for even warmer weather. Before we landed, the pilot announced we'd be delayed because crews were salting the runways. It was snowing.

While the snowfall was light and only a dusting was sticking to the ground, it was cold. So cold we shivered while getting into a taxi, and even in it, could see our breath. We dropped our bags at the hotel, pulling out extra layers of clothing to help stay warm while we explored. As we'd anticipated spring weather, we had little in the way of warm clothes; socks substituted for mittens, and decorative scarves became head covers. At least in the cold, we'd be able to fight jet lag more easily. It would be several hours before we'd be allowed to check into our room and rest.

The two most renowned sites in Istanbul, the Blue Mosque and Hagia Sophia, were a short distance from the hotel. The Sultan Ahmed Mosque, better known as the Blue Mosque, was built five hundred years ago. It features honeycombed domes and minarets reaching to the sky. Despite the cold, we stood outside admiring the unfamiliar architecture and taking in the enormity of it.

We stamped our feet and jumped up and down to keep warm. To take photos, we'd remove our hands from the socks, then replace them as fast as possible. While we lingered, a well-dressed man approached us.

"I am not official guide, so I do not need to charge you. But I am happy to explain the history to you. I know very much about this," said our would-be guide. We thanked him and turned away. We'd read that while these "pseudo-guides" can be helpful, they expect to be paid and can be both persistent and annoying. Our guidebook warned tourists should be firm about turning them away. Or, if interested, to negotiate a fee before going in with them.

He tapped Penny on the shoulder. "There is much about the Blue Mosque that books will not tell you."

"Thanks, but this is our first time here. We'll just look."

Within a minute of his leaving, we were approached by another man. "I would like you to enjoy your visit. Can I help you?"

After politely saying no and turning away, yet another potential guide appeared. And then another. I guessed that on this wintry day there wasn't much potential business. To escape them, and to warm up, we strode into the mosque.

The inside was as impressive as the exterior. The enormity was emphasized by the large empty space where the faithful kneel to worship. Lavish tiles in blue, turquoise, red, and gold covered almost every surface, especially on the inside of the main dome.

Since the portrayal of humans is prohibited in Islam, the decorations were floral or abstract patterns. Flowing calligraphy added to the design. I assumed they had religious meaning, but they could have been the name of the architect or directions to an administrative office. Below our feet, a red and gold carpet contrasted with the predominant blue. Weak light filtered through the stained glass that lined the top of the walls. Chandeliers twinkled, adding to the magic.

I didn't bother reading the guidebook because in my sleep-deprived state I wouldn't have retained any information. Just looking around made the visit worthwhile for me.

A short walk away is the Blue Mosque's tourism rival, the Hagia Sophia. It was built as a Christian basilica almost fifteen hundred years ago. I recalled that, since then, the function of the building had changed multiple times and that, at the moment, it had become a museum. (Since then, it has reverted to a mosque.) As with our entry into the Blue Mosque, a bevy of guides and wanna-be guides approached us. Getting more tired by the moment, we were less polite in shooing them away.

The interior of the Hagia Sophia appeared to have the architectural bones of a church rather than a mosque. However, there were no pews or other seating. I kept hoping I'd find a bench; every part of my body was fatigued. Dozens of low-hanging chandeliers provided the only light. On this dreary day, it was difficult to see any details unless we walked close to the walls. Between the dim lighting and tiredness, we spent little time there. We planned to return when we'd had some sleep.

On the walk back to the hotel the snow had subsided, but the wind had picked up and cut through my inadequate clothing. I couldn't wait to crawl into bed.

Two hours later, the alarm clock's insistent buzz drilled into my brain, and I groggily returned to consciousness.

"Time to go out," Penny said.

"Go away," I replied, refusing to open my eyes.

"If we keep sleeping now, we'll never get into this time zone." Penny poked me.

"Five more minutes."

"No, up. We're going out."

I opened my eyes and saw Maggie and Penny putting on layers. "Okay, okay. I'm moving."

Outside, it remained frigid. We window-shopped, admiring delicately painted ceramic tiles, plates, and bowls. The floral motifs reminded me of similar work I'd seen at the Victoria and Albert Museum in London. Other shops displayed glassware. The windows were filled with sets of tea glasses and saucers in vivid colors rimmed with gold, stained glass lamps, water pipes, and objects whose function wasn't obvious. We didn't enter any of the enticing shops, not wanting to buy anything.

"Come in. Get warm," a friendly voice called out as we looked in the window of a carpet shop.

"Thanks, we're just looking," Maggie said.

"You can look inside where it is warm."

"No thanks. We don't want to buy anything," I said.

"Just look. Come in, drink tea. We are very quiet; you can relax." The man spoke in a soothing, melodic tone. "No pressure, just look."

Maggie, Penny, and I looked at each other, shrugged, and followed him into the small shop. Tea, a warm place, and sitting down sounded good.

The young man led us to three plastic chairs. "Sit. Sit. First, tea." With his wavy black hair, a stray curl snaking across his brow, dark, deep-set eyes, and full lips, he could have been a model. We'd be looking at him as much as at the carpets.

He disappeared for a few moments.

Maggie whispered, "Don't let me buy anything."

"Or me," Penny and I chimed in.

Maggie continued, "Really, truly. Do NOT let me buy anything. In this state, God only knows what I'll come away with."

I thought, but didn't say, *Yes, you will. You're a shopaholic. I'll do my best to dissuade you, but I'll bet on you buying something.* On previous trips around the world, Maggie had often purchased so much that she needed to buy extra luggage to haul everything home.

The steaming super-sweet apple tea was served in beautiful garnet-toned glasses.

"I'm Kerem. Where are you beautiful ladies from?" His dark eyes shown with impishness. I realized we were about to be treated to a stage-worthy sales pitch.

After several more minutes of flattery and pleasantries, Kerem slid into the conversation. "I'm sure you'd like to see some carpets. Not to buy. Just look."

"Sure, why not?" We wanted to prolong the warmth and comfort as long as possible.

"Good, good. What colors do you prefer?"

"I like red."

"Blue or green, but show us your nicest designs."

"Of course. Of course."

Kerem disappeared for a few moments. Maggie repeated her plea, "Do not, not, not allow me to buy anything."

He returned with an assistant; each held an armful of rolled-up carpets. They placed them on the floor. Kerem pointed, and his helper picked one up and, with a flourish, unrolled it and placed it in front of us. The delicate pattern of intertwined leaves floated against a midnight-blue background. Then he unrolled a runner of deep green with scattered yellow and gold medallions. "Excellent quality wool," Kerem declared. He picked it up and held it so we could feel the dense weave.

More were unrolled until they surrounded us. So many my addled brain couldn't take it all in.

Penny pointed to a deep claret carpet with a midnight-blue border and four cream-colored diamond shapes in the center, filigreed with accents of the claret and blue. "I like that one, but it's too large. Do you have a similar one that's smaller?"

Kerem and his assistant left to find one.

"Penny," I asked. "What are you doing? Remember, we said no buying on the first day. We haven't been here twenty-four hours."

"I know. I know." She sighed. "But it is gorgeous and the exact right color for my guest bedroom."

"But, Penny. We'll be here for two weeks. Do you want to drag it around that whole time?"

"We'll be picking up a car. It's not going to be a problem."

After more glasses of apple tea, I was both exhausted and on a sugar high. All sense washed out of my system, and I succumbed to buying fever. In the end, after only a minor amount of bargaining, something at which we usually excel, all three of us purchased small rugs. I hadn't quite figured out the exchange rate and was relying on Kerem's conversion to dollars for the price. In my addled state, it seemed like a fair amount.

While his assistant wrapped our parcels, Kerem asked, "Where will you ladies have dinner?"

Penny, Maggie, and I looked at each other, uncertain how to

respond. We hadn't even thought about dinner. In our jet-lagged state, it might have been time for breakfast or any meal of the day.

"My cousin owns a wonderful seafood restaurant near the water. It is quite beautiful. Very fresh fish. Excellent food."

The three of us exchanged another glance.

"It is much loved by locals. Not touristic at all."

That would be good, I thought. Our hotel, close to the Blue Mosque and Hagia Sophia, was great for sightseeing. But the location also meant the neighborhood was touristy. My experience in similar areas was that nearby restaurants were usually overpriced and not terribly authentic. But as soon as he said his cousin owned the restaurant, my radar should have gone up. My radar was as tired as my body and brain.

"My assistant will bring your parcels to your hotel, and I will get a taxi to take you to his restaurant."

I shrugged. Maggie shrugged. Penny said, "Sure, why not." Having someone decide for us sounded easy. We'd get in a taxi and be whisked to a wonderful meal.

As promised, the restaurant was near the water. When we pulled up in front of it, the driver waved away our money. Kerem must have paid the driver. We didn't question it, simply thinking how thoughtful it was of him. Later, I chided myself. Kerem had clearly made one whopping profit on our carpets for him to treat us to a taxi.

The owner greeted us as old friends. "You are the Americans. My cousin called to say you were coming, and I must take extra good care of you." One by one, the portly man, who had a thick beard but not much hair on his head, swept each of us up in a bear hug. He smelled of exotic spices. "Please, please, enjoy yourselves. You are my special guests." He led us to a table covered in yellow cloth, surrounded by red leather chairs. "I am Efe. I will take excellent care of you. You are in for a wonderful evening."

Almost before we were seated, a waiter appeared with large crystal glasses filled almost to the brim with red wine. *Oh no*, I thought. *Jet-lagged and drunk, a terrible combination.* That didn't stop me from raising my glass as Efe toasted us for a full minute in Turkish. For all I knew, he might have been saying something like, "Thank you, Kerem, for sending these suckers my way." The reality was Kerem hadn't been wrong about the ambience or clientele.

"Let me choose our best mezze [appetizers] for you."

We nodded in agreement.

"You will eat fish, yes?"

We nodded again.

In what seemed like a blink of an eye—by this point all sense of time had washed away—enticing food filled the table.

"This is *bakla*." Efe pointed to a bowl holding a swirled creamy concoction topped with dill that looked a bit like hummus. "I think you name it fava bean." He then held out a basket of pita bread. "Dip the bread into it."

"Oh my God." I almost swooned. The texture was cloudlike, the flavor slightly nutty. I almost said, "Keep the rest of the meal; I'll only eat this."

"And this"—he pointed to a bowl of vivid red sauce—"is *muhammara*." I'd seen dishes like this before but didn't know the name. It's a mix of ground red peppers, walnuts, olive oil, garlic, onions, pomegranate, and spices. Efe squeezed fresh lemon on top. "Taste it. You will like." We did.

There was also hummus, baba ganoush, two different varieties of olives, bulghur salad, smoked eggplant, and *tarama* (a dip, also common in Greece, made from fish roe, lemon, and olive oil). It was a feast, and we hadn't gotten to the main course. Some foods were spicy, others briny or smoky, and one had a hint of sweetness. All had been freshly prepared by a chef who knew his way around a kitchen.

As we ate, all three of us felt better. Maybe it wasn't only jet lag. We probably needed food. When had we eaten last?

Wine flowed freely along with the mezze. I was past caring how drunk I became. Somehow, we'd find our way back to the hotel.

Efe came over often, checking to make sure we liked everything. "You are ready for the fish?" he asked. I'd forgotten these were the starters. More food? I wasn't sure I'd be able to consume another forkful. But yes, more food was coming. Despite being stuffed, we ate. I don't know what type of fish it was. The Turkish name meant nothing to me, but broiled and served with loads of lemon, it was sublime.

Hours had passed since we'd entered the restaurant.

"Coffee? Dessert?"

"No thanks," we replied in unison.

"An after-dinner drink? It is tradition." He disappeared for a moment and returned with a crystal decanter filled with deep red liquid. His assistant carried a wooden box that looked as if it might hold tea. After pouring the alcohol, Efe opened the box. "Cigar?"

I don't smoke and never have. And if I ever were to smoke, it wouldn't be cigars. My father smoked cheap stogies that stunk beyond belief. His habit had put me off of tobacco for life. Maggie and Penny didn't share that history and accepted Efe's offering. He ceremoniously lit their cigars. They puffed and sipped in delight. Efe hummed a tune, grabbed Maggie's hand, pulled her up, and danced her around the restaurant, much to the delight of the other patrons. Next, he waltzed Penny, followed by me.

It was well past midnight. I yawned and struggled to keep my eyes open. Time to settle up and head to bed.

I looked at the bill and pulled out a calculator. "This can't be right. What's the exchange rate?" Penny told me, and I reentered the amount. "Uh-oh."

"What?"

I showed her the amount. "Oh no." Maggie leaned over and looked. We all sobered up in an instant.

It occurred to me that we'd never looked at a menu or asked about prices. The total bill cost almost as much as the airfare had been. Fortunately, the restaurant took credit cards, or we'd have spent our vacation washing dishes.

I later found out we'd seriously overpaid for the carpets. We should have stuck by our rule of buying nothing on the first day in a new country. And, we should never, ever have gone to a "cousin's" restaurant and eaten without asking about prices. Still, it was a fabulous meal. Best we had in Turkey.

CULTURE CLASH:
LAS VEGAS, 1997

Right before I left on a business trip to Las Vegas, I'd read an article describing how the city had become a family vacation destination. When I'd been there before, in the '60s, '70s, and '80s, it had been 24/7 gambling, sex, and booze. Kids? I thought. Family friendly? I couldn't quite picture it.

A s I rode down the greatly expanded strip, I saw the transformation that had taken place. Next to porn palaces were amusement parks and arcades. Billboards for revues featuring overly well-endowed show girls were next to ones for Disney-type productions of pirate and animal shows. In the "Welcome to Vegas" tourist brochure, the best of fine dining from around the country competed with KFC and McDonald's. Ads for shops selling jewelry dripping gold, diamonds, and rubies were side by side with tacky souvenir purveyors.

A city that was already frenetic and disorienting appeared to be suffering a clash of cultures. I wondered what the Rat Pack and original developers of the strip would think if they could see what had become of their brainchild—this surely wasn't what they had in mind.

I was staying at the Mirage, which at the time was one of the most upscale hotels on the strip. According to the Zagat's travel guide, it was a "power" hotel. As confirmation of this, the convention when I was there was the National Governors Association conference. Governors and their aides from all fifty states were attending, and President Clinton was rumored to appear at any moment.

Despite the pedigree, the Mirage is, after all, a casino. Their business is to rev people up so that they will gamble and, if not gamble, at least spend a lot of money. But certain amenities one expects at upscale hotels didn't exist. There were long, inefficient check-in lines. The staff seemed too preoccupied with the governors to consider dealing with someone as insignificant as me. To get to the elevators, I had to walk past a gauntlet of gawkers, what felt like a thousand people admiring and posing for photos near an artificial tropical rain forest. Then there was an endless trudge, trailing luggage through a cacophonous casino and more casino and even more casino before I arrived at elevators up to the hotel rooms. On my return trip, there was literally no direct way to get from my room to fresh air without fighting my way through the casino—and the route, as sign-posted, was circuitous.

It was also disorienting that I was being paid to stay there. How absurd to conduct serious business in a setting that felt like an ongoing circus.

My first meeting was scheduled for early evening. I would moderate focus groups with local business owners at a location off the strip. With a free afternoon ahead of me and perfect blue skies, I decided to go for a swim. Getting to the pool required walking past the convention center. Because of the National Governors Association conference, politicos, the media, and security personnel (mostly men) in well-pressed, expensive suits flooded the hotel. I had to control my laughter at the sight of overfed tourists in swimming attire, some dripping wet, elbowing their way through a crowd of much-too-serious-for-the-environment conventioneers. A rambunctious little boy pulled away from his parents, ran full speed into the middle of a pack of conventioneers. Then, for unknown reasons, he dropped to the floor, began kicking his legs, and screamed at a volume that seemed impossible for someone so small. He was so loud he blocked out the roar from the casino. My initial misgivings about Vegas's new persona repeated like a mantra through my head. *Vegas? Kids? Conventions?*

Overflow from the conference—i.e., people who wanted to get away for a private conversation—huddled together, in their three-piece suits and red or blue ties, on chaise lounges around the pool. At the perimeter of the area, guys with ultra-dark shades and earpieces tried to be discreet. That was impossible.

The focus groups I moderated that evening should have been a normal evening's work. Au contraire.

The first hint that they would be unusual came when the participants introduced themselves and described the companies they owned. A few were the typical small businesses I expected—a hardware store, a restaurant, and a preschool. Then,

"I own a quickie wedding chapel, any religion, any time."

"Can you describe it a bit more?" I asked, not because I needed to know, but to fulfill my own curiosity.

"You know. Lots of people come to Vegas to get hitched. This is one of the easiest places in the country to get married fast." His face lit up as he continued, "And, of course, lots of people come and decide on the spot to marry." He paused for dramatic effect. "Often to someone they just met." Now he'd gotten everyone's attention. "All they need is proof of identity and age." He paused again. This guy's timing would have made him a perfect stand-up performer. "We don't ask many questions." Then, as if to soften the impression he'd made, he added, "We supply the witnesses, take photos, and, if they want, provide a bouquet. We're full service. Best in Vegas."

Next up was a woman listed as a talent recruiter. I couldn't wait to hear what kind of talent she was looking for.

"My talent agency mostly does work for the convention business. We get a lot of newcomers to Vegas and people who don't want to be tied down to a steady job."

Once again, I couldn't help but ask for more details. "What sorts of jobs do they do at the conventions?"

"Greeters. Impersonators. Demonstrators. Presenters. Crowd gatherers."

"Crowd gatherers?" I asked.

"If you want people to come to your booth, a shapely woman in a scanty outfit will definitely draw in conventioneers. They can't go topless, but they can be pretty close." Everyone in the room stared at this pudgy, plain-looking woman dressed in frumpish clothing. If you'd had to guess which one of the eight participants in the group owned the most risqué business, she would have been the last chosen.

Only in Vegas, I thought.

The businesses of the next few people could have been in any American city: real estate, carpentry, transportation. Then came the person I'd most wanted to hear from, the owner of a feather dyeing company. How many boas can any city need, even Sin City? Turned out, the guy has a thing for feathers, had figured out a unique technique for dyeing them, and sold them all over the world. I was disappointed; I'd been hoping for some exotic story.

Despite the inclusion of somewhat unusual businesses, the conversation about business loans was pretty mundane. Ditto for the second focus group, which again had some "only in Vegas" businesses, including a costume rental company (think about scantily dressed showgirls, not Halloween), a sports betting firm, and another wedding chapel.

The morning after the focus groups, I went to the Mirage's casual restaurant for breakfast. It appeared everyone from the convention and all the tourists arrived at exactly the same time. While waiting to be seated, I struck up a conversation with another woman who was by herself. To speed things up, we agreed to get a table for two.

Alice was associated with the National Governors Association conference, but not in any way I could have imagined. She rented specialty table linens and was providing a unique set of tablecloths and accessories for each of the conference's meals. I had no idea that this was a business or that anyone could earn a living doing so, but Alice assured me she did very well. My tax dollars hard at work.

"Oh yes, I do lots of top-level conferences all over the country. Plus, high-end weddings and parties, charity events. Anywhere people want to make an impression."

She then told me about the army of staff and vendors behind the scenes needed to make this conference as efficient and splashy as possible. "Think of all the tech support, lighting, video, and connectivity. Catering services, florists, and designers."

I told her about the woman who provided crowd gatherers for

conventions. "Does the governors' conference hire crowd gatherers?" I joked.

"No, but there are many people with strange jobs. Like showing attendees how to get to breakout rooms."

"There are people hired specifically to direct people to break-out rooms?" I asked incredulously.

"Absolutely. They get people to their meetings on time and to the shuttles that take them to the off-site events. And they're not doing the most obscure work here." I could tell she was enjoying my naivete about the conference business.

"Some people do nothing but work on procuring swag for the participants."

"The governors get gifts for coming here?" The more I heard about the conference, the more annoyed I was getting. This was an extravaganza at the taxpayers' expense.

"Probably not the governors, but definitely their staff." She thought for a minute. "I guess the one I'd give the prize to for the oddest job is the guy finding and displaying something to represent each of the fifty states. If he screws up, heads roll."

"What does he do the rest of the year?"

"I don't have any idea."

As I flew out of Vegas to Chicago, the next city where I'd be conducting focus groups, I thought about my twenty-four hours in the city. I was an unusual Las Vegas visitor. I wasn't there to gamble or attend a convention. I didn't have kids in tow or go to a show. The only thing that resembled other guests was that, apart from my time working, I never left the hotel. Within the confines of the Mirage, there was enough oddness for me to feel I'd experienced the new Vegas.

SEARCHING:
FES, MOROCCO, 1999

When traveling overseas, I'm generally more interested in meeting people who live in the area I'm visiting than in spending time with other Americans. But every so often, I will meet a fellow American who intrigues me. While in Fes for a sacred music festival, I met Rob, who was also in town for the festival.

Pure midwestern American, Rob dressed in a way that invited curiosity—a traditional white Moroccan djellaba and those yellow leather slippers that look like shoes for Santa's elves. But young men were attracted to him because Rob projected pure lust. He looked at every young man with a wolfish, appraising eye.

I'd met him in the bar of our ever-so-spartan hotel in Fes, after having endured an endless, dreadful bus trip from Casablanca. The bus ride felt longer than the flight from New York. It never exceeded forty miles per hour, and that was on the downhill stretches.

I drank a beer, gratefully pressing the cold bottle to my forehead. Rob sipped a club soda, a beatific smile on a flattish, square face that hinted at a Scandinavian heritage. Within the first few minutes, I learned that Rob, despite his sandy-haired, suburban, boy-next-door look, is a Muslim.

"When did you become a Muslim?" I asked. "And why?" I was trying not to be judgmental, but his appearance and demeanor screamed Lutheran to me.

"I had a crisis of faith about two years ago." He lowered his voice. "At about the time I came out to my family."

"But why Muslim?"

"Oh, I've tried a bunch of religions—Buddhism, Judaism, Hinduism. None of them felt quite right. Then a friend introduced me to Islam, and it seems to have stuck. But we'll see."

"Why is Islam more appealing than the others?" I asked.

"I'm still trying it out. It's one reason I wanted to come here."

I suspected Rob had chosen Morocco so he could experience Muslim "light." Pre-9/11 Morocco practiced a more forgiving form of the religion than Saudi Arabia, Yemen, Iraq, and other Muslim countries. In Fes, few women covered their faces; the atmosphere was relaxed and conducive to outsiders. And in Morocco, it was common to see men holding hands as they walked down the block. This had nothing to do with sexual orientation, only friendship. I suspected it made it easier for gay men to blend in.

Abdul, one of the many waiters hovering around the bar and closing in on our table, came over to see if we needed anything. Rob invited him to sit with us. Abdul was gorgeous. Slim and tall, he had what I think of as bedroom eyes, dark and piercing with long lashes. The three of us chatted amiably about life and love and religion. I asked a question that had been forming from the minute I'd entered the bar: "How come there's alcohol available here when the Koran strictly forbids it?" Rob and I stared expectantly at Abdul.

He tossed off, "Bars and alcohol are only for tourists. Muslims don't drink." We glanced around, noting that most of the men seated around the tables didn't appear to be tourists.

"But, Abdul, we saw lots of bars on the way over here. You'd have to increase the level of tourism a hundredfold to keep half of them in business."

He shrugged. We moved on. Rob got up to go to the men's room. As he walked across the light streaming in through the open door, I suppressed giggles and Abdul's stare was tightly focused. Rob had mastered the basics of Moroccan dress, but had failed in a few crucial details, like the fact that his lightweight white djellaba was transparent in bright sunlight. I could clearly see his paisley boxers and skinny legs.

When he returned, he had a tall, elegant woman in tow who he introduced. "This is Judith, my editor."

"Oh, you're a writer. What have you written?"

"You wouldn't have read anything I've published. Mostly, I've ghostwritten a bunch of memoirs."

Judith chimed in, "He's being modest. His book about the theater was very well reviewed and sold a lot of copies."

Seeming anxious to deflect any hint that he was a successful author, he said, "Theater people are most of the people I know. It didn't take much to put together a book." He waved his hands in the air as if clearing it. "The next one will be more difficult. I was assigned a project to write about the America's Cup, something I know nothing about and haven't a clue why they thought I'd be able to write it."

I looked at Judith, hoping she'd be able to provide an explanation. She raised her hands in a who knows kind of way.

Rob, Judith, my friend Maggie, and I were in Fes for a sacred music festival. It was getting close to starting time for the first concert. We reluctantly left the cool of the bar, met up with Maggie who had been resting, and ventured into the intense June sunlight and heat. The concert of Sufi chanters was held in a small, intricately tiled outdoor venue. The area was made fractionally cooler by the date palms and cedars that dotted the space. Fortunately, we sat in a shaded area, but the heat was still soporific.

There must be many people who find this type of music attractive, maybe even soothing, but for me, philistine that I am, it seemed to consist solely of wailing. Some of it was loud, some soft, some accompanied by drums, some unadorned. To my ear, it sounded like the keening of anguished souls. Each time I would begin to nod off, a crash of drums would startle me awake. The chanters went higher, lower, faster, slower. It was clear the audience couldn't tell when a song was finished. There was scattered applause each time the music slowed down. I would have wagered a lot of money that if the group repeated a song later in the program, no one would have noticed. The finale, all drums, wakened everyone in the audience. We staggered out in search of somewhere cooler, preferably with refrigerated air.

Over the next few days, Maggie and I made friends with other people attending the festival and saw Rob infrequently, except at the concerts. But my curiosity about him increased because every time I saw him in town, he was with another attractive young Moroccan man. He'd wave at me but wouldn't invite me over.

One concert was held near ancient Roman ruins. The musicians arranged themselves on a mosaic floor in front of marble columns. In the distance was a field of sunflowers. It was warm, not sweltering as it had been in the venues in town. There was even a gentle breeze. The scene could not have been more inviting.

I snagged a seat next to Judith. Before the start of the performance, we made idle chat about the concerts and Fes, noting that the music ranged from "fabulous, must buy a recording" to "oh my God, I never want to hear music like that again." Then I turned the conversation to Rob. "How's he doing in learning about Islam?"

She snickered. "He's got a lot of guys happy to teach him, but I don't think that's what they, or he, really has in mind." Shaking her head, she continued, "I'm happy I insisted on getting my own room. I'm also grateful that I like Fes a lot and am willing to explore on my own, because I haven't spent much time with him."

I invited her to have dinner with us, partially because it seemed the right thing to do, but also because I wanted to not so subtly learn more about Rob. I found him intriguing.

"Sure, I'd love to have company. The last time Rob and I spoke, he was rapturous about his new love, the hotel's bartender. I haven't seen him since then."

At dinner, Judith filled in her background and told us more about Rob. "I was first introduced to him by a mutual friend who enthused about his talent. That was about ten years ago." She paused to take a sip of wine. "He sent me some writing samples, and they impressed me. Despite his modesty, he's an accomplished writer. I agreed to meet him."

I sat and listened, not asking questions, just letting her tell the story in her own time.

"He's such a sophisticated author. I expected to meet someone polished and urbane. Instead, Rob was shy and seemed like a lost soul. But as he warmed up, I discovered he's very observant and has a wicked wit."

I'd noticed that as well. Some of his comments about the less appealing music we'd heard were hilarious. About one performance, he'd whispered to me with a straight face, "I want a tape of this. It's got to be better than my white noise machine." About a screeching group, he'd said, "Well, at least they've got good lungs and perseverance."

Judith continued, "This religious quest he's on seems to be looking for the wrong thing. It isn't religion he's looking for; it's acceptance. And not from strangers, but from his family." She sighed. "I wish I knew what I could do to help."

We talked more about the festival and our experiences in Morocco, but I figured she wasn't finished with the subject of Rob.

As we were getting ready to leave, she said, "I worry about him. He's considering living in Fes, at least long enough to write the new book."

That was unexpected. I asked, "Why? Where?"

"With the bartender. In his apartment."

"Oh."

When the last of the concerts was over, Maggie and I left Fes for the Atlas Mountains to go on a camel trek. Judith returned home. Rob remained in Fes.

I'd mostly forgotten about Rob until three months later when I received a brief email from Judith.

"I'm writing with very sad news. Rob will not be returning from Morocco. The house he was living in had a gas leak. There were no carbon monoxide detectors, and he perished. Contributions in his name can be sent to . . ."

The message shocked and saddened me. I doubted Islam was the answer he was looking for, but in pursuit of it, Rob was coming into his own, enjoying life, exploring, and experimenting. He had found the acceptance he craved when he pushed the boundaries beyond his comfort zone.

His was a life cut off too soon, in a place far from home.

DEEP-FRIED FROG WITH OK SAUCE: FOOD AROUND THE GLOBE

Eating new foods is one of the great joys of traveling. Sometimes the experience is extraordinary; at other times, it is all I can do to choke down a bite or two.

My nephew Greg looked askance as I ordered the cactus fries with avocado dipping sauce at a hole-in-the-wall restaurant in Sedona, Arizona. "Honest, they're great. You'll love them."

He didn't believe me. "They'll have prickly things on them. Ugh. And they'll be green. No one eats that stuff."

I agreed that where he lives on Long Island people don't eat cactus. "Not to worry, I'll eat them. You can stick with your burger." The truth was, I'd never eaten a cactus fry, but I wasn't about to tell Greg that.

When the cactus fries were served, he examined one carefully for any sign of prickles, then reluctantly bit into it. He proceeded to demolish the entire portion and asked if we could order more.

To me, this was an important lesson to teach him about being a traveler—you are often faced with unfamiliar, unappetizing-sounding, or smelly foods. Sometimes you might need to try food that you can't even begin to identify.

On one of my first trips to Hong Kong, I was handed a menu with items that simply baffled me. Though at the time Hong Kong was still British and many people spoke English, no one at the restaurant was able to adequately explain what these foods were. I copied into my journal the menu offerings that either totally put me off or defied my best imagining of what they might be.

- Ox's tripe with scallions and gin gin
- Fish snout with goose webs and wings
- Sautéed goby ball
- Meat floss on sticky bun with cinnamon blossom
- Broiled pig's tripe with crab's cream
- Deep-fried frog with OK sauce

As I pondered the menu (and settled on more familiar dishes), I reminded myself that to most Asians, the Western diet makes us barbarians. They wonder how we could possibly eat bacteria-infested, fermented milk emulsion (cheese), which to them stinks like a skunk.

On my earliest trip to Japan, visiting pottery studios, my friend Lisa and I stopped at a workshop that had been visited by our college professor Ken the year before. Showing the potter photos of us with Ken made us honored guests. Before our host showed us the workrooms and kilns, he led us to a small office. We all sat in silence since we didn't share a common language, smiling and waiting for something to happen. After a few moments, an assistant appeared with an elegant teapot and tea bowls. With great ceremony, the potter presented each of us with a bowl of tea.

The color, intense chartreuse, didn't seem natural but more like something artificially created to appeal to children. Bowing my head in thanks, I took a small sip of the foamy liquid. I nearly spit it out. The tea's astringency was shocking, reminding me of when I'd once bitten into an unripe persimmon. My mouth puckered, my lips burned slightly, and I had to fight hard not to gag. I managed to keep it down, but just barely. Drinking more seemed unthinkable, but I knew I had no choice. With great effort, I sipped my way through the whole bowlful and inwardly breathed a sigh of relief when no more was offered.

At the next studio, the second I saw the intense chartreuse poured from teapot to cup, I cringed but forced myself to smile, express thanks, and slowly consume the offering. Over the years and many trips to Japan, I have been served similar cups of tea many times and have come to dread the sight of that ceremonial welcoming drink. But to refuse the acrid tea, indeed, not to drink the entire cupful, would be considered the height of rudeness. I've learned to appreciate the symbolism of the tea, if not to like it.

In truth, I'm not fond of *any* tea. As a child, I was often ill with bronchitis and also had severe drug allergies. My mother's medicine of choice was tea laden with lemon and honey and occasionally enhanced with a shot of whiskey. To this day, a cup of Earl Grey or Lipton's is an unwelcome sight. But in many parts of the world, offering a cup of tea to a stranger is a way of welcoming them. Add yak butter and salt to the brew, as they do in Tibet, and for me, the ick factor increases exponentially. The combination of black tea and salty fat is thought to be beneficial in the high, cold altitudes of the Himalayas. As with my mother's home remedy, this tea is a medicine of sorts. When I was served a cup in Lhasa, the greasy black surface of the tea reminded me of an oil slick. The yak butter tasted gamey and slightly rancid, and the salt made me thirsty—for anything other than tea.

On the flip side, I've come to love lassi (an Indian yogurt drink), watermelon juice (Bali), and bubble tea (Japan), and often drink all of them in New York. I've gladly drunk many pisco sours (a strong, sweet alcoholic cocktail) in South America. In Bolivia, I tried Api Morado, a thick, warm concoction of purple corn, cinnamon, cloves, orange rind, and pineapple that is sweet and soothing. I wish I could find it closer to home.

The foods that are harder for me to swallow, literally, are the ones that once walked. As a city kid, I was never exposed to the butchering of the food I ate. I grew up thinking steaks came wrapped in cellophane and never thought much about a slab of beef as having once belonged to a large, friendly-looking mammal. So, seeing carcasses, often covered by flies, hanging in butcher shops across the globe made me think long and hard about my commitment to being an omnivore, at least in developing countries. For a couple of trips, I pretended to be a vegetarian, but the smell of cooked meat made me salivate no matter my resolve to eat only plant life. Finally, I came to peace both with my meat-eating urges and my squeamishness about its quality. Rationalizing that as lions kill for their food because it is in their nature, so, too, is eating a variety of foods natural to humans. And as long as the meat was well cooked, it wouldn't make me ill.

In Peru, I visited several people's homes. In the first one, as I sat chatting with my hosts, I noticed scurrying movement on the kitchen floor. I tried not to stare, but dozens of small, furry rodents darting about were impossible to ignore. My face, I'm certain, gave away my horror—I assumed I was seeing rats. My hosts had entertained Americans before, so rather than being offended, they explained that they kept cuy (guinea pigs), which were served at very special meals. I began plotting how to leave before I was invited to dinner.

At the next couple of homes I visited, I was less obvious about my discomfort upon seeing the skittering critters but still wary of being offered anything to eat.

Toward the end of the trip, my guide took me to a celebrated restaurant in Cusco, situated high on a mountain overlooking the red roofs of the city. He told me that it was a favorite of locals and tourists alike and, he promised, I'd have a very special treat. That phrase set off alarm bells. I downed one pisco sour, then another, preparing myself. A dish of appetizers was served. I wasn't sure whether to eat heartily, in an attempt to be full prior to the main course so that I could beg off of it, or to not eat at all in case I later threw up. I drank another pisco sour.

With great panache, a pair of waiters in crisp white shirts presented each of us with a platter on which sat a whole roasted guinea pig, head, tail, and tiny paws all still intact. Mine seemed to be grinning at me, as if to say, "*And you thought you were going to get out of this. Hah!*"

After the presentation, the servers took the platter back to the kitchen. *Thank God*, I thought. *They were showing me how it would be served if I were to order it.* But no, within minutes, the waiters had laid out in front of me a serving of cuy. I looked at the elegant plate, laid out with a sprig of parsley decorating a half rodent, one shiny black eye staring up at me. I sipped my pisco sour. I forced myself to take a bite. It tasted like chicken, sort of. Still, one bite was my limit.

Back in my hometown, in which there is a large community of Peruvians, I noticed a sign in my local supermarket offering for sale "flash frozen cuy." I was pleased that I knew what it was and even more pleased that I would never need to eat it again.

In other countries, I've been glad that I saw, but never had to try, the local food. The Masai of Tanzania primarily consume milk and fresh blood drawn from the neck veins of livestock. I was grateful for our supply of canned tuna. In Jogjakarta in Indonesia, I saw smoked bats for sale in the market. They were about three inches long and looked like dried mice. I didn't try them. Closer to home, seal flipper pie was for sale all over Newfoundland. It should have been a welcome relief from an endless, unvarying diet of cod. But I couldn't imagine eating any part of a seal—they're too endearing, not to mention endangered. Despite this, I remind myself that while I have the option to refuse these delicacies, for the locals, the foods are an important part of their diet. In fact, they are often considered a special treat.

Even when I don't choose to eat the more exotic foods in a country, perusing menus is always one of the fascinating parts of travel. If I can't read the language, I often try—with the help of a phrase book—

to figure out what the foods are. While this strategy has often been successful, sometimes what arrived wasn't what I thought I'd ordered. What I had translated as chicken in wine sauce turned out to be some other species of bird, swimming in cream. With similar confusion, I've eaten brains, liver, and other bits and pieces from familiar (I think) animals. On occasion, unable to read the menu, I've pointed at what someone else was eating and hoped for the best. Sometimes a kind server or owner has led me into the kitchen and let me choose from what was cooking. I can report mixed results, including some fabulous meals that I'll probably never have again, largely because I have no idea what I had been eating.

Traveling the world, I've learned to become an intrepid eater—not always happily and not always by choice. But I try never to judge. Even though I don't always open my mouth, keeping an open mind has become my definition of a well-seasoned traveler.

VISITING THE PAST:
USA, 2001

For my fiftieth birthday, I decided to take a sabbatical and spend a year traveling around the U.S., visiting places I'd always wanted to see and looking at my home country as if it were a new exotic destination. Guided by whim, local suggestions, and happy accidents, I discovered an America I never knew. I also sought out friends and colleagues from my past in an attempt to visit with my younger self. This part of my journey reconnected me with the potter I once was.

ALFRED, NEW YORK

The town of Alfred had changed little since I'd been there as a graduate student in 1976. It is small and isolated, not much more than the campus of the State University of New York. You *really* have to want to visit—it isn't on the way to anywhere and far from the closest highway.

Driving down Main Street, I noticed that there was still only one traffic light. The police used to stake it out late at night and nab unsuspecting drivers not bothering to stop on the traffic-less street. We'd all joked that those fines paid their salaries. I suspect that wasn't far from the truth. Because they were probably still supplementing their income with fines, I drove mindfully through town.

Near campus, I parked in front of a nondescript white clapboard house on Church Street. I had shared that house with Carol, a fellow ceramics grad student, and Bob, an undergrad in the agriculture school. The walls were thin, the rooms small and cramped, and our furnishings were a mix of Goodwill treasures and found objects. Carol and I spent most of our time in the ceramics studio. We thought of the house as a place to sleep and eat.

Bob, however, seemed to be at the house 24/7. I've no idea if he ever went to classes. The time we spent together can best be described as a lesson in patience. He had spent the previous year living in a tent in a remote corner of the Adirondack Mountains, doing who knows what. What I assumed were the aftereffects of that year included a general lack of basic hygiene, howling at each full moon at ear-blasting volume, making campfires on the kitchen floor tiles to prepare his dinner, and burning smudge sticks to ward off evil. And, because he was on a meager budget, he warmed and ate endless cans of mackerel, the cheapest protein available. His meals left the house reeking and attracted every cat in the neighborhood. I hadn't thought about Bob in decades, but the memories made me smile. He was more amusing in hindsight than he'd ever been in person.

After spending the night at a local motel, I entered the ceramics studio early morning. As a graduate student, it was where I'd spent almost all my waking hours. Entering the main workspace, the rows of potter's wheels, worktables, drying racks, and clay-spattered walls brought me back to days spent transforming lumps of clay into bowls, teapots, and casseroles. I was appreciating the work of the current students when I nearly banged into Andrea. She'd been a classmate of mine from the Kansas City Art Institute (KCAI), where I'd gotten my undergraduate degree. Though I hadn't seen her since 1974, when we'd graduated, I recognized her instantly and called out her name. She looked quizzically at me, then broke into a smile of recognition.

Andrea and her husband, John, also a former classmate of mine, were now co-chairs of the ceramics department. Andrea and I chatted, catching each other up on what we'd been doing for the prior twenty-five-plus years. When a student came by to ask her a question, she introduced me to him.

"This is Karen, a friend from the Kansas City Art Institute. I've known her for a long time, from before you were born." He looked at her, then me, incredulously. "Yep," she went on, "when you get to our advanced age"—she smiled—"you'll realize you've known people for twenty, thirty, or forty years."

It was true. And, at age fifty, my life as a potter simultaneously felt very distant and as if it had been only a few short years before. I had stopped making ceramics, even as a hobby, in my thirties. But the plates, vases, serving dishes, and mugs I had made and still use are a constant reminder of the years before I switched careers and became a marketing researcher and strategy consultant.

Andrea's husband, John, figures prominently in some of my clearest—and strangest—undergraduate recollections. I was a codirector of the college's (non) talent show—brilliant art students demonstrating that their talents were confined to the visual rather than performing arts. John was determined to take part and obsessed for weeks about what he might do. He eventually settled on singing a medley of advertising jingles. After a week, he'd come up with an ad for every letter of the alphabet except Q. When he hit upon Quasar (an electronics brand), he subjected everyone in the studio to endless recitals of Quasar's jingle. His performance was a highlight of the show. Stoned students cheered uproariously while John, dressed in a white spangled cowboy suit, sang his medley, accompanied by a friend wearing a black evening gown, playing a kazoo.

He'd once scared off a young man who'd come to the ceramics studio to proselytize. Pulling himself to his full six-foot-plus height, John bellowed, "Yes, I've heard of Hare Krishna. Have you heard of brute force?" The young man turned with amazing speed and fled, his saffron robes flowing behind him.

When I told Andrea I was sorry to have missed John, she sent me off to their home. Unfortunately, he wasn't around. But those memories fueled my determination to visit Kansas City and to track down other college friends.

KANSAS CITY, MISSOURI

Ken Ferguson was my favorite professor at the Kansas City Art Institute. He was a wonderful teacher and a talented, much honored artist. His work is in every major art museum collection of contemporary American ceramics. As chairman of the ceramics department, he'd created a global reputation for the college.

I hadn't seen Ken in more than twenty years and was nervous about visiting him. I wasn't sure he'd even remember me. Over the more than forty years he'd taught, he must have interacted with thousands of students.

Ken was a huge man—at least 6'5" and three hundred pounds. His presence was even larger; his personality filled any space, no matter how cavernous. When he spoke, his deep, growly voice dominated all conversations, and his laughter reached the far corners of the large ceramics building.

Though his exterior was daunting, inside he was a softy. I remembered a conversation he had with a student who wasn't doing well. He wrapped his bear-like arm around her tiny shoulders, pulled her close, and asked, "You're also studying fiber arts, aren't you?"

"Yes," she said in a barely audible whisper.

"Do you like it?"

"Yes," she murmured.

"So," he boomed, "how would you like to be doing a lot more weaving?"

All of us who overheard this exchange struggled to stifle our laughter, but Ken meant it sincerely, and the student knew it.

She whispered back, "I'd like that."

Ken loved teaching and loved his students. He instilled in me both a passion for the art and the most rigorous work ethic possible. When I wanted to visit ceramic studios in Japan, he encouraged me and helped me to achieve my plan.

About ten years after graduation, I visited KCAI while in Kansas City on a business trip. I entered the studio, dressed in professional attire rather than the clay-covered jeans and T-shirt that had been almost a uniform as a student. I'd been concerned he'd be upset about my career change. Instead, while the other teachers chided me for selling out, he asked, "Do you like what you're doing?"

Without hesitation I answered, "Yes, I love my career."

"Great. I always knew you'd do extraordinarily well wherever and whatever you decided to do." I didn't have the nerve or the opportunity to ask him why he thought that. For years I wondered what made him so confident about my future.

Ken had retired, but the alumni office had given me his home phone number. Ken's wife, Gertrude, graciously invited me to their home. As I walked to the front door, I saw that little about his studio and home had changed in twenty years. But, when Ken shuffled over to greet me, the changes in his appearance shocked me. Gaunt with pale, almost translucent skin and a pronounced stoop, he hadn't aged well and appeared to be ill. At a momentary loss for words, I struggled to say something neutral, but not idiotic. "You're looking great!" would have been greeted with derisive laughter. Ken had no tolerance for fools.

I needn't have worried. Ken, as always, took over. While *Jeopardy!* played in the background at a high volume, he told me about the current politics and staff at KCAI. Though no longer teaching, he still had inside knowledge on everything that went on at the college. In between calling out answers to the *Jeopardy!* questions—we had immediately become competitive—we reminisced about some of my fellow students, and he told me what he knew of their current status and whereabouts.

After *Jeopardy!* was over and Gertrude had shut off the TV, I got to the real reason for my visit.

"Ken, I've always wanted to thank you for everything you taught me. They were some of the best life lessons I've ever had, and I can't even imagine my career without them."

"Really? What does ceramics have to do with marketing?"

"Well, what I took from ceramics is that you must do everything thoroughly and in the correct order—A, then B, then C, then D. There are no shortcuts. If you don't prepare the clay properly, let the pots dry completely, and fire them correctly, they'll blow up.

But, within those rules, there is limitless room for creativity. That's how I approach my work now."

Ken shut his eyes and sat there, not saying anything for a long time. So long, I thought he'd dozed off.

His eyes opened, and he growled, "Gershowitz, I've never heard ceramics described that way. It's good. Very good. Can't improve on it. Wish you'd told me that years ago—I would have used it."

In return, he told me he had distilled his definition of what makes for success to three personality characteristics: intellectual curiosity, self-confidence—you need to believe you can do it—and dependability. Then, surprising me, he said, "I knew you had all three. You were going to do okay, no matter what."

He'd finally answered the question I'd had for so many years.

Ken Ferguson died two months after I visited him. I was so very lucky to have known him and grateful I had the opportunity to tell him how much I appreciated his guidance and support.

HELENA, MONTANA

A few weeks after visiting Ken, I drove with my college friends Diane and Willem to the Archie Bray Foundation in Helena. The Bray, as it is known, is a well-respected center for the ceramic arts. Ken Ferguson is strongly associated with the Bray: he was one of its first directors and for many years conducted workshops there. Many of Ken's former students followed his lead and became directors, resident artists, and workshop presenters at the Bray.

We arrived one week after a bash commemorating the Brays' fiftieth anniversary. Though the party was over, there were museum and gallery shows all over town. I was glad I hadn't been there for the celebration. Because I hadn't touched clay in decades, I would have felt like an interloper. It would have been interesting, though, to see some of my former classmates, many of whom had shown up for the event.

We spent most of the day exploring the grounds and looking at the best of the best contemporary ceramics. I was amused by the Bray's whimsy. Ceramics sprouted all over the property, often in unexpected places. A Bray tradition invites potters who work there to contribute pieces to the landscape. There was something magical about seeing fabulous bowls and plates randomly lying around in the flowerbeds and the grass, sculptural objects propped against buildings, and teacups wedged into corners.

As I looked at the anniversary exhibit and read the related materials, I was astonished at the number of well-known ceramic artists who had attended either the Kansas City Art Institute or Alfred University. At least a third of the ceramicists represented listed degrees from one or the other or both. The two-and-a-half-year period when I attended KCAI produced more than half a dozen celebrated artists.

At the Bray, far more than when I'd visited the studios at Alfred and Kansas City, I remembered the seductiveness of life as an artist. I recalled my connection to clay, the ceramic community, the joy of opening a newly fired kiln, and the pleasure of producing a beautiful and functional object. I also remembered why I abandoned it: the comparison to my peers proved I had neither the talent nor the drive.

The lessons I learned as an artist have served me well, and I'm glad I experienced that life. Reconnecting with my past reinforced my understanding that I'd made a good choice in my change of career. As I'd told Ken, I love what I do.

OFF THE GRID:
MONTANA, 2001

Lisa and I had studied ceramics together at college and spent a summer visiting pottery studios in Japan, but we hadn't been in touch for over twenty-five years. Hoping to reconnect, I sent a note to her at the Montana address provided by  our college alumni office before I left on my trip around the U.S. She immediately wrote back with an enthusiastic invitation to visit.

I couldn't locate Lisa's town, Harpole, on my large planning map, so I stuck a pushpin in what I thought was the general vicinity based on her description, "thirty-five miles west of Helena."

On June 14, two weeks before I was due to arrive, Lisa emailed detailed directions on how to get to her home. "Looking forward to seeing you after all these years. P.S. We've just had a second snow in June. That brings us to 20" for the month. Fortunately, it melts quickly." And, she warned, "Be prepared for somewhat rustic conditions," and went on to say that her family lives on a "compound off the grid," seven miles from town. "Compound" surprised me: it is a term I associate with the Unabomber and never expected to hear in the context of a friend. I wondered how a girl raised in a wealthy Main Line Philadelphia family had ended up on a compound in the middle of nowhere.

The drive on Highway 12 leading to Avon, the closest town to Harpole, was a perfect introduction to Big Sky Country. Speeding along at eighty miles per hour, I could see distant hills glimmering in the sun. In the foreground, fields of newly green grass were spattered with yellow and red wildflowers.

Once off the highway, I kept looking for something to announce the grand metropolis of Avon, but never saw any signs. The town is a single street of homes with a one-room schoolhouse at the end; there are no shops, no gas stations, no post office. For someone accustomed to the density of the Northeast, it was hard to think of it as a town.

Though I scrupulously followed Lisa's directions, it took several attempts to locate the rutted path that led to her property. At a snail's pace, I bumped and swayed for seven miles, sure the axle would break or a tire would blow at any moment. I shuddered imagining this drive in a blizzard. Despite my worries, the profusion of wildflowers and fresh grass helped keep me calm.

Rounding a bend, I got my first look at the compound—a cluster of low buildings stretched across a meadow. No vehicles were in sight. Lisa had told me she had some errands to do and that if I arrived before she returned home, to go into the house and make myself comfortable. As I pulled up onto a gravel patch near what seemed to be the main building, four dogs came bounding in my direction. Though I'm a dog lover, it took a few minutes to decide they were friendly and to step out of the car. After greeting the pooches, I made my way inside.

The living area was a large, beamed open space with a vaulted ceiling and walled-off sleeping areas. I poked around a jumble of books, artwork, ceramics, and musical instruments. A gleaming samovar sat on a low table. A long snakeskin dangled over the sofa, and a ski lift chair was suspended from the ceiling.

I was admiring her ceramics when I heard a car crunching over the gravel and went outside for my first sight of Lisa in almost thirty years. She remained compact and strong from years of hauling around sacks of clay and pots and looked much the same as when I had last seen her. With her fair complexion, curly hair, unlined face, and trim figure, she could easily have passed for twenty years younger. Only the glasses perched on the edge of her nose and a few gray hairs hinted at her age.

We hugged and made small talk about my journey and her errands. At the first opportunity, I asked, "So how'd you come to live out here?" Lisa explained she'd moved to Helena shortly after college for the thriving community of potters there. She'd met Tom, fallen in love, and married. Twenty years before my visit, Lisa and Tom moved to his family's homestead. Over the next decade, they refurbished and expanded it and had two children. The 150-acre property, originally a working gold mine, had been in Tom's family for generations.

Lisa took me on a tour of the structures scattered across the property. She explained that Tom was a skilled carpenter and had been adding buildings since they moved there. The first stop was her pride and joy, a cluster of small buildings housing her pottery studio, kiln, and showroom. In her finished work, I could see the influences of our trip to Japan so many years earlier.

Nearby was a modern, sky-lit building where Tom had his office, complete with a two-line phone and high-end computer. The lighting and heating, as in all the other buildings, was propane. Fascinated by this, I asked, "How is it you have a phone but no electric lines?"

"The state mandates that every rural property must have phone access. We pay for line charges, but not for getting the line out here. So, we had phone service almost immediately."

"But why no electricity?"

"It doesn't work like the phone. It would have cost us $20,000 to have the line installed, money we didn't have back then."

"But don't you want it now?"

"I suppose, but we're used to doing without it. Propane lights and refrigeration work surprisingly well." And, she went on, "With a few solar panels, we can charge our laptops and stereo."

She went on to explain that water was brought into her studio and the kitchen through a Rube Goldberg–like series of garden hoses and pipes. "Don't ever shut the water off completely," Lisa warned. "It will cause a plumbing catastrophe." She chuckled ruefully. "We've had more than a few floods." Over the next few days, I got used to the sound of slowly dripping water.

A short distance from Tom's office was a greenhouse, large enough to grow vegetables for the family, plus a surplus of herbs sold to restaurants in Helena. There was a tool shed larger than many Manhattan studio apartments. The buildings seemed to go on and on. Tom had built a guesthouse, a playhouse for their daughter, and an enclosed area for their son, where he and his friends had played basketball and ridden their bikes. I finally understood "compound." While there was a lack of conveniences that most Americans take for granted, like a microwave, TV, and hot running water, there was an abundance of space that few Americans ever experience.

During the tour, I was continually startled by the juxtaposition of simplicity and sophistication. A stack of *New Yorker* magazines was piled atop the propane refrigerator. Foreign-language videos were scattered about near the solar-powered VCR. Tom, a feature writer, had papered the outhouse with rejection notices from the *New Yorker, Smithsonian, National Geographic,* and other top publications. Ironically, in the years after receiving those letters, he'd been published by most of them.

Tom returned home late that afternoon. He seemed delighted that I was visiting, explaining that, apart from people who lived in the area, they didn't have many guests. "You have to *really* want to come visit," he said wryly.

In early July, so near to the solstice, it didn't get dark until very late. After dinner, Tom, not wanting to intrude on our reunion, excused himself. Lisa and I sat on the deck, downing bottles of Moose Drool, the local brew. At sunset, we watched an endless sky streaked with reds, purples, and golds go dark and reemerge as a dome of twinkling stars. They don't call Montana "Big Sky Country" for nothing. We reminisced about college friends and our journey to Japan. We caught each other up on our lives, having taken such very different paths. The flow of memories and ideas was stimulating and fun but also exhausting; I slept well that night.

The next morning, our conversation took up right where we'd left off; this time we sat with hand-crafted mugs filled with freshly ground brewed coffee.

I wondered where Lisa and Tom's son and daughter had gone to school. "In town, there's a one-room schoolhouse. The kids went there until high school," she explained. "They got a great education, lots of personal attention."

"And then?"

"We drove them into town. Then they had an hour ride to the high school."

"What happens in winter?"

"It takes longer." She sighed. "And in the worst of the winter, they boarded with friends in town." I thought about how long the winters must seem.

Lisa regaled me with stories about being isolated for days, needing to use a rope to get to and from her studio through banks of snow.

"One really bad winter, four years ago, I think, Tom worked as a volunteer EMT. During one particularly bad storm, we got a phone call about a crash on the highway just outside of Avon."

"How did he get to the highway in the middle of a storm?" I couldn't imagine negotiating the rutted path in blinding snow.

"In winter, he's always got a plow on the front of his truck." She laughed. "He's lived here for so many years he's like a carrier pigeon. He plowed through six-foot drifts to get to the crash."

"Yikes."

Even while gazing in awe at the beauty surrounding us, I couldn't help but wonder how Lisa lived in such an isolated, remote location without going mad. Tom often left for weeks on end doing research for his writing. Both kids had finished high school and lived away from home. And it's not as if she could pop over to the neighbors; the closest ones were miles away. When I asked her about this, she looked at me quizzically. It never occurred to her that this might be a problem.

"During the good weather months, I go into Helena a couple of times a week to deliver herbs and vegetables and visit friends."

"Okay, I get that, but what about during the winter? Which, it seems to me, is most of the year."

"I have my work and books and the dogs. Besides, it takes a lot of energy to keep this place going."

After a lifetime of living in cities and suburbs, I was incredulous—it really didn't seem to be an issue for her.

Her neighbors who'd lived on the adjacent property had moved into town a few months before. "They're in their eighties, and it was too isolated for them." She paused and added, "Guess I've still got a few years before I need to think about that."

That evening, after dinner, Lisa drove me to an area a few miles behind their home. A rocky dirt track wound through the tailings of abandoned gold mines, stands of willow, across a small stream, over cattle guards, and into open range. There were numerous downed trees, many newly fallen, blown over during a violent, windy snowstorm a few weeks before. Completely gnawed-through stumps were evidence of an abundance of beavers. At the end of the track stood a homestead that had been abandoned fifty years before, now slowly sagging and rotting away.

We explored the area a little before sunset. In the warm evening and glowing light, I could see how people might fall in love with this land. But I couldn't stop myself from wondering how, on a freezing, snowy morning in June, when she's putting on a down jacket to make her way to the frigid outhouse, Lisa manages to refrain from screaming, "That's it; I've had it!"

Later that evening, after more bottles of Moose Drool, Lisa admitted she'd like indoor plumbing, but after twenty years, the lack of it had become routine.

On my third day, I got to see Lisa at work, preparing for a gallery show. We talked intermittently while she trimmed and glazed pots. The focus she applied to the work was Zen-like—skilled, steady, calm, and deliberate. I hadn't done any of those tasks in years but was happy to lend a hand where I could.

I even got my hands into the clay and threw some pots. The

ooze of slurry between my fingers and the act of coaxing a vessel from a formless lump was magical. My pots weren't very good, but after more than twelve years of not touching clay, I was delighted that, like riding a bicycle, the basics of the craft had come back immediately. It felt comfortable doing these once-familiar tasks.

Over the next two days, I fell into the rhythm of Lisa's life, working in the studio, driving into Helena to deliver herbs, and going about the endless chores required by the property. One evening her daughter and some friends from town visited, and there was an impromptu barbecue and a lively game of horseshoes. At every spare moment, we sat with glasses of wine or bottles of beer and talked. I would have been happy at times to sit with a book, but Lisa wanted to take full advantage of having company— there would be plenty of opportunities for her to read once I'd gone.

On my last morning, I sat on the front steps of the house. From that vantage point, I admired Lisa's studio, looked across gentle hills to distant mountains, watched the antics of four dogs, and listened to a squadron of birds twittering in the nearby trees and the echoing drilling of a distant woodpecker. Above my head, another flock of birds repeatedly visited the eaves of the house where, I noticed, they were industriously yanking out insulation, probably a rare and prized nest-building material. Mostly I looked at the sky, a field of pale blue streaked with wispy clouds.

Over the five days I had spent with them, I'd noticed both Lisa and Tom seemed to be in a state of constant awareness and appreciation of the subtle changes around them—their lifestyle encouraged, even demanded this. It's what kept them safe. I tried to imagine what it would be like to have an always-present awareness of my surroundings, to wake up each morning with such vast beauty at my doorstep and have a pottery studio a hundred yards away. Then I thought of the cold, darkness, and isolation. Despite the loveliness and serenity, I knew I could not possibly live this way.

A small peony bush grew next to the steps; the first blossom, white with the faintest hint of pink, was beginning to open. There were two other buds. After that, the show would end. The peony around the corner had cried "uncle" after the latest snowstorm and produced no buds at all. In early June, give or take a few days, the peony bushes in the front of my house in New York always explode with blossoms—often, there are as many as one hundred blooms on the oldest of the plants. Here, for Lisa and Tom, the altitude and harsh winters made the three blooms more precious than my ostentatious display.

THE CABIN DOCTORS:
WYOMING, 2001

The Devil's Tower, a massive rock formation in Wyoming, is a key feature in one of my favorite movies, *Close Encounters of the Third Kind*. I've seen it dozens of times. Ever since my first viewing of the film, I'd wanted to visit the Devil's Tower. When I was planning my yearlong trip across the U.S. to celebrate my fiftieth birthday, it went to the top of the list of must-visit places.

I came upon the following snippet in a travel magazine and knew where I'd be staying.

Every summer for the past 12 years, the Devil's Tower KOA Campground in the Northeast corner of Wyoming has shown the same film outside on its big-screen TV, and no one ever complains. That's because the movie is *Close Encounters of the Third Kind*, and during the climactic scene campers can look up and see the actual 865-foot-high rock formation, shaped like cat-in-the-hat headgear, that served as the landing dock for the mother ship.

It was thrilling, at long last, to be in the presence of the Devil's Tower. Deep in a remote area of flat grassland, the rock formation was larger, steeper, and more impressive than I'd imagined.

The prospect of setting up a tent was less thrilling. Friends who'd traveled with me in other areas of the country hated the idea of camping, and the cumbersome four-person tent I'd been shlepping around hadn't been used once. While checking in at KOA, I discovered cabins were available. An extra $10 to avoid hauling out the tent and setting it up was a bargain.

"You have bedding, don't you?" asked the receptionist.

"No worries. I've got a sleeping bag and pillows."

"Great, then you're all set. Here's a map of the campgrounds." She pointed out the bathrooms, showers, and general store. "And here's where we show the movie every night after sundown."

She didn't need to explain which movie.

I'd never been to a KOA campground before and didn't know what to expect. It was larger and less dreary than I'd imagined. It also smelled wonderful, a mix of fresh pine with a hint of something I couldn't identify.

Following the map to the cabin, I passed dozens of enormous campers that appeared large enough for a family of ten. Many had set up tables, chairs, grills, awnings, and other paraphernalia to make their site homier. They looked as if they planned to stay for a while.

The cabin was larger and more cheerful than I'd anticipated. Not five minutes after settling in, two muscled women in paint-covered work clothes knocked at the door. They looked tired and hot, their faces flushed and speckled with bits of sawdust.

"Did you just arrive?" one of them asked me.

"Just got here," I replied.

"Hi and welcome. I'm Deb, and this is my sister Marianne." She wiped away a rivulet of sweat trickling down her cheek. "We're carpenters and painters. We just finished the repairs on this cabin, and there may still need to be a few finishing touches." She poked her head through the door and gave the room a once-over. "Let us know if there's anything you need."

"Seems great to me. It's very cozy," I answered. "But if I notice anything, I'll let you know. Will you be around for the next couple of days?"

They told me they were preparing the cabins for the coming season. And would be working at this campground for another week. Marianne handed me their business card, "the Log Cabin Doctors."

"Sit down for a minute. Take a break." They glanced at each other, and I thought they might refuse. I'd been on my own for several days and wanted some company, so I added, "I've got lots of cold water. Have a drink with me." With that, they dropped onto the bench at the picnic table outside the cabin. Before saying another word, each one chugged down a full bottle of water. I handed them each another bottle. Their bulldog, Tyson, hunkered down in a shady corner and lazily watched us. I rummaged through my things, found a bowl, poured water into it, and set it down near Tyson. He lapped at it greedily, sloshing water in all directions. When the bowl had been emptied, he lay back down, closed his eyes, and started to gently snore.

It was obvious the two women were sisters. They shared the same muscular body type, curly dark hair, round faces, and deep-set brown eyes. They were in their late twenties. I started thinking of the two of them as a unit; I quickly forgot who Deb was and who was Marianne, even though they weren't twins.

One or the other warned me they planned to work late into the night—or at least as late as they could saw and hammer without disturbing everyone. "You mean you're not going to see the movie?" I joked.

"We've been here almost two weeks and haven't seen it yet. But we plan to before we leave." She swiped at another stream of sweat.

I asked how they came to be working at the Devil's Tower. They explained they spend most of the year on the road. In their well-equipped van, they drive to different campgrounds, usually in remote areas. For a few weeks, they work nonstop rebuilding and repairing cabins. They shore up sagging foundations, replace rotting floorboards, rebuild beds, reshingle roofs, do whatever it takes to get the cabins into shape.

"Is there enough work to keep you busy?" I asked.

"We've got more work than we can handle. Sometimes we work for commercial campgrounds, sometimes for the government," one sister said. The other chimed in, "We could use clones. How good are you with a hammer?"

"Disastrous."

"Too bad. You could earn some quick cash. We're behind here. There's a campground near Arches National Park we're supposed to be at next week." Deb and Marianne looked at each other and sighed. "This week is going to be tough."

I found them intriguing. "How did you get into this?"

"A friend of ours owns a campground. He was looking for someone to do repairs. Couldn't find anyone."

The other sister took over. "Most guys like to build cabins, but they're not real keen to fix them up."

The two sisters ping-ponged their answers. "We don't mind. In fact, we prefer fixing up the cabins."

"It makes for shorter projects."

"So, we get to see a lot of different places."

"And we don't have to worry so much about materials."

I broke in and asked, "So you started doing this work for a friend. How did it become a full-time business?"

"One satisfied campground owner led to another, and then word about us spread across the country." She took a long swig of water. "What's so great about this is that we take time off between jobs to explore the area. We couldn't afford to do so much traveling if we weren't doing this."

That sounded great. They were self-starters who'd figured out a way of earning money while traveling around the country. One thing roused my curiosity. I wondered where their home was; their business card listed only a phone number.

"Where's your home base?" I asked.

"We don't have one." Her sister nodded in agreement.

"What? But . . ." My voice trailed off. That was not the answer I was expecting. I was speechless for a moment. I'd assumed they worked in the spring and summer, then went home to reconnect with family and friends. Much as I love traveling, I also love being home. My home is a comfortable place where I can totally relax. It's filled with things that have great meaning for me. When I'm on the road, I also cherish knowing that when I've had enough, I can retreat there. But getting into those issues seemed to be too deep, given that we'd just met. So, I focused on practical difficulties.

"What do you do about mail? If nothing else, you must get some bills or bank statements."

"Our mom's pretty good about sorting that out for us. Once or twice a year, we stop by her place and hang out."

"How long have you been doing this?"

"A few years, I guess." I must have gasped.

Her sister chimed in, "I think we're going on our fourth year."

Before I could find out more, they excused themselves and went back to work. Tyson trailed sleepily behind.

That night, I watched *Close Encounters of the Third Kind*. One minute I'd be watching a flickering image of Richard Dreyfus sculpting a mound of mashed potatoes to look like the Devil's Tower. Then I'd glance over at the real thing to see how well he was doing. A minute later, there'd be the distant sound of hammering, and I'd wonder about Deborah and Marianne. How did they maintain friendships when they were in locations with almost no pay phones and the chance of getting a cell phone signal is nil? While on the road, my cell phone was a lifeline. I talked daily with family and friends. I couldn't imagine being cut off from everyone I care about for extended periods of time. The website I'd created specifically for this trip to allow family, friends, and colleagues to follow my adventures had kept me connected. Frequent responses to my posts made me feel even more in touch.

When the movie was over, I went back to the cabin. I fell asleep to the sound of hammering.

The next morning, the sisters joined me for breakfast. I told them about the movie. They asked about me, curious about a single woman traveling alone. When they heard about my travel history and that I'd be crisscrossing the U.S. for a year, we swapped stories about places we'd visited and travel tips. Then I asked them more questions. I was burning to understand how they managed their business and their life.

"We've got a phone line and answering machine at our mom's home. Every few days, when we have phone access, we'll call in and pick up messages." They explained that campground owners understood they were probably somewhere remote and didn't expect an immediate response.

"What about friends?"

"We've met lots of great people." That wasn't at all what I'd meant but knew I shouldn't pry further.

"How long do you plan to keep working and traveling like this?"

"Till we tire of it. But look around." She motioned to the Devil's Tower, the trees, the blue sky. "They're paying us to be out here. All summer and autumn we'll be in other places, all as spectacular. Then we'll head south."

I could see her point but persisted. "Don't you get tired of moving around so much, not having a home to go to?" She explained that, once a year, they took a vacation for a month or so.

"We return to somewhere we loved when we were working," said her sister.

"We settle in, don't go anywhere, or do anything, just relax. That's all we need," the other sister added.

I realized that, much as I love to travel, I need a lot more.

SPUD-TAC-ULAR—ENORMOUS OBJECTS:
NORTH AMERICA, 2001

The Potato Hall of Fame is a small museum. Even the most inventive people would have a tough time filling a large space with tater-related stuff. But Idahoans are determined folk and successfully filled a few rooms.

My introduction to enormous objects came about in the early '70s, while a student at the Kansas City Art Institute. A professor of sculpture had been commissioned to create a monumental Canada goose for a provincial park. Designing and building the goose took months, but eventually a proud steel and fiberglass goose emerged from the hangar-sized studio. It looked as sleek and smart and elegant as a Canada goose can look, far more handsome than the ones who congregate in my local park.

I wondered how this bird with a seventy-five-foot wingspan would wing its way to Canada. It was too large for any conventional form of transportation, and its construction didn't lend itself to moving it in sections. But not to worry, we were told a Canadian government helicopter would arrive on campus to fly it north.

On flight day, most of the student body partied on the sloping lawn in front of the dorms while we waited for liftoff. The helicopter hovered above the statue, dipping and rising as workers carefully lowered and cinched supporting chains into place, the goose tentatively hopping from foot to foot. Then the goose slowly rose into the air, accompanied by the hooting and applause of a few hundred stoned-out students. As it rose higher and higher, we lost sight of the helicopter and could only see the largest bird ever, majestically flying.

I always imagined some farmer in rural Iowa looking up, then screaming, "Marge, come out quick. You've got to see this." She, of course, wouldn't make it outside in time to see the bird. For the rest of their lives, she'd swear he'd been hallucinating.

It was the drive from the Apostle Islands in Wisconsin to Minneapolis, Minnesota, that set me off in search of encounters with enormous objects on my road trip around the United States in 2001.

At the local tourist office in Bayfield, I was told the main attractions along the way were places to sample cheese, unless I was interested in fishing. The tourist brochures didn't indicate much of anything else unique to the area. I set out anticipating pretty scenery, cows and farms, and some small towns that had an antique shop or two worth poking through.

Given the emphasis on dairy production, the first hour of the drive wasn't quite what I expected. There wasn't a farm in sight. Instead of meadows, the county was heavily wooded. In early June, the roadsides were festooned with wildflowers. Though I didn't see any water from the road, in any given mile there were at least two or three signs indicating turnoffs to public access to a lake or river. Sprinkled liberally through the sparse traffic were muddied 4X4s and vans towing boats. Pretty soon, I started coming across sign after sign for bait and tackle. As I was told, this is a big fishing area.

I pulled into Hayward, an attractive small town, to stretch my legs and see whatever there was to see. All around me were shops selling hardware and fishing equipment and, somewhat surprising to me, a slew of shops geared toward tourists. Not much about Hayward seemed like a place that would bring in tourists, and it is hours from any major city.

After inspecting the wares at a couple of shops, I got it— Hayward is where you go after a day on the lakes to reel in a souvenir. If you hadn't caught anything, or even if you had, these shops offered more lasting mementos of your fishing expedition. You could pick up a hand-carved wooden trout or a set of trivets adorned with bass. Fish T-shirts, pajamas, hats, playing cards, and bed linens—anything that could be adorned with a fish likeness was for sale. I began to get an inkling of how far this zeal for fishing went. While I don't share this passion, I was entertained by the thought of some grizzled codger lounging in trout pajamas, sipping coffee from a muskie mug, while flipping through rod and reel catalogs.

What made me look twice were the postcards displayed in every store. Card after card featured what appeared to be truly gargantuan fish. In response to my questions, a shopkeeper gave me directions to the National Freshwater Fishing Hall of Fame.

The main attraction at the Hall of Fame is a series of gigantic replicas of freshwater fish, each hundreds or thousands of times life-sized. The pièce de résistance is a half-block-long, four-story-high concrete, steel, and fiberglass statue of a leaping muskie. Inside the sculpture are exhibits of hooks, reels, and prize catches. But, for me, the real fun was hovering outside and watching people hang out of the muskie's open jaw and make faces at everyone below. I longed to have my friend Maggie traveling with me. Over the years, I've conned her into posing with any number of strange items, like standing behind a decapitated Greek statue so that Athena now sported red hair and shades. But since neither Maggie nor any other friend was with me, I took dozens of photos of people I didn't know. The sight of so many folks, from kids to senior citizens, letting down their inhibitions, making goofy faces, and getting into silly poses was irresistible.

After that encounter, I knew there was no way to journey around America and not take notice of enormous objects and keep track of them. As an art student, I'd always been intrigued and amused by the work of Claes Oldenburg, the artist who created sculptures of everyday objects, like spoons and clothespins. His notion of raising the commonplace to "high art" brought up questions of what is important to us. Throughout history, societies have created monuments to what they value. Inca temples and European cathedrals reached toward God and the heavens. In modern cities, our largest and most costly objects are office towers, contemporary signals that business is king. The fish in Hayward indicated to me that when local communities erect oversized objects, these are done not simply to amuse but to honor what they care about. The fact that they are so silly, and prompt silliness in observers, is a bonus.

Leaving Hayward, I set out looking for more supersized local objects. As I am a methodical sort, I set some rules for myself. The best objects, naturally, were the ones I stumbled upon. A mention in a tourist brochure or a recommendation by someone I met were also acceptable methods for sightings. But anything found on the internet or in a guidebook was out. As an aside, there are several internet sites devoted exclusively to giant-sized objects. But using them felt like cheating to me.

When I entered I-dee-ho, where license plates read "Scenic Idaho, Famous Potatoes," and there were signs pointing to the Potato Hall of Fame, I knew I'd find a giant potato. Sure enough, outside the entrance to the "spud-tac-ular" Potato Hall of Fame in Black-foot is a huge spud looking just like, well, like a ten-foot-long lumpy brown potato. It looks sad in my photo, with no one posed in front of it, but that's because I was the only one there. Once again, I needed Maggie, though I would happily have conned anyone into standing in front of it. But not many folks that day wanted to spend their vacation time learning about potatoes.

Since I was there, I figured I should look around. From this museum and its cousins, I learned that it is possible to create an exhibit dedicated to almost any topic, no matter how arcane, outrageous, or dull. It's even possible to learn something while visiting these museums, though I don't imagine that the knowledge will ever come in handy unless you're planning to become a contestant on *Jeopardy!*.

From the Potato Hall of Fame, for example, I learned that $1 out of every $7 generated in Idaho is related to the production of potatoes, and the most common brand of potato harvesting and processing equipment is "Spudnick." As a bonus, I got to see the world's largest potato chip, now sadly cracked. On my way out, I was given a sack of "free taters for out-of-staters."

As I drove west, I encountered a slew of other colossal objects. Based on what the citizens of Duncan (Victoria, British Columbia) have chosen to glorify with oversized sculpture, the town has multiple loyalties. In the First People's Cultural Center, master carvers work on and display totem poles. These magnificent and truly gigantic objects honor animal spirits and ancestors.

At the other end of town, honoring Canada's national obsession, is a gigantic hockey stick. I learned about the hockey stick from the concierge at my hotel in Victoria. While he described it, he seemed both proud and somewhat dismayed. He told me the hockey stick had "Put Duncan on the map. People all over Canada now know about us" Unfortunately, according to him, the cost of the hockey stick had been proportional to its size, money the town could ill afford.

My search turned out to be fruitless, without a photo to show for my efforts. I followed the directions to the high school where the stick was displayed. I drove up and back and around the school but couldn't find it. I got out and walked around the building, wondering how I could miss an object described to me as over one hundred feet long. As it was the middle of July, the school was closed, and there wasn't a soul nearby to ask. I was about to declare defeat and drive away when a woman walked out of the building. I ran over and asked if this was the right school, and if so, where was the hockey stick? She pointed up. Sure enough, there it was, right above me. The hockey stick, while of gargantuan proportions, is displayed high on a wall behind a tree. Appropriately, it is visible only in the winter when the branches are bare.

As I experienced more and more giant object sightings, I discovered that what's important to a town spans quite a range. These objects can be animal, vegetable, or mineral, natural or man-made, real or imaginary. Most are quite logical for their setting, though not necessarily what one would think of first. Along the Northern California coast are oversized statues of sea lions, saltwater fish, Paul Bunyan and Babe the Blue Ox. Gallup, New Mexico, displays a fifteen-foot-high Navajo-style ceramic pot and a Navajo warrior that looks like a ginormous cigar store statue. North Carolina, a major center for furniture manufacture in the U.S., displays the largest chest of drawers as well as several chairs and tables fit for a giant. In Leamington, Ontario, home to a Heinz production facility, there is a tomato capable of producing a lifetime's supply of ketchup for the town. Detroit boasts a Ferris wheel–sized Uniroyal tire. Springfield, Massachusetts, the birthplace of Dr. Seuss, displays a huge Cat in the Hat.

The AAA guide cited Cannon Village in North Carolina as the home of the Fieldcrest/Cannon factory and mentioned that the visitor center displayed the world's largest towel. Maggie was traveling with me, and as we drove thirty miles out of our way to see it, we fantasized about the towel. We imagined a circus tent–sized towel capable of encircling the entire population of the town. Or that it was displayed with an equally oversized chaise lounge, sunglasses, and bottle of suntan lotion. I mentally drooled over the possibilities for outrageous photos now that Maggie was with me and looking forward to posing.

We entered the visitor center in eager anticipation, only to discover that the so-called world's largest towel is a mere five feet by ten feet. We groaned in unison, our fantasies shattered. Hanging on the wall, it appeared to be hardly larger than a typical beach towel, and as a backdrop for an outrageous photo was a total bust.

There are places that really should have a larger-than-life signifying object but don't seem to. Seattle could use a humungous steaming coffee mug at the center of the city, leaning up against a supersized laptop computer. I never saw a giant ear of corn in Iowa, crawfish in New Orleans, or horseshoe anywhere in Kentucky.

All the tourist information about it proudly proclaims that Wenatchee, Washington, is the home of the apple industry in the West. On my way there, I listened to the local radio station, AppleFM, while cruising through endless orchards. I figured that somewhere in Wenatchee, there had to be a giant apple. I didn't spot one, and there wasn't an Apple Hall of Fame. To try to track the elusive giant apple down, I went to the Apple Marketing Board Visitor Center.

The souvenir shop had apple paraphernalia by the bushelful: aprons, pot holders, corers, and recipes. There was a movie about the apple industry, apple paintings, and life-sized replicas of each variety grown locally. You could even sample some apples for free. None of that was what I was after.

The elderly woman at the desk in the shop looked ever so slightly like one of those dolls whose head is made from a dried apple. I asked her, "Is there a giant apple in town?" She pursed her lips, thought for a moment, and replied, "The biggest ones are about a pound, but the crop isn't in yet." I explained again, this time elaborating on what I meant by "giant." "You know, nine or ten feet high, a sort of symbol for the town?" Her response was, "Why?" I wasn't quite sure how to respond, though I stumbled through an awkward explanation of giant objects as symbols of what a place really cared about. She looked at me impassively, slowly shook her head no, and turned away.

Because I never did find a giant apple, I offered the suggestion on a tourist comment card that they should consider building one. While leaving town, I came across a gigantic hamburger, fries, and Coke on the top of a fast-food takeout place. It was hardly the same thing, but then maybe I misjudged what was important to Wenatchee.

DANGER, DANGER:
WHITE SANDS, NEW MEXICO, 2001

I'm fond of seeking out the weird when I travel. So, when I was traveling in New Mexico and read about White Sands, it seemed worth a detour to check it out. In terms of bizarreness, when I visited in July 2001, White Sands exceeded my most outrageous expectations.

The White Sands National Monument is about seventy miles from Las Cruces and is notable for two reasons. First, it is the site of one of the world's largest aboveground gypsum deposits. Gypsum is a widely used mineral found in cement and drywall, as well as ordinary items like toothpaste and dinnerware. In New Mexico, the deposits form miles upon miles of powdery white dunes. It is also home to the White Sands Missile Range, one of the major explosive test facilities in the United States since 1945.

To visit the monument, you must drive through the missile range on Highway 70. The park service brochure warns, "White Sand Missile Range completely surrounds the park. For safety reasons both the park and U.S. 70 between the park and Las Cruces may be closed while tests are conducted on the missile range. These closures occur on an average of twice a week. They generally last from one to two hours."

Fortunately, they weren't testing while I was there. When I entered through the park gates, the landscape looked identical to the featureless desert scrub that I'd been driving through for miles. However, I could see patches of white in the distance. As I drove farther into the park, these mounds of white grew and grew until they engulfed the entire area. In many areas, it was white-hot, shimmering reflected light, as far as I could see in all directions. While it sounds and is a harsh environment, it is also breathtakingly beautiful.

At the visitor center I watched an introductory film. Most national parks offer this as a guide to wildlife, vegetation, and the most beautiful and geologically notable areas. This one, however, focused more on warnings than animals, geology, or botany. There were strident warnings about not picking up any strange objects (call the park rangers or police immediately!!), bringing a compass if you are hiking off trail because it is easy to get disoriented and lost, having sufficient water, and protecting yourself from the heat and sun. I was surprised they didn't make me sign a waiver saying they weren't responsible if I was injured or killed.

Hiking and nature trails led out onto the dunes. Some were dotted with cacti and other desert plants; some were pristine white. The white was so bright that despite dark sunglasses and a full-brimmed hat, it was impossible not to squint. Once out on the dunes, there was absolute stillness. There were no sounds, no breeze, nothing but shimmering heat until, repeatedly and abruptly, pairs of supersonic jets screamed across the sky. These pairs of fighters came by every five or ten minutes. They would be gone in an instant and peace would return until the next flyover.

As I walked, my feet sank into the powdery gypsum, leaving behind footprints until the slightest wind kicked up. Then all traces would be erased like footprints along an incoming tide. It was easy to see how visitors could feel adrift and get lost. Though I've got a good sense of direction, I hadn't thought to carry my compass, and the dazzling white disoriented me. The tall, prominent trail markers were the only thing keeping me from mild panic.

When the sun was moving directly overhead, it was time to find somewhere cooler. A ride through the park in an air-conditioned car seemed a great idea. The circular tourist road is paved for the first five miles or so. It then becomes a track of packed-down gypsum. At that point, the white is nearly blinding as the road loops through the dunes. It could have been snowbanks glaring reflected light.

Out in the middle of nowhere, there were picnic areas; rows of metal sheds over picnic tables randomly placed. I could imagine how the metal heated the air beneath it until the shelter would be a perfect rotisserie to roast a chicken, but not a safe place to seek relief from the heat.

While I walked and then drove, I didn't see a single other person—no one else was as crazy as I to visit midsummer. And then . . . I saw a family wearing bathing suits perched at the top of a dune, sunning on beach towels and picnicking from a large wicker hamper, no vehicle in sight. It was as if they had been magically whisked away from some oceanside beach, found themselves in this odd place, and decided to simply go on as if nothing had happened. Or they were a mirage. Was the relentless white making me hallucinate?

But no, on second and third hard looks, there really was a family there. I considered climbing the dune to ask why they were there and if they were enjoying themselves. Then I thought, *No, it's too damned hot. And because they're crazy doesn't mean I have to be nuts too.*

I continued on my way, following haphazardly posted signs that pointed "this way out" back to the visitor center.

There, a prominently displayed poster advertised the White Sands Missile Range Museum. As it was directly on my route back to Las Cruces, I had to visit it. As soon as I got off the highway, there were warning signs: no photography, no stopping, don't pick anything up, explosive trucks stop here for inspection, and so on. To enter the museum, I needed to go to a registration office for a vehicle pass. That, too, had a lengthy warning, including such phrases as "significant areas of the Range are known to be contaminated with unexploded ordnance" and "these areas present a very real hazard to personnel moving around the Range." They definitely made their point—go to the museum and don't even think about going anywhere else.

The museum consists of an outdoor area where dozens of missiles (presumably disarmed) are displayed, along with a description of each, including length, diameter, weight, propellant, range, when first fired, and most oddly, a description touting its key destructive features. For example: the SRAM could "launch the missile even when traveling at supersonic speeds," and Honest John could "carry either conventional or nuclear warheads." Going through my head was a whirl of, *How many billions of dollars does this display represent? They're all peeling and rusting. Why don't they take care of them better? These certainly are phallic looking; no wonder men like them so much. The destructive power of these things is almost inconceivable.* And, most often, *What the hell am I doing here looking at this?*

Inside were more strange displays, including the Missile Range Hall of Fame and an explanation of how all missile parts were sprayed with shark liver oil so if they exploded, the pieces could be tracked by specially trained dogs.

If the Air and Space Museum in Washington, D.C., represents the finest in aviation and exploration, the White Sands Museum stands for the worst humanity can create. I was happy to drive away and not look back.

OFF SEASON: SICILY, 2003

After seeing many areas of mainland Italy, I wanted to see the country's two largest islands, Sicily and Sardinia. Both are popular summer vacation destinations, so I scheduled a trip to Sicily in April. Sardinia would wait

for another time. I like to travel during the shoulder season, April and October, when most tourists stay home. Museums, archeological sites, and shops tend to be uncrowded during those months, and the weather is generally good. On off-season trips, I'd leisurely strolled through places that at the height of tourist season would have induced a red-alert level of agoraphobia.

My friend Maggie and I only made reservations for our first few nights in Palermo, planning to "wing it" for the remainder of our two-week stay.

After a few days in Palermo, the capital of Sicily, we picked up a rental car at the airport outside the city. I'd insisted on an automatic transmission. On earlier visits to northern Italy, I'd faced manic Italian drivers. This time, I wanted to make our touring as easy as possible. Driving in Sicily would be a challenge, according to the guidebook. It reported that in some towns, if you make a wrong turn, you're likely to face stairs that you must drive up or down. The encouraging phrase, "be brave, you can do it, and besides you don't have any choice," scared the hell out of me. I had visions of blowing tires, damaging the underbody, or even flipping the car. The guidebook listed Agrigento, our first destination, as one place where driving on stairs was likely to happen. All I could think of was, *Oh shit.*

The directions to Agrigento had been simple: take the autostrada for 128 kilometers, exit, and you'll be there. What we hadn't read in the guidebook or been told by the car rental agency is that the autostrada ends abruptly in the center of Palermo before it picks up again a few kilometers out of town. Those few kilometers were put-gray-hairs-on-your-head frightening. Drivers paid no attention to the lane markings. They darted and dashed into any opening, no matter how small. Tiny snub-nosed cars that looked barely big enough to fit two people snugly—clown cars as I thought of them—putt-putted along, forcing other, larger, more powerful vehicles to swerve around them. Trucks and buses used their superior heft to go wherever they liked. Motorcycles wove through traffic at top speed. Pedestrians blithely walked through the craziness. It amazed me we didn't see any accidents. I tried to imagine what traffic would be like in August when tourists invade the island. That image made the madness we were experiencing seem almost calm.

Once away from Palermo, the roads became more manageable. I loosened my white-knuckle grip and began to enjoy the rocky terrain and small, ancient villages.

As we entered the outskirts of Agrigento, we could see the archaeological site in the distance. Next to the ruins, and far from the center of town, was a small hotel. Without a thought to price, we pulled in and got a room. My anxiety level dropped, and that after-noon, I was able to marvel at the ancient architecture, mosaics, and wildflowers springing up everywhere. The photographs from that day are spectacular—perfect blue skies and not a soul in sight.

We ate in the hotel restaurant that evening, unwilling to go even a short distance in the car at night. Besides, in Palermo, we'd discovered that it is almost impossible to get a poor meal in Sicily. We were the only diners and had the full attention of the waiter. He told us he'd bring us "the best we have in the kitchen." In this un-prepossessing eatery, he delivered a huge plate of antipasti—creamy burrata cheese, olives, paper-thin slices of smoked ham, prosciutto, grilled artichoke hearts, sardines, roasted eggplant, figs, and chunks of hard and soft cheeses, served with a warm loaf of crusty bread.

We took our time savoring this feast as we looked out a picture window at the spotlit ruins. They were awe inspiring.

While we ate, Muzak played in the background. The playlist would have been perfect in a Macy's elevator.

"'Raindrops Keep Falling on My Head' has to be part of this mix," I said. Sure enough, it started a short while later.

"'The Girl from Ipanema' or a bad arrangement of a Simon and Garfunkel song," Maggie guessed. She, too, was correct. We guessed more than a few correctly.

"It's so sad that people around the world are listening to the same mundane music. It's especially sad in contrast to this setting and the food."

When we finished dinner, the waiter cleared the table and pre-sented us with dessert—orange, vanilla, and pistachio cannoli—and a cordial made from pistachios. Despite feeling like overstuffed piglets, we managed to eat and drink it all.

The next morning, no longer on the autostrada and away from

the threat of making a disastrous turn onto a staircase, I could breathe while we drove east toward Castelgirone.

In Castelgirone, a town known for ceramics, there's a broad stairway going straight up for about two city blocks into a residential neighborhood. Because the stairs weren't crowded, we stood at the bottom and had an unimpeded view of the colorful, hand-painted tiles that adorn the front of each step. At the bottom of the steps there were dozens of shops open, all of them bereft of customers. In one, we admired and then bought plates, bowls, and tiles decorated with fruits and flowers in muted tones of blue, gold, pink, and green. While the proprietress wrapped our purchases, we asked her for a restaurant recommendation.

"Not many places in town will be open."

"Is it too early?" I asked, thinking that 1:00 p.m. might be considered an unlikely hour for lunch.

"No, this is when people eat. But this time of year, most restaurant owners don't open because there are few tourists. This is when they take their vacations."

"So, no suggestions at all?"

"Let me think." After a minute, she picked up her *telefono*. She chattered in rapid Italian and a smile emerged. She nodded at us while she continued speaking. "You're in luck. My friends are at their restaurant. It's one of my favorites. You'll love it." With that, she drew a map and wished us, "*Buon appetito.*"

After getting lost several times and climbing steep flights of stairs, we entered a large, high-ceilinged room. Originally, it had been the reception area for a palazzo. The walls were covered in pink silk brocade. Tables were laid out with silver and damask, each with a candelabrum. But the most impressive part was the domed ceiling—a confection of floral murals high above us. Apart from two other diners in a distant corner of the room, we had the space and staff to ourselves.

The owner and waiter spent a lot of time at our table, helping to translate the menu and pointing out dishes they thought we'd especially enjoy. While we waited for our meals to be prepared, the waiter chatted with us as we sipped glasses of pinot grigio. He told us stories of the palace in its glory days and unobtrusively kept our glasses brimming with the sublime wine. By the time they served my wild mushroom risotto, I had more than a slight buzz. Maggie was nearly orgasmic over each bite of her light-as-air seafood pasta. As a finale, the proprietor brought over dessert—a multilayered extravaganza of sponge cake, cream custard, and lacework spun sugar on a pool of tart orange sauce. When the owner asked how we'd enjoyed the meal, Maggie placed her hands together in a gesture of prayer and bowed, then kissed him on each cheek. For the next several days, we fantasized about being the owners of the palace and having staff to attend to our every need.

On other trips, we had discovered that traveling off-season means restaurants aren't crowded, the locals have time to spend with us, and prices are often less expensive. But on this trip, we learned that, in April, most Sicilian restaurants were closed. When we could find an open one, the hours appeared to be limited and somewhat random: lunch from two to four or three to four thirty, and dinner whenever the owners felt like being there. Almost every day included a long hunt for meals. In part, this was because there weren't many restaurants outside of major cities. We surmised Sicilians don't eat out very much; theirs is a culture of family and friends and home cooking.

We had the same problem with lodging. Occasionally we lucked out. We stayed for a couple of nights in an Agriturismo (a farm that hosts guests for the night—think of it as a bed-and-breakfast with extra benefits) in the middle of a citrus grove. The property was almost deserted, and we had lots of attention, including a special tasting of local wines. Dinner was prepared with ingredients grown on their land, lamb, baby carrots, and salad in a tangy, citrusy dressing. In the morning, I savored a tangerine I'd picked from a tree outside our door. In another town, we stayed in a villa surrounded by a profusion of wildflower-filled fields. Our luck didn't always hold. It became a game to find somewhere to stay as early as possible so we wouldn't worry about where we'd be sleeping that night.

One morning, while on our way to the medieval town of Noto, we found a room in a B&B on the very top of a hill. Milleventi had 360-degree panoramic views of the countryside. Vincenzo, the young owner of the B&B, explained, "The name of the house and mountain means 'the Thousand Winds.'" It was easy to understand why. At what we referred to as the Wind Tunnel Hotel, we could barely go outside without being knocked over. We held onto whatever was available to keep from being buffeted by the ever-blowing wind. This was on a day Vincenzo said, "lucky for you, it's a bit calm today." Despite the presence of a radiator in the room, there didn't seem to be any heat.

Arriving in Noto, a UNESCO world heritage site, I drove through a labyrinth of alleys that were just wide enough for one car. The road rose and fell at alarming angles, and the warning about encountering a staircase spooked me. Though I like driving on winding back roads and roller coaster–like roads, these streets caused my anxiety level to rise. Cars followed right on my tail, beeping impatiently as I crept along. People darted out in front of me. Motorcycles appeared out of nowhere. Maggie, trying to navigate, couldn't figure out which direction we should be going. I was ready to pack it in when we found a parking spot. I thanked my father for teaching me how to parallel park efficiently. Rattled, I was glad to get out of the car and be on my own two feet.

Noto turned out to be a fascinating place, well worth the stress. Streets were lined with baroque buildings decorated with elegant curlicues and statuary. The main gate to the city, the Porta Reale, resembled a triumphal arch. As we wandered, we noticed groups of people walking toward a wooded area and followed along to see what was happening. Through a high arch, along a path canopied by a line of trees, was the start of a religious procession for Good Friday.

Participants walked from a church at one end of town to a church at the opposite end. Marchers moved along slowly for several minutes, accompanied by a band playing hymns, and would then stop while a priest spoke. From the little I understood, they were re-creating the Stations of the Cross. Many marchers were nuns and priests. There were also pilgrims dressed in medieval robes holding banners or carrying lamps, children in altar robes, and ordinary folk walking along with the procession. It amused me that beneath the robes, most people, including the priests and the nuns, were wearing jeans and sneakers. Some people in the crowd had faces that came straight out of the Middle Ages. I recognized noses, chins, lips, and eyes from paintings I had studied as an art history student.

There was only one restaurant open in the city, a pizzeria. Hard to believe, but the pizza was awful, burned, and too sweet. It was the only bad meal we had in Sicily.

That night, at the B&B of the Thousand Winds, we tossed and turned as the howling wind rattled the windows and fingers of frigid air attacked us.

In the morning, we were happy to take our leave and head to the Greek ruins at Palazzolo Acreide. The drive there was through an area that looked exactly as I expected Sicily to look. It was rocky, rocky, and rockier. To get stones out of the fields, Sicilians build walls. Sicily has been cultivated for close to twenty-five hundred years, so there are a lot of walls. There were areas where perfectly straight, parallel walls, at twenty-foot intervals, went for miles on end, sometimes as high as seven or eight feet. Stone guardrails lined each side of the road. Open areas, which hadn't been cleared for farming, seemed to be growing rocks. In fact, everywhere I looked were stones except for the houses, which were built from wood and concrete. Not a single one appeared to be built of stones—an oddity, I thought.

When we reached Palazzolo Acreide, the archaeological site, we brought in a lunch purchased at a small food shop. We ate bread, cheese, and fruit amidst sun-drenched Greek remains from the 3rd century BC.

A few days later, we headed to Taormina, a town known as the seaside gem of the island. Exiting the autostrada, we were thrown into the madness of Sicilian traffic. Though it was April, long before the start of prime tourist season, the roads were clogged as we inched along narrow streets. What little we saw of the views was magnificent. But we couldn't find anywhere to park so we could properly take in the gorgeous Mediterranean setting or have a meal. Despite hotels of every description jammed in, up, and down the mountainside, we couldn't find a room. Most hotels were closed. The ones that were open were under construction, dreary and smelling of mold, or absurdly expensive.

Given that we weren't smitten with the place, we pressed on, thinking there might be something available along one of the less renowned beaches north of the city. We gave up after the second town. As in Taormina, almost every property was locked up tight, and the open ones looked like construction zones. Rather than spend more money than we wanted to, we headed inland toward the circular route around Etna.

We stopped at a restaurant we thought might have rooms for rent. It turned out not to have rooms, but one of the restaurant employees told us of an Agriturismo close by. She phoned the owners of Arrigo, and confirmed we could get a room. Her hand-drawn map allowed us to find it with no difficulty, though it was in the middle of nowhere. It was one of the few places we visited in Sicily that had great signs. We took that as a hopeful omen.

When we arrived, the gates to Arrigo were padlocked, and no one was in sight. We honked the horn, rattled the gate, and drove up several dead ends, thinking the building we saw was an annex. We walked around the area to kill time, hoping the owners were on their way. Down the road was a wonderful view of Etna spewing steam. Then, concerned that dusk was setting in and that we'd get stranded on the slopes of Etna with nowhere to sleep, we got back into the car to resume our now desperate search for a bed. As we pulled away, a car approached, honking frantically at us. The owners apologized profusely—at least that's what we assumed since we couldn't understand a word of what they were saying—then unlocked the gate and led us inside.

They offered us a choice of several lovely rooms for the lowest price we'd paid anywhere in Sicily. We were delighted, congratulating each other for our persistence. Of course, by that point, we would have settled for anything upwards of a dungeon. The room we chose had a cathedral ceiling with long hewn beams, wrought-iron bedsteads, an elaborately carved armoire, lamps, chairs, and an ultra-modern blue-and-white-tiled bathroom. Heaven on earth. The room was chilly, but there was an electric heater that our hostess switched on.

Using lots of sign language, she explained about the locks and keys and handed us the keys. She then showed us a public room with coffee and tea-making supplies, snacks, a TV, and comfortable furniture to lounge on. They bid us arrivederci, locked the gate, and took off. In all my years of traveling, that was a first—I'd never been left in such elegant lodgings on my own, holding a set of keys.

Maggie and I explored the house. Old photos of harvesting and stomping on grapes were scattered through the rooms, providing a clue as to the building's origin as a winery. Old kegs and grinding wheels had been skillfully crafted into attractive and comfortable furniture.

We returned to the restaurant that had directed us to Arrigo and faced a table groaning from the weight of the buffet: caponata, cheese pies, mushrooms sautéed in wine, greens, multiple varieties of salami and prosciutto and cheese, spinach pies, deviled eggs, bean soup, calzone, pizza, sun-dried tomatoes, grilled eggplant, red peppers and zucchini, baked and fresh ricotta, and other foods I've since forgotten.

Back at Arrigo, the room was bitingly cold, though we'd left the space heater running. We could see our breath, and despite layers of warm sweaters and jackets, it felt as though we'd been running air-conditioning at full blast rather than heat. And, if the bedroom was cold, the tile floors in the bathroom made it feel as if we were stepping onto the North Pole.

Fearing frostbite or hypothermia, we raided the other bedrooms, collecting space heaters and down comforters. We covered the bathroom floor with purloined towels and piled blankets on the beds. Once again, we slept fitfully. The next morning, we didn't bother to help ourselves to coffee. We dressed as quickly as possible, went to the car, and blasted the heater.

We spent the day driving around the foothills, playing tag with Mount Etna as clouds covered, then cleared, the view. When we had a clear view, the snow on Etna glistened. The mountainside terrain varied from steep, grass-covered, treeless swathes to heavily wooded areas. Herds of sheep and goats grazed in the green meadows, their bells tinkling. But those same slopes showed evidence of landslides, vast areas where the land had shifted ten or twelve feet. We were later told they'd had a very wet winter, and these slides were the worst they'd had in decades. In several places, slides blocked a full lane of the road or the road had collapsed where the land below it had given way. This made for some white-knuckle driving when a collapsed road or mudslide was right before a turn, and we couldn't see what was coming from the other direction.

Our hotel guide listed an Agriturismo outside of Nicosia, a town from the Byzantine era. We arrived, drove up, down, and through the town looking for signs. There were none. At the police station, a police officer gave us directions in rapid Italian. He was trying to be helpful, and we sort of got it, but not quite. We drove in circles, then stopped to ask a guy filling bottles from a spring. In an avalanche of Italian, he gave us directions. We made a U-turn and backtracked. No luck. Our next advisor was a woman walking with her daughter. Her directions included a landmark, left at the first restaurant along the road. Of course, when we got to the corner, there were two choices. We made the wrong one. Another back-track. A fork in the road, another wrong turn. By the time we arrived, I would have slept in a barn if it meant I could have gotten into a supine position and not moved for a while. Fortunately, it was a pretty place with a comfortable bed. Within five minutes of getting into the room, I was sound asleep.

When I awoke and went for a walk, I met the farm's donkeys, geese, and sheep. The owner's son spoke English well, so we could communicate. When we said, "You really need signs," he replied, "Yes, we do." He laughed and said, "I'm surprised you found us." Another chuckle. "Most Italians have a tough time, and they can understand the directions."

"So why don't you get signs?" I asked.

"The signs," he said, "are on order."

I suspect that had been the case for years. He also told us there are no other hotels or any other type of lodging in Nicosia.

When we left the Inn of No Signs, we headed to another town known for ceramics, San Stefano Di Camastra. Camastra is in a gorgeous coastal area in the northern province of Messina. The main road through town is lined with shops selling ceramics. Despite the lovely setting and obvious tourist attraction, there wasn't a single open restaurant, trattoria, or sweet shop anywhere, even on the major shopping street. By that point on the trip, we'd created a cache of emergency food. We needed to dip into it often. I've been back to the area recently and there are now several restaurants to choose from.

Fortunately, the ceramics were lovely. We wandered through the shops, admiring platters, tabletops, vases, and delicate bowls in a whirlwind of styles, patterns, and vivid colors. Each shop had a different take: bright sunflowers, swirling red, blue, and gold paisleys, some featured classic patterns, others contemporary designs. The contrast to the drabness of the town was startling.

At the edge of the business district, there was a broad promenade facing the sea, lined with palm trees. In most seaside towns this would be recognized as a perfect site for benches, cafés, and shops. In Camastra, there were two iron benches and a row of concrete apartment blocks, every window covered by a metal shutter. Nothing was remotely attractive, except for the view.

Looking back, the gorgeous scenery, nearly empty tourist attractions, and locals not yet jaded by hordes of tourists made our visit to Sicily a delight. But what made it most memorable were our searches for food and shelter. Who could forget our panic at the prospect of sleeping in a tiny car in frigid temperatures?

Sicilians didn't seem to have the tourism thing down, despite the wealth of things to do and see—beaches, churches, baroque, Norman, and medieval towns, mosaics and pottery, Greek and Roman ruins, not to mention Etna and the coast. In most parts of the world I've visited, even in remote places, the locals have realized that tourists bring in money. Consequently, they've done whatever possible to encourage tourism. In Sicily, quite the opposite seemed to be true. In most areas, there were few hotels, restaurants were difficult to find, and they had limited hours. Taormina represented the other end of the spectrum—overbuilt and overcrowded. It felt as if Sicilians wanted to herd all tourists to a single location and keep them away from everywhere else.

The Sicilians we met were gracious and helpful, but I always had a feeling they resented our being there in April. It was as if they were savoring their alone time before the great wave of tourists crashed onto their island.

Perhaps they've been very smart, not encouraging tourists to come in and disrupt their way of life, at least not during the off-season. But given the relative poverty on the island and its natural beauty, it could attract significant tourist money all year round to help raise the economy. But when I reflect on it, I realize I'm thinking like an American, not a Sicilian.

VIETNAM ENCOUNTERS: 2004

I'm of the generation who thinks of Vietnam as a war zone. Horrific images of napalm and bombings are permanently lodged in my brain. When I started reading accounts that described the country and people in a positive light, I wanted to see it for myself.

While my friend Maggie and I were traveling through the country, there was no way we would have considered renting a car. Traffic in Saigon (Ho Chi Minh City) and Hanoi was a whole new level of crazy. Traffic lights and stop signs didn't exist. Battalions of cyclists, motorbikes, cars, trucks, and buses moved at top speed on wide boulevards. Making a left turn required perfect reflexes and nerves of steel. Drivers seemed to know the rules of the road, but to me, it looked like a free-for-all. Walking around the city, I was so terrified of crossing the boulevards I willingly paid a taxi to get us across.

Some of the areas we wanted to see would have been difficult, or even impossible, to reach on public transportation. So, we arranged for day tours.

Our first trip was to the Mekong Delta. The Mekong Delta is a network of tributaries between Saigon and Cambodia. During the Vietnam War, some of the fiercest fighting took place there. Images of the dense jungle, soldiers in camouflage, burned crops, and bombings were shown almost nightly on TV. Though the war had ended nearly thirty years before, I anticipated seeing remnants of the bombing.

Our group of eight boarded a minivan in Saigon and headed to the Mekong River. There, a motorboat awaited us for a tour through the lush valley. The water was murky brown, contrasting with an intense green shoreline. On the first leg of the journey, we passed small islands, fertile fields, other tourist groups, and commercial boats loaded with produce heading to markets. The guide told us that the delta is where most Vietnamese agriculture is situated. Endless varieties of fruit and vegetables, as well as rice, grow there. It was a peaceful, almost idyllic environment. There wasn't a trace of combat.

We stopped at one of the islands for lunch. As we sat at a table in a verdant garden, our small group chattered in a mix of fractured English. There were Europeans, Asians, Australians, and a Canadian. Maggie and I represented the United States.

I became intrigued by the Vietnamese Canadian man seated next to me. I guessed him to be in his midseventies. He wore brand-label clothes and carried an expensive camera. Cuong and I bonded as we spoke. The rest of the group talked on their own, and it was as if Cuong and I were alone. After some idle chitchat, I asked him questions about his life.

"This is my first time back in Saigon since 1980."

"What do you notice most about how it's changed?" I asked.

"It's modern, busy, affluent." He described the many construction projects he'd seen in Saigon and the abundance of material goods. "Last time I was here, there wasn't much to buy. And now! You can get anything. From anywhere."

"And the traffic! I'm afraid to cross the street." He patted his chest. "It's amazing an old man like me doesn't get a heart attack!"

As I gently probed, his story came out. He lived in the North as a child and into his twenties. When the French pulled out of Vietnam in 1954, he moved south. In Saigon, he married and had six children. He worked as an electrical engineer. When the Americans pulled out twenty years later, Cuong attempted to get himself and his family out of the country.

"What happened then?" I asked.

"The authorities captured us." His face drooped. This was a tough story to tell. "I ended up in a reeducation camp for five years. My family was in the same camp, but in a different area. I saw them, but not very often."

"That must have been awful."

I wondered, but didn't ask, what he thought of the American pullout. I also wondered if he'd been tortured by the Viet Cong. On his own, he offered some insights into his time being held by them.

"I worked in the fields, mines, building streets, anywhere they sent us." He paused and cleared his throat. "When I wasn't working, they sent me to 'reeducation classes' to teach me proper respect for the government."

Their attempts to brainwash him didn't take, and in early 1980, he and his family escaped to Laos. From there, they traveled to Malaysia. He then moved alone to Ottawa.

"Why Ottawa?" I asked.

"I didn't know anything about Canada, and that's where the aid organization arranged for me to go. I didn't object. I just wanted to get to North America." He looked wistful. "I thought I could get a good job, and within a year or two, send for my family."

For three years, he lived alone in Ottawa. He couldn't have chosen a less hospitable place weather-wise, though he said people were friendly and helped him to acclimate. Early on, he suffered in the cold, lonely for his family, working menial jobs, and learning English.

"One snowy night, I had worked the night shift at a restaurant. I was waiting for the bus in the freezing cold, standing in snow that came up to my knees." Cuong shivered, as if reliving that night. "I cried, feeling lonely, freezing, miserable. I thought about my wife and children. I remembered my life before the war and wanted it all back." He shook his head. "But I knew it wasn't coming back. I cried some more."

While I'd read memoirs by so-called boat people and had some impressions of difficult immigration from war zones, his story shook me. Hearing directly from someone about his lived experience made the ordeal very real. Since then, with every news headline of war zones and migrants fleeing their country, Cuong comes to mind. I ache for people caught in poverty or political fights, who must give up everything and start again.

I was relieved that Cuong's story had a happy ending. Eventually, he brought his whole family over to Canada.

"We have a good life in Ottawa. We all learned English. I got a good job. My kids are all doing well." He swelled with pride. "My son is a doctor. He'll be joining me here next week." He gave me a thumbs-up. "I can't wait to hear what he thinks about all the changes."

Two days later, Maggie and I took another tour to a different area of the Mekong Delta. In My Tho, a motorboat picked us up, and we went into a smaller tributary of the river. We stopped several times at sites designed for tourists. At the first stop, we walked through a grove of coconuts and got to experience the humid but perfect growing conditions. A woman who worked in a candy-making operation offered us coconut candy and demonstrated how they made it.

We were served tea and cake in a different small village, as local musicians performed Vietnamese folk tunes. In a wildlife sanctuary, they invited us to pose for a photo with a python wrapped around our shoulders.

Next, we transferred to a small boat and paddled deep into narrow canals. This was the Vietnam I imagined from the 1970s. The vegetation was thick and looked as if it would have been easy for soldiers to hide in. Though it was hot and humid, I shivered, remembering scenes of soldiers in the jungle during the war.

Our final stop was a Buddhist temple. It looked garish to me, and with loads of tourists wandering around, not peaceful. Maggie and I were disappointed with this tour. It felt too planned, too perfect, with no opportunity to interact with anyone. We only saw a particular slice of life that seemed staged. I was ready to return to lively, chaotic Saigon.

Before our departure back to the city, we walked into the temple's inner sanctuary. Moments later, a monk, an old gentleman with an affable expression, stopped Maggie and me. With Hang, our guide, as interpreter, he asked, "Are you sisters?"

"No," we told him. "We're friends."

Hang translated, "You have kind faces. You are good, compassionate, loving people."

The monk turned and looked deep into my eyes and whispered a few words. Hang leaned in to hear and told me, "He said, you help the world. You feel sad when there is poverty and injustice in the world."

Digging deep into the folds of his robe, the monk pulled out something. He leaned in even closer and whispered even more softly, this time in English, "I have a gift for you." As he slipped a bracelet of prayer beads onto my wrist, he bowed his head. I did the same. I was stunned by both the gift and his English. Before I could thank him, he turned and walked off into an area marked by a sign in multiple languages that read, private.

I asked Hang if it was common for monks to approach tourists. "No," he said. "I've never seen that happen before." Hang looked at me more closely, as if trying to determine what the monk had seen in me. I wondered the same thing.

COOKING MY WAY AROUND THE GLOBE—
PART 1: UBUD, BALI, 2004

As I knew from my first trip to Bali, daily offerings are made to appease the Hindu gods and deities the Balinese worship. After rituals have been performed, the festive food is eaten. Nothing goes to waste. The preparation of festive food is labor intensive, done communally, and always beautifully displayed. While touring, I saw several feasts laid out for locals to enjoy. The food looked fabulous. If I'd had more nerve, I would have invited myself, but that seemed culturally inappropriate.

I joined a tour of the local market. I visit markets often during my travels, but frequently don't know what I'm looking at. This time I could find out.

"What is that green goop?" I asked the guide.

"An herbal drink meant to make you strong. It's got great medicinal properties. Pregnant women drink a cupful every morning during their last trimester for an easy delivery."

I tasted a bit. It was bland, and the slimy texture was tough to swallow.

At another stand I asked, "How do they get that food so pink?"

The guide replied, "The pink is from artificial food coloring. Pink foods are much beloved by the Balinese. But you should avoid all pink foods."

I thought about the red dye that was routinely used in American foods and thought it couldn't be much worse than that.

We tasted half a dozen Balinese fast foods: sticky rice with cane sugar scooped into a banana leaf cone and eaten as a sweet snack on the run; sweet corn mixed with coconut, vanilla, and cane sugar—a crunchy, sweet snack. There were a dozen of us on the tour, and whenever we'd see something interesting, someone would buy a bag for a thousand rupiahs—about eleven cents—and share it around. Just enough for a good taste of each.

We stopped at a spice seller's booth and bought fresh nutmeg, cinnamon, vanilla, and long pepper. At the vegetable stands, there were tiny eggplants the size and shape of a tangerine, snake squash that looked very snakelike, various tubers used like potatoes, mangosteen, white mangoes, rambutans, snake fruit, and dozens more exotic fruits. There were also apples imported from Washington State—used only for ceremonial occasions.

Along with the edibles were offering trays—small boxes made from banana leaves filled with flowers, fruits, nuts, and incense. They're used to appease the gods. They are placed daily in front of every building, on shelves of items for sale, on doorsteps, just about anywhere. In addition to the small boxes, every building has an offering box high on a wall for gifts to the higher gods. I saw hundreds of them during my stay in Bali.

At the end of the tour, I wandered through the tourist section of the market, picking up a few items here and there, then wandered off to have a cool drink. I became addicted to watermelon juice on my first visit to Bali. During this trip, I became more adventurous, drinking any combinations offered to me. Mango and lime became a new favorite.

Since I wouldn't be eating with locals, a cooking class seemed the next best thing. The class was taught by Janet DeNeefe, founder of one of the best restaurants in Ubud, Casa Luna, and author of *Fragrant Rice,* a memoir about her life in Bali. She's an Australian who had lived in Bali for twenty years. The class took place under palm trees on wooden tables; cooking outdoors is traditional in Bali. The shade and a subtle wind cooled off the area on what was otherwise a hot, sticky day.

To begin, Janet explained that traditional Balinese food has complex customs, rules, and regulations. These dictate what may and may not be eaten in a specific place, time, and situation. While she adapted the menu to our Western tastes, she told us that the Balinese will eat almost anything that won't kill them. Besides a wide variety of plants, they will eat most things that crawl, fly, swim, or walk.

A "festive" meal made sense for a cooking class. Our group of twelve worked together, chopping, mixing, boiling, frying, and then plating the prepared food. All of this was accompanied by Janet's gentle instructions and a lot of laughter.

When we first showed up, baskets filled with spices, leaves, and shoots were artfully laid out on a table. Before Janet arrived, we attempted to guess what each was. With twelve of us in the class—the majority Australians, the remainder American—we only identified a little over half the ingredients. Once Janet explained the foods, it was clear why we didn't know more of them. They don't exist in our parts of the world.

Fortunately, in the handout with recipes, she included substitutions. For candlenut, we could use either macadamias or cashews. Long pepper, which, when dried, looks a bit like a small pine cone, could be replaced with mild white pepper. For Pandan leaf, which is used in either sweet or savory dishes, Janet suggested using vanilla beans for the former and macha or cilantro for the latter. Salam leaf is like bay leaf, but with a curry undertone.

We smelled and tasted four different varieties of ginger, each with a distinctive aroma and taste, from sweet and mild to hot and spicy. Every Balinese dish includes at least a small amount of sweet, sour, hot, and salty. Even using identical ingredients, by changing the proportions, the taste is different. In addition to the spices, we smelled and tasted a couple of dozen other ingredients, including veggies, fruits, and nuts. Then the cooking began.

Our menu included:

- hibiscus tea
- *lawar paku*—fern with spices
- *rujak*—sweet and sour sauce
- *sate lembat ayam*—chicken sate with coconut
- *buncis pelecing*—beans and coconut milk
- *bregedel jagung*—sweet corn patties
- *gado-gado*—vegetables in peanut sauce
- *nasi kuning*—fragrant yellow rice

Using a stone mortar and pestle, we ground spices to be used in sauces. With a rough blade, we grated coconut, then mashed some of it. Everyone had a hand in the preparation. We sautéed, fried, and steamed. Then Janet demonstrated the proper way to plate the final dishes.

I'd never before cooked a full meal in the open air in such a communal way. It brought together a group of people in a shared activity, with everyone contributing to the effort. I understood why, with its almost perfect weather, this is a mainstay of the Balinese culture.

The reward for our efforts was a fabulous feast; each dish was fragrant, distinctive, and delicious. We sat at tables surrounded by palm trees and flowers, drank our hibiscus tea, and ate what we had cooked. My favorite was the spicy fern dish—lawar paku. I ate it there and have never had it again, yet I can still remember the taste. The fern fronds were fresh and crunchy, the coconut sauce sweet and spicy, and the ground candlenut added additional texture.

It is embarrassing to say, but since that class, I have never again prepared any of the dishes, despite the well-written, clear recipes Janet provided. I'm not even certain why. I've cooked foods I've learned in other classes. But with complex ingredients and many steps, I guess Balinese cuisine isn't top of mind for me.

ODDBALL WISCONSIN, 2005

I'd been collecting outsider art for about ten years when I began to hear about fantastical environments created by untrained artists. Often, they start out as minor projects, then the creators become obsessed.

The work grows until it consumes years of their lives and acres of land. Typically, the sites are in remote locations. To see them, you must travel far from cities and major tourist attractions.

I read about art environments in Wisconsin in two different guidebooks, Oddball Wisconsin and Weird Wisconsin. It became clear the state is a gold mine of art environments—my kind of place. So, off I went to Wisconsin to hunt out these treasures.

M y first stop in Madison was at Ella's Deli. It was tough to find a parking spot, but once I got into the restaurant, it was easy to understand why. While the food was mediocre, the decor was amazing, an art environment of sorts. Oversized Spider-Men and Popeyes, grinning ten-foot-high bananas, seahorses and elephants dangled from the ceiling, mixed in with mirrors and ornate chandeliers.

Each table had a recessed area filled with a collection of silly items covered by glass. Mine displayed Cracker Jack prizes. At the next table were Pez dispensers, and on the other side, staplers and tape dispensers. You'd think the place was designed for kids. But there were twenty packed tables with no children in sight.

It was visual overload. I could imagine stoned college students hanging out there, gazing around and saying, "Oh wow, man!"

Before leaving Madison, the waiter gave me excellent directions to Sid's Sculpture Yard, a local folk art environment. He was excited that I was heading off to see "a place that rivals Ella's."

Sid Boyum died more than ten years before my visit. But, according to *Oddball Wisconsin*, wonderful handmade sculpture filled his backyard. The property was overgrown and in disrepair. I tiptoed through towering weeds for a look over the fence. A towering man-eating mushroom, a potbellied beaming Buddha, a pagoda, torsos, and wondrous faces filled the yard, and peeked through the overgrowth. It pained me to see this lifetime of artistic expression abandoned. I hoped that the Kohler Foundation—yes, the Kohler of tubs, sinks, and toilets—would help restore the property. From my research, I learned that locating, restoring, and preserving folk architecture and art environments in Wisconsin is a key mission of the Kohler Foundation, whose headquarters are in the state.

My next stop was unplanned. When I saw a hand-painted sign for "spectacular sculpture," I followed a series of signposts like a hound in hot pursuit of a bone.

There was no mistaking which property contained the "spectacular sculpture." A sign at the head of the driveway read sculpture by Paul Bobrowitz. A herd of flying pigs constructed from scrap metal flanked the sign.

The road led through several acres of Paul's scrap metal creations—a flock of delicate birds, ten-foot-tall bears, faces, hands built in abstract shapes. At a building that appeared to be his studio, I parked and got out to wander. First, I ducked my head into the workshop to try to locate someone, but got silence in response to my "Hello??"

I set off to explore. I'd start up one path to see a sinuous reclining figure, only to be distracted by a pair of masked faces that attracted my attention. Then I'd spot giant insects with mischievous grins that hinted at their intent to sting a new victim. I lost track of time, mesmerized by the variety and whimsy of the sculptures.

About thirty minutes into my walk, I met Paul, the artist. He was putting a new coating on the floor leading into his gallery. He was a gentle soul with a soft voice and a mysterious quality. Paul told me he'd always made sculpture for fun, but until ten years before, he'd worked as a carpenter. At that point, he had enough people buying his work that he could afford to be a full-time artist.

One of the great things about visiting a working artist is that they're always happy to see you, chat about their work, and try to sell their work to you. But even if you buy nothing, they are uniformly gracious.

I repeated several times how much I liked his work.

He asked, "Why?"

"Because you so clearly follow your instincts, and aren't tied to any particular style. You follow your heart."

He said, "Honey, that's what I keep getting flak about. The critics say that I don't follow a single style long enough to develop it."

"I think what you're doing is fine. Stick with it."

A few minutes later, he mentioned he was planning to move. Thinking about the number and size of the pieces, I couldn't even begin to imagine this. I asked, "Why would you do that?"

"I'm running out of space."

"Really? Seems to me you've got a lot of land."

"While this seems like a big place, things are getting more than a little tight in my studio. I need a lot more space to work in and store materials."

"How long will it take you to move everything?"

"Well, I figure it all got here one piece at a time, so it will go out one piece at a time."

"How long have you been living there?"

"Oh, about fifteen years."

"And how long do you think it would take for it to all get moved?"

"About a year and a half."

Had I enough money and a way to haul more of Paul's work home, I could have done some real damage. Instead, I got a mere two figures, each about eighteen inches high. One had a cocky expression and outstretched arms. The other was waving as if to get my attention. They both seemed to be pleading for a ride.

Back on the road with my hitchhiking purchases, I drove through rolling countryside dotted with silos, cows, and farmhouses with wraparound porches. In a couple of hours, I arrived at my next destination, the Fiberglass Animals, Shapes, and Trademarks Corporation, or FAST, located outside of Sparta. For anyone who likes large roadside objects, this is the mother lode. It is the place where Big Bob figures, giant cows, and life-size dinosaurs are born.

On my fiftieth birthday trip, I'd seen the 145-foot-long muskie at the Freshwater Fishing Hall of Fame in Hayward, Wisconsin. The size and detail of the colossal creature awed me.

While I didn't see any sculptures emerging from their casting molds, I got to wander through the company's mold yard. The folks at FAST didn't mind visitors but warned everyone not to touch anything because of sharp edges.

"And be careful as you walk around. There are sometimes wasps' nests in the grass," one employee told me.

Behind the factory was a vast field that at first glance appeared to be strewn with junk. Looking more closely, I realized the property was littered with the molds of FAST's creations, scattered about like wrapping paper on Christmas morning. I carefully picked my way through the odd shapes—a twenty-foot-high head and torso of a knight, two giant frog water slides, a smiling hippo face, a Viking, a swan, and Big Bob.

I later asked and was told that they reuse molds to save money; they never throw anything away.

Before I left, I visited the office where they gave me a catalog, should I wish to purchase a giant turtle, knight, or duck at some future date.

Next up was the Wegner Grotto, a folk-art site restored and maintained by the Kohler Foundation. Built by Paul and Matilda Wegner, a farm couple, it was a project to keep them busy during retirement. First, they built in their front yard a twelve-foot replica of the *Bremen*, the ship they had emigrated on from Germany to the United States. Then they kept going—an American flag, a re-production of their fiftieth-anniversary cake, fences, arches, a prayer garden, and birdhouses.

As with so many other untrained artists, they used materials at hand and a ton of imagination. Constructed from concrete, they studded the structures with shattered pieces of glass to catch sun-light. Glints of light lit up the area. The contrast to the surrounding farmland made it seem as bright as Times Square at night.

Outsider art sites are true environments. Walking into them is entering a different realm. They are one-of-a-kind, personal artistic statements. The outside world melts away, and you begin to live inside the creators' vision.

I thought about the Kohler Foundation and wondered why and how they chose to preserve folk art environments. It's not like they draw crowds or were likely to bring them positive PR. I concluded that someone in the foundation, like me, had a personal love of this art. I sent them kind thoughts and much appreciation.

The next morning, following information in *Weird Wisconsin*, I headed to Mount Horeb. The town had become a tourist attraction for two reasons, the Mustard Museum and the Trollway. No, not a toll way, a Trollway. Mount Horeb is proud of its Norwegian heritage, and its main street is lined with large, carved wooden trolls.

Every store offering food displayed signs reading homemade lefse. Not knowing what this was, I entered a restaurant to ask. By luck, I picked a great place with a tin ceiling, cozy wooden booths, a tiled floor, and a soda fountain. The proprietor, Mr. Leslie, was an old-timer, very chatty and eager to fill me in on *lefse*.

"Potato cakes. Think crepes or flat bread made from potato puree. You must try them."

"I just ate breakfast."

"Doesn't matter. You can't come here and not try lefse."

"Okay, I'll come back after I've looked around town."

He wasn't taking that for an answer. Paying customers had to wait while the proprietor, Mr. Leslie, rambled on. I got a long commentary on lefse, trolls, Norway, tourists, and mustard.

After several minutes, I persuaded him I'd return in an hour.

"Okay, but sign the guestbook. That way, I'll be able to track you down if you don't come back," he said with a wink.

I signed the guestbook.

The Mustard Museum was hopping. The museum is half shop, half exhibit, of all things mustard, no other condiments permitted, and a slew of free samples. I sat through a video showing how founder Barry Levenson had his epiphany to start the museum. It had something to do with arguing a case before the U.S. Supreme Court. He was a district attorney who had a bottle of mustard in his pocket that he had taken from a tray in a hallway of his hotel. He won the case. Sure that the bottle of mustard had brought him luck, he started collecting mustard in earnest. It was a wackier story than any I'd heard about the outsider artists.

After tasting a half dozen mustards, I was ready to take on lefse. Mr. Leslie welcomed me back like a long-lost friend. He brought over a plate of freshly prepared lefse and stood there watching me eat it. The lefse looked a bit like a soft tortilla. The plate had a stack of rolled lefse, accompanied by strawberry jam and cream.

"These are delicious." I didn't have the heart to tell him I preferred mustard over lefse.

I'd saved the best stop of the day for last. Grand View was built in the 1930s, '40s, and '50s by a farmer, Nick Engelbert. After his death, his decorated house and garden sculptures fell into a state of disrepair. As with so many other environments, the Kohler Foundation discovered, repaired, and preserved the statues Englebert had created. Life-sized, the statues were made from concrete embedded with shards of glass and pottery, beads, buttons and seashells.

Engelbert had a sense of humor. I laughed at the man holding a bottle looking ready to take a swig, while a monkey stood close by watching him as if to discourage his drinking. A statue of a young boy reading captured the essence of being absorbed by a great story. A Viking standing in a boat conveyed satisfaction in discovery. As with the other environments I'd visited, I was alone as I strolled through the grounds. I thought of Grand View as a monument to artistic vision, passion, and sheer joy of life.

Frank Lloyd Wright was one of my mother's heroes. She had earned a degree in architecture in the 1930s, a time when women were a rarity in the profession. Because of her devotion, I'd visited many Frank Lloyd Wright sites. Taliesin, in Spring Hill, is the mother lode. This is where he spent most of his time, for most of his life. It embodies his vision over many decades. By the way, Taliesin is Welsh for "shining brow," as in the hill's brow. Wright thought a house should never be situated on the top of the hill, but embedded in it, a natural part of the surrounding environment.

Though Wright was certainly not an oddball, I took a tour of his home and studio. Wright's one-hundred-year-old designs look contemporary. His influence on architects worldwide has been extraordinary. Every time you experience cathedral ceilings, a cantilevered structure, or large picture windows, you can tip your hat to his genius.

I was taken with the sweeping lines of the buildings, both inside and out, and his attention to detail. He designed everything from the doorknobs to the overall landscape plan. All the little bits combine to create a cohesive environment.

Though I was glad to see Taliesin, the primary reason for visiting this area was to see the House on the Rock. I had heard about it from the proprietor of the UCM Museum in Louisiana. He'd been inspired to create his oddball museum because he loved the House on the Rock so much. Based on his recommendation, I read about it. It sounded like a bad acid trip come alive.

The visit started with a long driveway lined with leering gnomes, winged dragons, and other weird and wonderful figures.

On my way out, those same sculptures looked commonplace, if not tasteful, compared to the rest of the estate.

Alex Jordan, the architect and owner of House on the Rock, built it perched on top of an enormous rock, complete with a glass-paneled room projecting far out over the mountain that allowed for a commanding view of the valleys surrounding it. In part, he did this to thumb his nose at Frank Lloyd Wright, who had—depending on which story you listen to—either rejected his application to become an apprentice or fired him from his apprenticeship. Remember, Frank Lloyd Wright had a fondness for building on the brow of a hill, never on top. Jordan was out to get back at him. The house was down the road from Taliesin, and Wright would have seen it almost every day.

Jordan hired workers from Madison, luring them to the construction site with promises of money, food, and whiskey to blast away the top of the hill. It doesn't say in the guidebook how many people got hurt doing this, but the combination of dynamite and whiskey sounds pretty risky to me.

The site of the house allows a bird's-eye view of the valley, but visitors have only one opportunity to see it. Once you start on the museum path, it's a 2.6-mile forced march, first through the house, then through barn after barn filled with stuff. Dark hallways connect the buildings and you're never certain where you are, how far you've come, or more importantly, how much farther you have to go. An hour into this extravaganza, I'd heard kids whimpering, "It's dark. I'm dizzy. I'm tired." Too bad, once you're in, you're in.

The decor is a testament to bad taste. It makes Graceland look refined, nearly aristocratic. Big replica Tiffany lamps abound. I figured he'd bought a truckload. They're held by ships' figureheads or hang down in strange places, like six inches above a carpeted floor.

Each room is a different garish color. Describing every room and object isn't possible, nor is a list of the highlights. That would go on for pages. The man collected everything, and all of it was on display. He didn't care whether it was good, bad, or indifferent. It just had to be.

He was an early enthusiast of animatronics, half of it predating Disney. Moving people and objects lived in every room. Push a button, and figures came to life; drums banged, cymbals crashed, bows scraped, oboes blew, and violins sang out. If that weren't enough of an auditory overload, in every room a recording boomed. The soundtrack throughout this entire adventure was true audio hell: off-key renditions of marches, opera, and popular tunes played at ear-splitting volumes.

In the Tribute to Nostalgia Room were Burma-Shave signs, guns, and circus paraphernalia. Nearby, in a glowing red room, there was what is reported to be the world's largest carousel, spinning at the far end. You'd think this would be great fun for kids, but a small boy of five or six years ran shrieking through it, trying to hurry his parents along.

Unfortunately, visitors can't ride the carousel. But then again, by that point in the tour, people would probably come flying off from dizziness and exhaustion. Instead, people stand clutching the protective railing and watch mermaids, giant dogs, frogs, pigs, goddesses, and dozens of other figures spin past. There are no carousel horses. Those line the walls. Overhead, dozens of mannequins fitted out with angel wings float languidly. It felt like a nostalgic visit to my college days in the '60s, hallucinogenic images minus the drugs. Throughout this journey, I felt a sense of being stoned, though I was straight and sober.

When at last I pried myself out of this room, I was practically running, desperate to get out, breathe fresh air, and see natural light. Instead, I was forced through rooms of circus stuff, jewelry, additional animatronics, armor, dollhouses, organs, and more, much more. After what felt like days, I was spit out into the gift shop.

The following morning, it was off to Prairie Moon, another of Kohler's restorations. On the way, I made a quick stop at the Rock in the House, where an enormous boulder had crashed into a home. It was pretty amazing, considering that only one of the windows was broken when it rolled into the house. Given the proximity to the House on the Rock, it made for a catchy tourist attraction.

At Prairie Moon, a fence of native stone and conical posts surrounded the sculpture garden. In the garden there are rockets, a Hindu temple, dinosaurs, and more. The guide quotes Herman Rusch, the artist, as saying, "I kept on building. You don't ever know where it will end up when you start."

It was an apt quote for the creations of all the artists I visited. In total, I saw ten outsider art environments. They all displayed that same sense of wonderment and compulsion.

All artists are driven by a need to try something new, push the medium a bit further, express a new idea. I remember days in a ceramic studio when ten hours would pass in what felt like no time at all. I suspect that for these artists, similar days would pass into weeks, months, and years of creativity. And, unlike those seeking fame and fortune, these individuals, in their remote homes, were creating for the joy of it, for themselves. Art in its purest expression.

FOR COD'S SAKE:
NEWFOUNDLAND, CANADA, 2005

In Newfoundland, puffins outnumber humans. Moose wander through towns. Located on the easternmost tip of North America, it is far more remote, less touristy, and much wilder than almost anywhere on the continent. Though "the rock," as

locals call the island, is less than a three-hour flight from New York, there is but a single direct flight a day from the U.S. That service started one year before I visited.

In New York City, where I grew up and now live, nothing stays the same. People from around the world move in and out constantly, introducing us to new foods, clothes, music, and ideas. Buildings go up and come down regularly. Every time I walk on a street I haven't visited in a while, there are new restaurants to try and stores to shop in—I thrive on change. I assumed that Newfoundland traditions would be deep-rooted and the culture rock-solid. It sounded like a place where time has stood still. On days when the frenzy of New York was too much, it sounded idyllic.

One evening during a walk on a beach in Rocky Harbor on the west coast, I started a conversation with a guy painting his boat. He told me he was working on his boat so it wouldn't look shabby when it was confiscated.

"Confiscated? Why would it be confiscated?" I asked.

"I plan to fish for cod."

"Right. So why would they confiscate your boat?" I repeated, puzzled. I'd eaten cod at least five or six times by that point; it seemed to be ubiquitous.

"Illegal. I'm not allowed to catch even one damn fish for my own use. That isn't right." Then he began to really get worked up. "Damned politicians. The cod are so thick out there you could walk across the bay on them. But can I catch even one to eat? No. I can't." I shook my head sympathetically but thought, that couldn't be right. Where was all the cod I'd been eating since I arrived coming from? He went on, "They're a thousand miles away. What the hell do politicians sitting in their nice offices know about cod? Not a damn thing, that's what!"

Twenty minutes later, I finally managed to extricate myself. He could have gone on all night, ranting and cursing the fools in Ottawa who were making the lives of Newfoundlanders miserable.

For the two weeks I traveled around Newfoundland, cod came up in conversation several times a day. I was never the one to bring it up. "We've all become outlaws," one man told me. "We're the new generation of pirates," said another. A woman from Ontario staying at our B&B told us that she'd gone on a boat with relatives and spent her time peering through binoculars on lookout duty. "My uncle wanted me to taste fresh cod, but he was really nervous, convinced the patrols would catch him, and he'd be fined." She paused, then added ominously, "Or worse." I found out later people could land in jail for repeated offenses.

In restaurants located outside the main towns, menus are limited.

Usually there's some combination of fish and chips, sautéed cod, cod cakes, baked cod, cod stew, cod au gratin, cod with broulis (cod drenched in a sauce made from onions fried in bacon grease and topped with bacon chips), cod tongues, or cod chowder. The only thing missing was cod sushi. Occasionally salmon, scallops, or shrimp found their way onto a menu, sometimes a burger or chicken breast, but that was it. After a few days I began to crave pasta, a great salad, a taco.

Even in the most settled areas of Newfoundland, the towns are small, self-contained, and several miles apart. In more sparsely inhabited areas, one town can be many dozens of miles from the next. All hug the water's edge. The province's interior is mostly empty. Steep hillsides surrounding some seaside villages make grazing animals and even rudimentary farming a near impossibility. It's a stark, rocky landscape. Key to the success of a settlement is a secure harbor for cod fishing boats. No safe deepwater harbor, no cod, no town.

Remoteness and the harsh living conditions have been part of Newfoundland's heritage since the establishment of villages four hundred years ago. Cod fishing is why the land was originally settled and the only reason for staying there. Cod controlled wealth, politics, even survival. That was in the 1600s. Not much has changed. In the face of the cod fishing prohibition, locals have tried to hang onto traditions. They didn't want to change, or couldn't.

The guide on a whale-watching expedition told me that his father, grandfather, great-grandfather, and generations going back to the 1600s had all been fishermen. "It's my birthright," he told me. "In 1992, the government declared that the waters were being fished out and shut down all cod fishing." I learned later that efficient fishing methods and overseas ships working in the area had led to the near extinction of the once plentiful fish. The decree meant about thirty thousand people were put out of work. Then he told me, "They offered fishermen $90,000 to stop catching cod. Permanently." To the guide's family, who were barely managing to get by, that seemed like a fortune. They took the offer, as did most Newfoundland cod fishermen. After a few years, the money ran out, and they had no way to earn a living. His relatives began to leave the area. He was one of the few to stay behind. It is a struggle.

Once again, I wondered where all that cod I'd been eating was coming from. When I asked, people told me many different stories. Individuals were sneaking out at night and bringing in fish. Nova Scotians were selling cod from Newfoundland waters back to locals. Cod was bought illegally from factory boats operated by the Japanese or Norwegians. A minor amount of fishing was permitted, but strictly controlled by the government. The only story that sounded totally implausible to me was that they were still using frozen fish hoarded away at the time of the ban. I never did learn a definitive answer.

Where I live, cities are growing taller and expanding into suburban areas at alarming rates. In contrast, Newfoundland's small population is shrinking, with the decrease especially rapid in small, remote fishing villages known as "out-towns." After cod fishing was banned and other fishing severely curtailed, there wasn't much for people to do in the villages. As the guide told me and others confirmed, much of the younger generation has fled. They've moved to the capital, St. John's, as well as other areas such as Ontario and Saskatchewan. Several people told me that there are more Newfoundlanders living in Saskatchewan than people who were born there. I don't know if that's true, but it makes for a great urban myth. Still, after the guide's story and learning that the children of several of our B&B hostesses worked in Saskatchewan, there could be a kernel of truth to this myth.

I understand leaving an area to find better work opportunities. People often don't have the skills, finances, or other resources to develop new industries. But it baffled me that with cod so hard to come by, the Newfies that remained didn't switch to chicken or burgers or some other source of protein. Then it came to me: as Newfies see fishing for cod as their birthright, so is eating it. It's a fundamental part of their culture. They're clinging to whatever they can.

I've traveled to nearly ninety countries but have never been to a place where a single *anything* is so pervasive in people's lives. Perhaps among the Inuit in Alaska, where seal hunting determined survival, the same single-mindedness exists.

I was happy to return home to New York City and appreciative of its countless options, from food to entertainment to work opportunities. I occasionally complain about the energy needed to make the many decisions in my life. But my time in Newfoundland renewed my love of choices and change. It also made me understand that I make my choices. They aren't imposed on me. I've never been forced to give up my career, my home, my connections to my birthplace.

If I had grown up in Newfoundland, how would I reshape my life? To a Newfoundlander, cod is king. At least it was. Now what?

CONTRASTS:
LOMBOK, INDONESIA, 2006

When I visited Bali in 1991, the main beach areas of Kuta and Nusa Dua were busy, but not overly so. The pristine beaches in other coastal areas were not yet built up, while inland remained quiet. Then swarms of Australian tourists began arriving and things got a bit out of hand with excessive drinking and rowdy behavior.

Bali's population is predominantly Hindu, people who were tolerant, if not overly happy with this change. Indonesia's faction of orthodox Muslims were appalled that such immoral behavior was happening in their country and vowed to end it.

A bomb planted by an al-Qaeda-inspired group exploded in the heart of Bali's tourist area shortly before I revisited the island in 2006. Tourism was way down, and the economy was hurting. While I wanted to spend a few days there to see the changes, I decided to spend most of my time on Lombok, the island to the immediate east of Bali. I'd been told by several people that it was an unspoiled paradise. "Why don't more people go there?" I asked. "Bali is better known and more set up for tourists. Some people are concerned about spending time in a place that is predominantly Muslim," were the answers I got.

My accommodation on Lombok, Puri Mas, was described as a "boutique hotel." It was affordable only because the economy was in distress. My private villa overlooked the sea and was decorated with the finest local handicrafts. There were no TVs, radios, or internet to distract me from the beauty of the surroundings. The grounds were lush, awash in tropical flowers, sculpture, colorful fabrics, and fountains. I'd never stayed anywhere so luxurious.

My first night, the manager told me there were four other guests at Puri Mas, a property with twenty villas. It was so spread out that I didn't see any other guests until a few days later.

Awake before sunrise, I lay in bed listening to the early morning sounds in the dim light. In the distance, a chorus of roosters crowed. Water from the previous night's rain dripped off the roof, trees, and bushes. A lone frog croaked loud and clear for a few moments, stopped, then minutes later started again. Small birds sang close by. There was an undertone of waves crashing at the shore.

I heard what sounded like a loud "uh-oh!" It seemed as though the noise came from the bed. I pawed through the sheets and blanket looking for whatever made the noise. I found nothing and drifted back to sleep. A few minutes later another piercing "uh-oh! uh-oh!" bolted me awake. I couldn't locate the source, but later found out it was a gecko. I never knew they made sounds at all, and certainly not as loud as what I had heard. I was also told they are much beloved by the Sasak, the Lombok natives, because they eat insects.

I started the day with a swim in a pool that would be hard to surpass for loveliness. An odd free-form shape with sparkling blue water, it had broad steps leading into it and was deep and long enough to do laps. Surrounding the pool was a carefully tended garden of crotons, orchids, bamboo, and hibiscus in intense pinks and purples. Traditional Hindu statuary of Ganesh, Hanuman, and other gods and goddesses peeked out from manicured foliage. It was like no pool setting I'd ever experienced. I swam alone, thinking how lucky I was. After every few laps, I stopped to take another look at the surroundings and thought, *This is how the ultra-rich live.* I also thought how odd it was to be in a place that decorated with Hindu symbols, rather than Muslim, the predominant religion on Lombok.

Breakfast was at a table on a patio a few feet from the Lombok Strait, the water that separates the two islands. Across the water is Agung, the towering volcanic mountain on Bali. Though it is about one hundred miles away, it looked deceptively close, as if one could swim or paddle over in a few minutes. That morning I ate banana pancakes and drank papaya, pineapple, and banana juice. In Indonesia, they make fruit juice and smoothies out of whatever is at hand. While at the hotel, I had a different juice at every meal—combinations of watermelon, mangosteen, honeydew, passion fruit, ginger, turmeric, mango, avocado, pineapple, banana, lemon, lime, papaya, and dragon fruit. The possibilities were endless.

Before I'd gotten through more than a few chapters of the book I was determined to read, Ma came by. She was a sweet woman who I thought of as The Pamperer. While her English was limited, Ma knew enough to convince me to allow her to give me "full treatment." I didn't know what "full treatment" consisted of, but her smile and gentle manner, and the price (less than $20), convinced me to say, "Yes, sure."

For the next few hours, I was manicured, pedicured, massaged, had a facial, and my eyebrows plucked. While she massaged me, I could hear waves at the shore, later accompanied by a gentle rain drumming on the roof of the bungalow. It was relaxing beyond belief, and simply being in the presence of this kind spirit was peace-inducing. By the time she was done, I was mush.

Though I could easily have remained ensconced in this magical place, I wanted to see Lombok, not some luxury hideaway. At reception, I arranged for a tour of the Sasak villages in the island's interior. Then I got a ride into nearby Senggigi.

Senggigi used to be the main tourist area on Lombok, stretched out along the beachfront just north of the capital, Mataram. In the late 1990s, Lombok was hyped to be the next Bali, and a building boom began. But the bombings on Bali kept people away from both islands. Tourist numbers plummeted, and construction projects halted.

What a sad place Senggigi was now. There were abandoned shops and hotels everywhere. Although it wasn't bombed, Senggigi was still a victim of the terrorist attacks.

The walk around town became an exercise in avoiding street hawkers. Several followed me, desperate for business. While I felt their pain and need to sell me something, they had nothing I wanted. What would I do with beaded bracelets, poorly printed T-shirts, or frightful sarongs in blazing neon colors? I wasn't up for a knockoff Rolex.

At the art market, my main destination, there was booth after booth of second-rate handicrafts, cheap jewelry, crude ceramics, key chains, magnets, T-shirts, and souvenir mugs and plates. I was nearly the only tourist there, and no one looked as if they'd sold anything in ages. The vendors didn't even try very hard once I made it clear I wasn't planning to buy anything. My heart went out to everyone, but there wasn't much I could do for them. World politics, Muslim religious fanatics, and fear of another bombing had kept tourists away and destroyed their livelihoods.

Returning through the gates at Puri Mas was entering a different world. Walking to my villa, I discovered new gems: a perfectly placed piece of sculpture, a carved wooden arch over a doorway, a pink orchid peeking through a palm frond. Calm returned, though the contrast between these surroundings and what I'd just experienced in town gnawed at me.

The following morning my driver/guide, Safei, arrived. A tall, slender man who I guessed was in his early thirties, he had delicate features and long fingers that punctuated everything he said. He made sure I'd brought an umbrella because it rains for about an hour every afternoon, and off we went in the villa's van.

Our first stop was at a local pottery village that Safei explained was a cooperative. Most potters in Lombok are women. They make the pots in their homes, then bring them to this facility for firing and selling. A few of the women prefer to work together creating pots at the gathering place. When enough pieces have been made and thoroughly dried, they use coconut husks and rice stalks to make a raging blaze and fire the pots.

I was curious about the religion of the women.

"They are all Muslim," Safei told me.

"Why no head coverings?"

"Too hot."

That surprised me—it wasn't hotter here than in Saudi Arabia. "Do they hold to other parts of the religion?" I asked.

"Oh yes. Like me. Very faithful," was all he had to say on the subject. I dropped it.

Given my training as a ceramicist and my love of trying crafts in other countries, I wanted to attempt making a pot. Safei was surprised by my request.

"This is the first time anyone has ever asked to do this."

"Is it okay?"

"I'll ask them."

The women cleared a space, gestured for me to sit, and chattered with each other. I thought I heard some discreet tittering in the distance. I suspected they were anticipating a disaster.

The clay was very soft, far softer than I'd ever used. Safei and the women watched closely as I rolled the clay to form coils and slowly built up a reasonably decent-looking small vase. They seemed pleased I'd done such a good job. Then one of the women demonstrated their technique. I was amazed that she could build large structures using such wet clay, yet before my eyes, she constructed a two-foot-high vase. Her technique was to add flattened-out pieces, then smooth them into the existing wall.

Many of the completed pieces were earthenware in simple, striking shapes with smoke marks from the firing. Unfortunately, they were very heavy. Rather than buying a piece I really loved, I picked up a small gecko candleholder as a memento.

After the pottery village, we headed to a traditional Sasak weaving village, Sukarara. The tiny village was populated by kids, women, and chickens. Most men were in the fields working. Women sat with backstrap looms, methodically weaving cloth, hour after hour. The shopkeeper, speaking more than passable English, explained the fine thread was made from local silk and cotton. He translated as I admired the craftsmanship and asked questions.

"When do girls learn to weave?"

"From a very young age. They start with coarser thread and make small pieces."

"Do men ever weave?"

The shopkeeper explained that women weave songkat, a one-sided fabric used for wedding dresses and other festive occasions. The men weave ikat, or double-sided fabrics used for everyday garments as well as bedspreads and other household items. Songkat is finer, more intricate, and harder to produce. Ikat is woven on a large loom, but there are fewer colors, the weaving is much looser, and pieces take less time to complete.

The patience to produce such fine fabric far exceeds anything I could ever muster. I can't begin to imagine sitting for literally hundreds of hours throwing a shuttle back and forth, back and forth. I watched the women weave, took photos, then went to the showroom. It was a simple space, filled with exquisite fabrics. The weaving method may be hundreds of years old and done using very basic tools, but the finished results are anything but simple. The material was soft with intricate bands of color, unlike anything I'd seen before.

Safei and the shopkeeper dressed me in a wedding outfit and had me pose for photos. They served me a bottle of iced tea, then got down to business. Safei had told me this would be a good place to shop, as it is owned by the villagers. He said I could get reasonable prices, and the money would go directly to the people rather than a middleman. Piece after piece of fabric was lovingly unfolded. Black flecked with gold, white, blues, and greens. Burgundy shot through with patterns in yellows and white. Blues, greens, oranges. Then came a white piece with a design in purple, turquoise, gold, and a dozen more subtle shades. I knew that one would be going home with me.

With much friendly chatter, I eventually selected three pieces. Then the bargaining began. "Good price for you, good price for me." I don't know where the shopkeeper got that line, but he repeated it often. Lots of figuring and handing the calculator back and forth. I kept getting confused. At 9,250 rupiah per dollar, it was easy to add or subtract an odd zero. Eventually, we settled on a price of about $130 for three pieces of fabric. I hadn't bargained very hard, since my purchases represented at least a couple of months of work. The guidebook said the weavers make three or four dollars a day. At $130, they were not getting rich.

As we drove out of the village, we passed a dozen more weaving shops, all glitzier looking. "Not good places," Safei said. "Workers get less money." I was glad I'd gone to a place that was "good for me, good for them."

We continued driving south out of the lush flatlands to the drier areas south of Mount Rinjani. At the sleepy beach town of Kuta, we had a lunch of satay and rice, then drove up over the mountains to the lagoon at Mawm. Along the way, we passed villages that were small and poor. According to Safei, they had no electricity, running water, or medical care, and were largely left to fend for themselves by the government.

Mawm was a perfect white sand cove in a forgotten corner of the globe. I walked to one end, passing a group of children who had constructed, out of sand, leaves, branches, and pods, a beach village, complete with rice paddies, houses, and palm trees. A young woman with a child walked with me. Her teeth, which pointed in a dozen directions, were stained bright red from chewing betel. Her eyes were large and sad, but she stood tall and straight. She lifted her son's shirt to show me bright red bug bites and scratch marks nearly covering his back. They didn't seem to bother him; he smiled at me beatifically. I guessed that this woman, who was twenty-two or twenty-three, maybe twenty-five, had seen more hardship than I would have in my lifetime.

The poverty I saw all day tugged at my heart. I wished I could do something but had no idea what to do. Like many middle-class Westerners, I give to charity and work pro bono for causes I believe in. I do what I can. It isn't enough. Not nearly.

I have good food, sanitation, medical care, a well-appointed home, and a thousand luxuries, small and large. As I've seen during my travels around the globe, most of the world's population has none of this.

The next day, I went off with Safei for another excursion. We stopped first in Mataram, the capital of Lombok, to buy an audio-tape of a singer that Safei had been touting: Megi Z. He's a famous actor and singer who, from Safei's description, seemed like a sort of Indonesian Tony Bennett.

While we drove, I asked Safei a lot of questions about his life. He told me he was the main decorator of Puri Mas and several other resorts, but since all the troubles, he'd taken to doing whatever work he could get.

"Are you married?" I asked.

"Soon. My family will find me a wife."

"So, marriages are arranged here?" I asked.

"Either arranged or couples elope."

"That's an interesting choice."

"If the couple can't afford a traditional wedding, which is very expensive, or if you find a love partner, it is okay to elope."

That surprised me. It didn't seem in keeping with what I knew about Islam.

Safei continued, "Mostly Sasak people do elope." He turned to point out a building with a lovely garden. Our discussion about marriage was over.

Shops and restaurants in Mataram served the local population and were busy. I was relieved it didn't feel haunted the way Sengiggi had.

Now that Safei determined I was really into crafts, he took me to a wood carving village, one tiny shop after another lining a dirt road. In the workshop we visited, young men and women worked in semidarkness, cutting, placing, and polishing fragments of mother-of-pearl into mahogany chairs, tables, and bureaus. It was hot, dark, and, to my Western eyes, brutal. I wondered if, locally, these were considered good jobs. Safei told me yes; I didn't believe him. The showroom was equally dark and dusty—two floors jammed with baskets, bowls, boxes, and furniture. It was hot! I was a bit overwhelmed. In the end, I bought two small pieces, mostly out of guilt.

For lunch, we stopped at a street-side tempeh vendor, "the best on Lombok," according to Safei. The owner used to be a chef at a Sheraton on Bali but decided he preferred to return home to Lombok and work at his own business. A cauldron of boiling oil, fresh ingredients, and a warming cart had made this guy a success. A constant stream of cars and motorbikes stopped to pick up a bag of freshly fried tempeh, soybean chips, fried banana or veggie fritters. For about 40 cents, I got a good-sized portion of tempeh, plus a handful of chilis. The standard procedure is to take a bite of the tempeh, then a bite of the chili, and wash it down with beer. It was great.

After a few days of relaxing in Puri Mas's tropical paradise, I took my final excursion with Safei. He was quickly becoming a friend, who seemed to enjoy my company as much as I enjoyed his. This drive took us north toward the coast. The road snaked first along a hilly coastline. Around every bend was a view of coconut palms, rice paddies or corn fields, and untrammeled white sand beaches. I could happily have stopped at any one of the beaches and gone beachcombing for a couple of hours, but we had a mission and didn't linger.

We stopped at the Saturday market, a bustling place that underscored Indonesia's reputation as the Spice Islands. There was ginger, turmeric, tamarind, garlic, onions, peppers, cilantro, chilies, shallots, saffron, multiple varieties of peppers, cloves, nutmeg, and others I couldn't identify. The sellers were all very friendly, holding things up so I could look at them closely and smell them. A few shopkeepers offered me a taste.

Some of the women in the booths were gorgeous. In other circumstances, they could have graced the cover of *Vogue* or *Harper's Bazaar*. We may not have been able to converse, but we smiled a lot. The ones who spoke any English thanked me for being there. One commented about how horrible the terrorism had been and how it was making life difficult for everyone. Though it hadn't been bombed, Lombok was a place where the terrorists had won. Tourism had disappeared.

Back in the car, we went farther up the coast, then turned inland through the jungle. Our destination was the starting point for treks up sacred Mount Rinjani. Tourists can do a four-day trek up to the lake at Mount Rinjani, or a soft trek overnight to the rim of the mountain. I did the fluffy version, a walk down concrete steps to a long, powerful waterfall. There were plants and flowers I'd never seen. Butterflies fluttered around me. Once at the waterfall, the mist from the falling water was delightfully fresh. The walk back up the steps was hot, hot, and hotter. Each step was about twenty inches high. By the time I got to the top, I felt as though I'd worked out in the gym for hours. But after a cool fruit juice under a shaded platform, I was ready to move on.

We retraced our route to the coast, then turned back inland on another road. Safei stopped to show me a coconut processing operation. The company collects coconuts from all the local villages, takes off the outer husk, loads the nuts onto trucks, and transports them to Java, where they are crushed into coconut oil. The piles of coconuts were like mini mountains. I was given fresh coconut to drink and eat and chatted with the owner. His first words were to thank me for coming. He told me how much everyone on Lombok hated the terrorists. It was a sentiment I'd heard from a lot of people.

Next, we went on a drive through a monkey forest to the peak of a low foothill of Mount Rinjani. There was a tiny, traditional guesthouse where we stopped for fresh banana pancakes with cane sugar syrup and sprinkled with fresh coconut. There was also a sideshow of chickens and stumpy-tailed cats scrounging for scraps.

When Safei asked her, the proprietor walked to the jungle and called the monkeys, making a high *ee-ee-ee* sound. Within minutes, there was rustling in the trees, and a family appeared—one enormous male, a couple of smaller males, and a harem of females, each holding a baby. We fed them peanuts and coconut. The family was very well behaved and polite. Great fun to watch and play with.

After spending a week relaxing and learning about life on Lombok, I flew back to Bali. At the airport I heard a rumor that a tsunami had killed ten thousand people in Indonesia, Thailand, and Sri Lanka. It was the first I'd heard anything about it. Lombok is a thousand miles away from where it struck.

All along the street, people were selling copies of the *International Herald Tribune*. The articles were terrifying and sobering. Forty-five thousand dead from the tsunami, with the number rising quickly. Fears of cholera and starvation. I read that tectonic plates under the ocean shifted, creating a wall of water that plowed through coastal areas.

In addition to the horrible loss of life, people feared what additional damage the tsunami would do to the struggling economy. It would be yet another reason for tourists to stay away. Terrorists and nature conspiring to make life miserable for millions.

I stopped in an internet café to check my email. There were a slew of messages asking if I was okay. Several people said they had put my name on the list of missing people. They didn't realize how far I was from what had happened. I sent reassuring messages to everyone I could think of.

The enormity of the disaster and the fact that I'd spent time on Sumatra during a previous visit to Indonesia made it very real. I could easily picture the small villages that were swept away in the path of the tsunami. I thought about the people who perished in this disaster, as kind, hardworking, and peaceful as those I'd spent time with on Lombok. They were individuals to me, not some distant, faceless, anonymous people.

The Balinese and Sasak were still reeling from the terrorist bombings. Given that people in the West don't understand Indonesia's geography, I feared they would stay away from Bali and Lombok, islands heavily dependent on tourism, in even greater numbers. I pictured the poverty in Lombok's remote areas and abandoned tourist towns and wondered how much worse it might get.

After all these years, I have perfect memories of both Puri Mas's luxury and the poverty I'd seen. The contrast still haunts me.

HOMESTAY: CHINA, 2007

As part of a tour of China, the itinerary included a homestay. It was one of the reasons I opted for that particular tour. Our group of sixteen Americans would stay at homes in a small farming village ninety minutes outside of Xi'an, the city known for the  terracotta warriors. While I didn't know what to expect, I was looking forward to the experience of seeing how ordinary people lived.

I t was clear that Xi'an was succumbing to urban sprawl. As we drove out of the city, new homes and commercial spaces surrounded plots of farmland. In ten years or less, the town we were visiting would likely be a suburb of the city. The rate of building in China was frenetic.

Once off the main road, we entered a different, slower-paced world. Our first stop was a grade school. It was old and a bit ramshackle, with faded paint and well-worn floors and furniture. We sat on benches as our guide gave an explanation about education in China. It's compulsory to grade nine, and free. But the family must pay for books and materials, which makes it unaffordable for poor families. I'm still not sure how they justified the conflict between "compulsory" and "you must pay." However, the government had recently decreed they would pay all expenses through grade nine, a step in the right direction.

Shortly after the explanation, the PA system crackled, and a Strauss waltz blared. Classroom doors flew open, and kids poured out, running and yelling their way to the yard behind the school. It was recess time. While I knew Western classical music was popular in China, the choice of a Strauss waltz seemed an unusual one to announce school periods.

Change the setting and music a bit, and it could have been New York City. The kids wore tracksuits or T-shirts and fleece pants and sneakers. The littlest ones played patty-cake or jumped rope, both the regular kind and what I've always called Chinese jump rope. In Chinese jump rope the rope isn't turned. Instead, two children stand apart with a rubber band rope around their ankles. The jumper takes leaps over the bands in specific patterns. I enjoyed seeing kids in China using what seemed to be the same rules that my friends and I had used. Four little boys were engaged in a game that looked like rock, paper, scissors. Whoever lost got hit or pinched by the winner. Older boys played basketball or Ping-Pong. Some raced around playing tag and what looked like statues. After twenty minutes, another Strauss waltz crackled on the PA and the kids trudged back to their classrooms.

We visited an art class of eleven-year-olds. The teacher invited us to sit with the kids at wooden tables burnished from years of use, surrounded by narrow benches. The lesson for the day was drawing lotus flowers. An assistant distributed drawing paper to each of us, students and guests. I sat with a small girl, and we shared a box of pastels with the other children at the table. When I drew a lotus, my training as an artist helped me to draw a realistic-looking flower. The kids were fascinated, stopped what they were doing, and watched me intently. When I finished, they clapped. I think I blushed.

At the end of class, the kids presented us with their drawings as a gift. Then they sang the Chinese national anthem and the ABC song in English. To reciprocate, we demonstrated that we could count to ten in Chinese, with some help from our guide.

I wondered what they'd remember after having foreigners come through their classes. It was an experience that had never happened when I attended school. I tried to think how I might have felt at that age if a group of Chinese tourists had visited my class. I suspect I would have been quite uncomfortable around any group of unknown adults, much less those from another country. It made me consider if this had been a great social exchange or if it was somehow exploitative. I still can't decide.

Leaving the school, we walked through the old village, now mostly abandoned. In 1994, a new village, the Chinese version of a condominium complex, was built. Ninety families lived there around a central square. The guide divided our group of sixteen among three families. She introduced us to our hosts, who led us to their homes. It was a pleasant village, each home with a small garden filled with flowers and vegetables. The houses were all similar and surprisingly large. They typically housed several generations.

Mrs. Jong, our hostess, gave us a tour; on the main floor, there was a living room, bathroom, two bedrooms, a large entry hall used as a dining room, and behind that, a kitchen divided into several small rooms. Upstairs were more bedrooms and another bathroom. The rooms were filled with family photos, paintings, Buddhas, porcelain and cloisonné vases. Apart from the antiquated kitchen and bathrooms, it looked very comfortable.

She seated us at a round table and served tea. Since we couldn't chat because we spoke no Chinese and Mrs. Jong knew no English, we showed each other photographs. It was interesting to see how similar Chinese and American pictures of families are. Smiling parents, grandparents, and children, often with a family pet. Some were casual, others from celebratory occasions such as weddings, birthdays, and graduations.

Our guide had provided us with sheets of phrases in Chinese and English: Useful Phrases One and Useful Phrases Two. Each phrase was numbered. On one side of the page, the text was in English, and on the flip side in Chinese. To communicate, you'd look for a phrase you wanted to share. Then you'd find the same number on the Chinese side and show it to the host. She'd then read the Chinese translation. Both our small group and Mrs. Jong kept confusing page one and page two. For example, looking at the page in front of me I'd suggest to another guest that she point to number 23 to tell Mrs. Jong, "Thank you, you're a very generous host."

The other guest would look at her page and say, "Why would I want to tell Mrs. Jong, 'Now we will make pickled vegeta-bles?'" (Number 23 on the other sheet.)

Mrs. Jong would flip back and forth and point to something like "what beautiful children!" while she looked at a photo of a guest's cats. We were all continually in stitches.

We moved to the rustic kitchen for our cooking lesson. On a table constructed by balancing a board on sawhorses, Mrs. Jong's mother-in-law demonstrated noodle making. She was a rotund, gregarious woman who every so often tilted her head back and let out a prolonged giggle. With motions that had been practiced for decades, she dropped a baseball-sized ball of kneaded dough onto a wooden board. In under a minute, using a plain wooden dowel, she'd rolled it paper-thin. She then loosely folded it over and over until it looked like a long, layered pastry. With a sharp cleaver, she chopped through the layers of dough to make linguini-thin noodles.

I marveled at her skill. Then came my chance to knead, roll out the dough, and chop. The elder Mrs. Jong had been merry during her demonstration; while I attempted to duplicate her motions, she bellowed a room-shattering guffaw. Though I am skilled with rolling and shaping clay, which made it easy to do with dough, chopping was an unfamiliar task. The cleaver was heavy and looked lethal. My first attempt produced a bedraggled-looking noodle. Mrs. Jong's mother-in-law came behind me, put her hands on my mine, and together we slammed down onto the cutting board with a resounding *thwack*. My end product was wider and thicker than those made by the expert Mrs. Jong, but they'd definitely be edible. When I finished, she gave me a big thumbs-up, then hugged me and posed for a photo.

While the noodles dried, we moved onto preparing vegetables for the wok. Mrs. Jong assigned each of us a different veggie: carrots, string beans, cabbage, squash, mushrooms, and more. Then she demonstrated the proper way to cut each one.

While we were chopping, they set water to boil in a large cooking pot on a coal stove. They tossed the noodles into the roiling water and then almost immediately scooped them out and put them into a bowl. Next to the coal stove was a gas stove. Another guest was invited to sauté the veggies under Mrs. Jong's watchful eye.

At that point, we were shooed out of the kitchen so they could properly serve the food to us.

Dinner was a feast, simple but delicious. There was fried bread, cauliflower, peas, squash, our noodles, and scrambled eggs mixed with the vegetables we'd chopped. Everything was tasty, fresh, and perfectly cooked. Mrs. Jong offered us beer and a shot of the local fire water. It tasted like raw alcohol.

After dinner, we were each handed a large, colorful paper fan, no explanation provided. I presumed the translation sheets simply didn't cover the next activity. We tried to guess what we'd use the fans for. Cooling ourselves off in the warmish evening? As a few of us were menopausal women, were they meant to help us with hot flashes? It was after Mrs. Jong led us a few blocks to the village square that we learned their intended use. Our guide met us at the square and explained that every evening after dinner, the women of the town congregate to socialize and dance.

At 8:00 p.m., a PA system crackled to life, and traditional Chinese music poured from loudspeakers. At first, it was only our guide, hostesses, and us in the square. Soon, women from the community and the other members of our tour trickled into the brightly lit area until there were forty or more of us. Each of us clutched a large, bright fan in our hands. As the songs changed, so did the dances. There was a circle dance that resembled the hora. There was one performed in neat rows that required intricate steps. Another emphasized lots of fanning our partner and other dancers and waving our fans in smooth motions that emphasized the grace of the dance. The tempo changed for each, though most were upbeat if a bit discordant to my Western tastes.

No matter their age or looks, the men in my tour group were in high demand as partners for the village women. That's because, other than the men in our tour group, all the dancers were female. The local men prefer to stay home to watch TV, drink, smoke, and play mah-jongg.

The townswomen each adopted someone from our group and led us through the dances. I'm not a great dancer, but my partner was forgiving of my klutziness. I eventually gave up trying to imitate the steps and had a good time moving around with the group. As long as I was enjoying myself, they didn't seem to mind. Two young girls from our group did a version of the electric slide, which the locals tried to imitate, some with more success than others. I felt vindicated when they had as much trouble as I'd had learning a new dance. The women couldn't have been friendlier or more hospitable, proving that lack of a common language wasn't an impediment to a good time.

Back at our host's home, we prepared for bed. There was a nice, fluffy comforter and a pillow filled with buckwheat or beans. I slept well, although it was—as every bed in China had been—hard as a rock.

Congee, rice porridge, is a mainstay of Chinese breakfasts. It was offered on the breakfast buffet of every hotel I had stayed at. I'd tried it, but to me it was tasteless, with a texture I associate with baby food. It's typically served with a selection of toppings like peanuts, tofu, pickled vegetables, and crumbles of hard-boiled eggs. After the first hotel sample, I switched back to Western foods in the morning, though the rest of the day I was eager to eat local options. Here it was congee or nothing. The homemade version didn't alter my opinion. In deference to Western preferences, Mrs. Jong served us coffee. For that, I was grateful.

At our parting, we each presented Mrs. Jong with a small gift representative of our hometown. I'd brought pot holders with a design featuring NYC sights. They had probably been made in China. Still, for a place where we'd spent time cooking, it seemed an appropriate gift.

On this trip to China, I saw the Great Wall, giant pandas, the Forbidden City, the terracotta warriors, cruised on the Yangtze, and visited a slew of other "must-see" destinations. They were impressive. But the day spent in this village was equally memorable.

As I'd hoped, this was a far cry from a typical tourist excursion. I was appreciative of the arrangements made by the tour company; it was something that would have been difficult to arrange on my own. The experience felt like a win-win: The locals got some extra cash and the opportunity to spend time with Americans. Because I stayed overnight, it was a chance to meet local people and learn about their lives in a relaxed way.

BLUE ICE:
PATAGONIA, CHILE, 2009

My client had raved endlessly about her trip to Patagonia. "It's one of the wildest places on the planet. You're such a traveler. You have to go." I'd been thinking about visiting there, and after hearing her enthusiasm, decided now was the time. I looked through tour information on both the Argentinian and Chilean areas of Patagonia and found a trip that appealed to me. In addition to seeing other parts of Chile and a lot of hiking, the tour included a five-day cruise through the Chilean fjords. The brochure photos were breathtakingly beautiful.

When I arrived in Chile, I met the other travelers in our tour group of eight. On an introductory walk around downtown, we saw both the good and bad of Chile's capital, Santiago. Beautiful architecture, art, and parks fill the city. We also saw destruction caused by earthquakes, which are a constant threat. In front of a few buildings, we heard about the awful history during the time of General Pinochet. Under his regime, the junta had jailed, tortured, and executed thousands of Chileans.

Over the next few days, we toured the area around Santiago, going to several justly famed vineyards and the beautiful Pacific coast. We then spent a few days in the lake district before flying to Patagonia, where, for me, the real journey began.

In Torres del Paine National Park, dramatic skies changed minute by minute. Dark clouds that scudded across the sky created a constantly evolving patchwork of sun, clouds, and swirling mist as the backdrop to towering mountains. Part granite, part sedimentary rock, these two-toned gray and brown giants with jagged peaks, sharp ridges, and sheer rock faces dominated the park. Strong winds on the lower rolling hills set fields of willowy, golden grasses swaying, like waves moving toward the shore. Clusters of pastel pink and purple lupines were a gentle contrast to the imposing mountains.

One side of the mountain range is wet, the other arid. The dry side is home to thousands of guanacos, a large native deer with expressive eyes and thick fur that helps them survive the fierce climate. We visited in January, at the end of calving season. It's the time when young guanacos, all long gawky legs, scampered about.

After an easy, brief hike through the grassland, we picnicked near an intensely blue waterfall. The roar of the water, powerful from springtime glacial runoff, obliterated most conversation but was a fabulous soundtrack.

On the rainy side of the mountain range, the wind was violent. Our guide, Jorge, told us the wind often gusts up to eighty miles an hour. I'm certain the blasts of air we experienced were close to that. It felt as if I were being attacked by an air gun. We hiked through a densely wooded area to Grey Lake. At the beach's shoreline were icebergs that had split off a glacier. The water was aquamarine, the icebergs glistening white. If the winds had died down a bit, I could have stayed there for a very long time. But the gales were biting, and even with several layers of clothing, the cold seeped in.

Hiking back, I had to brace myself against the wind, which had changed direction and was rushing toward us in a fury. One of our group, a thin young woman, got blown over; fortunately, she didn't hurt herself. Jorge grabbed her arm to steady her and prevent her from getting blown over a second time. The trail that had taken an hour to hike to the lake took nearly two hours to retrace. As we got back to the van, the skies opened, and it poured torrentially.

When we returned to the lodge, the rain stopped, and a brilliant rainbow materialized. It arced completely across the sky, each band bright, distinct, and anchored in a mountain. It was the kind of rainbow that inspires searching for the pot of gold at the end. I rushed to take photos, sure it would disappear any moment. Two hours later, it was still there.

The next morning, we drove deep into the park to hike. The trail meandered through rolling hills covered in a golden-yellow carpet of grass and wildflowers. It was punctuated by porcelain orchids that were translucent white and closely resembled the material for which they are named. We skirted turquoise lakes, a color I associate with the Caribbean and Mediterranean, not a frigid climate. As on the previous day, the wind whipped the clouds in a peek-a-boo dance with the sun and snow-covered mountains.

Our first stopping point was a waterfall with volume, speed, and power that rivaled Niagara Falls, though it was much narrower and shorter. We were marveling at the waterfall's intensity when Jorge yelled at us, "Brace yourself when you see the wind." That puzzled me—how do you see wind? But seconds later, I learned. Powerful gusts of wind hit the water in the lake, lifting gallons and gallons and carrying it across the surface. It barreled in our direction. The spray from the river soaked us. The gusts were so strong we all stopped walking, braced ourselves, and waited for them to subside. When we resumed walking, we were all on high alert.

Even during high tourist season there are almost no people in this part of the world. Other than at the lodge, we rarely saw other cars, buildings, or humans. It felt remote and isolated. The national park is the most visited place in the area, and tourists only come during a four- or five-month period. The rest of the time, it's left alone. I tried to imagine what it would be like in winter and concluded you must be a special kind of human being to want to spend any time there at all. The weather is brutal.

After the hike, we drove toward Puerto Natales for the start of a cruise through the Chilean fjords. We stopped along the way at a tiny town for a rest break. It was like visiting the Wild West. On the narrow, dusty street that was the business district, I watched a person trot up on horseback to pick up groceries. The one side street was a rutted mud lane. Two little restaurants seemed like outposts at the end of the world. I had to muscle my way out of a small shop because the wind kept slamming the door back.

Late afternoon, we boarded *Skorpios III*, our home for the next five nights. The captain, Constantine, was of Greek descent—hence the name *Skorpios*. It was a small cruise ship with a capacity of ninety passengers, but on my trip it was less than half full.

Within thirty minutes of leaving Puerto Natales, there wasn't a house or boat in sight, and I guessed correctly we wouldn't encounter another until we returned to port. The national park had been cold. Being on open water heading toward glaciers was colder.

If I wanted to go outside, even for a quick photo, I put on layers of clothing.

The scenery changed radically every few minutes. It transformed from blue sky and snow-covered peaks to intense rain and forested areas streaked with waterfalls, and then back again. The gentle motion of the ship and mesmerizing views nearly put me into a trance. Life in New York seemed a million miles away. I stood staring at the view until another guest came by and said, "You're turning blue." I hadn't even noticed the cold.

The next morning, I woke to the sound of muffled banging. My eyes flew open, and I leapt out of bed to see what was happening. I parted the curtains to see a small flotilla of mini icebergs sliding gracefully past, with a few crashing into the ship. I dressed and was on the top deck in two minutes flat. *Skorpios* was approaching the Pio XI glacier, the largest in South America. It's three miles wide and twenty-eight miles deep and one of the very few on the globe that wasn't receding. It was advancing.

On deck, I was greeted by a monumental wall of blue and white. Intermittent sounds like cannon booms were followed by ice crashing into the water below and a violent spray of water. It was hard to take in the enormity of the glacier. I found myself braving freezing-cold temperatures and bone-chilling winds to stand on deck and stare at it. I had a lot of company.

Our morning excursion was on small motorboats to get closer to the glacier. From the *Skorpios*, the glacier looked massive. From the motorboat, it was truly awesome. Half as high as the Empire State Building and nearly three miles wide, it dwarfed the boats we were in. I felt as if we were Lilliputians against the enormity of the ever-changing, ever-moving monolith.

Up close, the structure reminded me of an ice-blue Bryce

Canyon. Peaks, crevasses, valleys, and knifelike edges glinting in the sun made it clear we wouldn't be walking on this glacier. When the sun angled against a particularly sharp edge, it looked as though it could slice through ships or anything else that dared to come close.

At the far end of the glacier, as the skiff navigated through a field of icebergs, each one larger than our little boat, there would periodically be a thunderous boom. A car-sized chunk would fall from high on the glacier, and we'd watch it tumble into the sea. The resulting wave would rock our small craft violently. Though the shaking rattled me a bit, I never felt in serious danger. It was obvious the crew were skillful and had done this excursion many times. I did wonder how they knew where to go to avoid being hit directly or flipped by a wave.

Frigid air radiated from the wall of the glacier. Five layers of clothes be damned, I shivered. Chattering teeth around me became particularly noticeable when a large cloud swept across the sky, blocking the sun. A brief but heavy rain drenched us. I was happy when we returned to the *Skorpios* and were handed a glass of mulled wine. It took a long time to thaw out, but the experience had been worth every shiver.

The crew scooped large chunks of glacial ice onto the deck. The behemoth ice blocks were carefully stored under tarps. When more ice was needed for drinks or cooling, the crew went up and chiseled off a hunk. After seeing that, I ordered every drink "*con hielo*," "with ice," because I got such a kick out of it. The ice was clear, pure, and ancient.

The highlight of the cruise was a four-hour journey in a small ice cutter through the iceberg-strewn waters of a fjord. Because there were so few passengers, we all managed to squeeze onto the small ship. The bow was narrow and sharply pointed and looked quite battered. Unlike most ships, ice cutters have reinforced hulls and very powerful engines that allow them to break through ice. I saw this demonstrated as we crashed through sheets of ice, shards pummeling the sides, creating a narrow path.

The sounds of the engine and ice were deafening. I had earplugs, earmuffs, and a hood—and the noise still rattled my brain. Though the boat was covered and there were space heaters, the sides were open, and the spray and rain soaked all of us. Though it was midsummer in Chile (January), it was brutally cold.

Nothing prepared me for the experience of bobbing in the middle of an ice sculpture garden nestled between towering rock walls and deep blue glaciers. There was no green, red, or yellow. We'd entered a perfect blue and white world.

The visual images were so compelling I didn't have time to focus on the discomfort. I now know the meaning of ice blue, which spans a hundred shades from crystal clear to near white to iridescent pearl to deep ultramarine. The relentless wind sculpts the ice into graceful forms, some reminiscent of Brancusi or Henry Moore or Barbara Hepworth. Others resembled ice dunes. Every few minutes, we'd pass another glacier oozing down to the sea. Sprinkled across the glaciers were hundreds of waterfalls.

Deep in the middle of the ice field, we slowed down while the crew scooped out chunks of ice. It was the clearest ice I'd ever seen. The blocks were like fine Steuben glass. Compacted by thousands of years of pressure, there were no ice bubbles. Using a chisel, crewmembers broke up the ice, distributed it into cups, and poured an amber liquid into it. Captain Constantine told us we'd be drinking "thirty-year-old scotch with thirty-thousand-year-old ice." He raised his cup for a toast. "Here's to the ends of the earth."

TASTE OF THE SEA: HOKKAIDO, JAPAN, 2012

Post-retirement, my friend Judy spent a year in Japan, something she'd wanted to do for years. Before she left the U.S., we'd arranged to meet in Hokkaido about halfway through her stay. I'd chosen Hokkaido, the northernmost

island of Japan, because on my previous trips to Japan I'd never ventured that far north. We would spend a week exploring this remote area and then fly to Korea for a week. We divvied up research and planning—Judy would cover Hokkaido, and I would handle Korea, a country neither of us had ever visited.

D uring the long layover in Tokyo, before boarding the flight to Sapporo, I was jet-lagged and exhausted. I couldn't read or focus on much of anything. Trying to remain awake so I wouldn't miss my connecting flight, I walked around the airport, drank several cups of coffee, and wrote a list of everything I knew about Hokkaido:

- Site of the 1972 Winter Olympics
- Gets a lot of snow and is extremely cold
- It is a large island
- There is a big winter ice festival
- Principal city is Sapporo

That wasn't much information. I trusted that Judy researched where we would go and what we would do.

The first few days in Sapporo cured my jet lag but weren't enthralling. It's a large, modern city that's less frenetic than Tokyo or even Kyoto. To me, Sapporo lacked personality. It seemed the Japanese equivalent of a small, modern, nondescript U.S. city. During winter, Sapporo may come alive because of the cold weather activities. In summertime, the architecture, shopping malls, and even the parks seemed bland.

While delicious, the sushi and other food we ate looked and tasted similar to what is available in New York City.

Judy had studied Japanese for a couple of years prior to her trip. This meant she was our official translator, though she confessed, even with all the lessons and six months in the country, her language skills remained limited. Since I speak only about ten words in Japanese, I was impressed that she spoke well enough to acquire our train tickets to Wakkanai.

I was looking forward to seeing Wakkanai, the northernmost city on this northernmost Japanese island.

The train ride was a little over five hours. As we traveled north, the landscape changed from urban to suburban to farms and eventually uninhabited, uncultivated land. I'd traveled through much of Japan on previous trips, and this was the least developed area I'd seen. It was misting as the train pulled into Wakkanai. The pervasive gray seemed mysterious and fitting. The effect made ordinary structures and greenery resemble woodblock prints.

At our hotel, the desk clerks spoke only Japanese. I was grateful Judy could communicate with them. Though the mist was now a steady drizzle, we ventured out for a walk. Within minutes, we were searching for the source of incessant drumbeats. We caught up with a parade snaking through downtown streets. A troupe of women in matching, bright kimono jackets performed choreographed dances as they moved ahead. Their broad smiles and vigor demonstrated they were undeterred by the now steady rain. Equally intrepid marchers and performers followed them. Parade viewers all wore heavy jackets and stood under umbrellas, cheering them on. Everyone seemed to take the rain for granted. It diminished none of the joy. We never found out the reason for the parade, but in all ways, it was a grand welcome for us.

A stroll through the fish market at the port made me salivate. Crabs, packaged in neat bundles, resembled huge baseball mitts. I'd never seen so many in one place, nor such large ones. Whole fish were arranged on ice in artful patterns. When one was sold, they rearranged the display to ensure it remained appealing. Three-foot-long dried squid sealed in plastic competed with fresh and dried fish bits and pieces in bright packaging. I had no idea exactly what type of fish were on display or what was in those packages, but I imagined sushi chefs going bonkers at the market. I couldn't wait for our first meal.

At the ferry terminal, we inquired about day trips to Rebun Island, home to a national park known for wildflowers, hiking trails through rugged mountains, and dazzling views. While Judy bought tickets for the next morning, I looked around and realized most signs were written in two languages. They were not the expected

Japanese and English; instead, they were Japanese and Russian. A few featured all three languages, but they were the exception. The Kuril Islands, administered by Russia, are less than two miles away. Sakhalin, Russia's largest island, can be seen from Wakkanai on a clear day, and several ferries a day transport people and freight between the two.

Dinner that night was at a tiny restaurant with seating for about a dozen people. I felt like a celebrity as we sat at the counter. We were the only non-Japanese. It impressed waitstaff and other diners that Judy spoke Japanese, and everyone seemed eager to ensure we enjoyed our meal. Watching chefs skillfully slice and arrange plates of sushi and sashimi was like seeing a beautifully choreographed dance. There was no wasted motion.

The chef asked Judy a question. She translated, "Do you want to try this?" She pointed to the thick slab of marbled pink fish the chef was holding.

"What is it?"

She asked the chef, then turned to me. "I don't have a clue what he said."

"Can you tell him I'm allergic to shellfish?" Then I added, "I really don't want to go to the hospital here. Not an experience I need to have."

She told the chef, who nodded and told Judy he'd only prepare fish.

"Okay then, I'm game. I'll try anything he offers."

We ate seafood we couldn't begin to identify. This was about the freshest fish I'd ever eaten. Some of the sushi was so delicious and different from what I am familiar with, I wished I knew what it was. Without a name, I'd never be able to order it again. Then again, it was probably local fish, unavailable elsewhere.

The next morning was clear and bright. Rebun was faintly visible from the ferry terminal. As the ferry neared it, we saw a series of gentle slopes and a single tall mountain peak dominating the small island. It was intensely green.

One road led away from the ferry terminal in either direction. We walked along the one that appeared to go toward the hiking area. Small homes dotted the shoreline, each with a boat or two tied to a dock. There were few cars. Scanning the area, we located the trailhead leading to the mountain's summit. There was a faint path. This was not a heavily used trail. I lasted for about an hour, walking through tall grasses and a profusion of wildflowers before my back began to scream.

I knew the sharp pain would be even worse walking down the mountain, so I turned around. Judy proceeded up. The walk down was excruciating. Any slight misstep or slide downward sent a blade through my lower back. So, I walked sideways at a snail's pace, careful to maintain my footing. To distract myself, I looked carefully at the flowers and grasses and took a zillion photos. I was familiar with the deep red wild geranium, rich purple and blue anemone, and pale-yellow primula that grew interspersed in the tall grasses. But I couldn't identify many of the others. I later read that Rebun is famous for the alpine flowers that bloom there at sea level, a rarity on the globe.

When Judy and I met up again, we headed back to "town" in search of a meal. The only place we could find was in the ferry terminal. Not what I was hoping for, but there were no other choices. I anticipated the Japanese equivalent of fast food sold at the Staten Island Ferry terminal in New York City. That is, processed, precooked, bland food.

My eyes opened wide when I looked at the menu. There were

photos of a large variety of fish, both as sushi and cooked. What made me gasp was a picture of a bowl of orange-colored salmon roe. I am mad for salmon roe, *ikura* in Japanese. At sushi places in New York, I always try to order something that is topped with it. But even at the best, most expensive restaurants, the portions of ikura are measly. It is as if the roe is meant as decoration or a flavor enhancer, the equivalent of a truffle in French cooking. Here was a white porcelain bowl filled with nothing but ikura. There was no question about what I would order.

Each tiny glistening morsel was perfect. I nearly swooned with the first bite. It was like biting into the sea: sweet, creamy, briny liquid surrounded by a thin membrane. I savored each bite, knowing I'd be unlikely to have this much roe again at a single meal. I wanted to enjoy the experience and fix it in my memory. Judy observed me closely. "I've never seen anyone enjoy something so much."

"You have to have a bite of this. It's extraordinary."

Judy took a morsel. "It's great."

"Want some more?"

"No, just wanted a taste."

I couldn't believe she was turning this down. It was the freshest, most delicious food I'd eaten in a very long time, including the fabulous meal the previous evening.

The following morning, we had breakfast at the hotel. A long buffet was laid out. I checked out the extravagant offerings. On the table were large bowls of rice, hard-boiled eggs, tofu, and various soups and broths. Brightly colored pickled vegetables sat next to steamed vegetables. There was bread, curry, and assorted shapes and colors of seaweed. I was nearing the end when I stopped in disbelief. Perched on a bed of crushed ice was a jumbo bowl of lustrous ikura. Forgetting every other offering, I transferred one heaping spoonful of this treasure onto my plate, spooned out some rice, and returned to the table. This was heaven.

After I'd finished eating, and refrained from licking the plate, I considered getting more. Judy encouraged me to go for it. Close to the display, I observed a Japanese guest filling the equivalent of a soup bowl to the rim with roe. Okay, I wasn't the only person being greedy. I couldn't even begin to imagine what a bowl of ikura that size would cost in New York, or even in Tokyo. He stuck around as I followed his lead.

"You like roe?" he asked in perfect English.

"Oh yes, it's nearly my favorite food."

"Mine too. My wife and I come up here every year for this."

It surprised me that he spoke English so well, and I asked him about it. He told me he taught English at a university. I was happy to talk with him as he was the first Japanese person I could communicate with easily since I'd arrived in Hokkaido.

"Where do you live?" I asked.

"Near Kyoto."

We continued talking as we moved away from the buffet so other people could get to it. There were lots of people eyeing the bowl of ikura.

"Do you have relatives in the area?"

"No, we come for the ikura. This is where you get the freshest ikura in the country."

"It's worth traveling from Kyoto just for this?" I asked.

"We also eat the crabs. And *uni*, sea urchin." He rubbed his stomach with his free hand. "Because the water is very cold, salmon, urchins, and crabs are plentiful here. Nothing else tastes like this."

We walked over and sat down with Judy, chatting while we each slowly indulged in our bowl of ikura. He was pleased we'd been to Rebun and suggested other sights in the area. "But the best part of being in Wakkanai is that bowl in front of you."

Over the next few days, we explored the cold, windy tip of Japan. Hillsides of tall grasses shimmered, mimicking waves in the sea. At Cape Soya, we posed for photos at the monument identifying the northernmost point in Japan. In the sea, whitecaps and waves skidded along the surface and crashed into the shore. On a warmish sunny day, we wore heavy jackets, scarves, and hats to protect ourselves from incessant blasts of frigid air. Everywhere we went felt fresh and unexplored, as if the wind made everything new each day. Unlike Sapporo, this northern landscape was captivating. It felt wild, untamed, and filled with energy.

But with all the wildness of Wakkanai, the professor from Kyoto was correct—eating that ikura (and several more bowls of it) was the most memorable part of being in far north Japan. If I close my eyes, I can still conjure up the roe's intense flavor of the sea.

WHO KNEW?:
SOUTH KOREA, 2012

I have two fine arts degrees in ceramics, a bachelor's and a master's. Throughout my education, the Japanese were held as the gold standard of Asian ceramics. But as I read about Korean potters, my admiration for their craftsmanship and design grew.

When the opportunity arose to travel in South Korea, I was excited about seeing the area where ceramics are produced. I'd heard a tale of an ancient town not far from Seoul where houses are built from thrown pots, and nearly everyone in the area has a family history in the craft, reaching back many centuries.

Home to Samsung, Kia, LG, and Hyundai, I knew Korea had a reputation for being high-tech and very competitive in the global market. Beyond that, I was curious about the culture, about which I'd gleaned snippets but didn't feel as though I understood with any depth. It was my favorite kind of adventure—a focus on something I love and a lot to discover.

My friend Judy and I arrived in Seoul at night, so glimpses out the taxi window didn't reveal much beyond the lights and highways of a standard-issue Asian city.

Our hotel was anything but standard issue. Our room was decorated with an enormous strawberry painted on the wall. The bathroom had a glass wall that went opaque with a flick of a switch and a slew of baffling gadgets. Our favorite was the toilet, which did almost everything but pee for you. When flushed, it sang out a little tune to cover the evidence of having been used.

On our first morning, we ventured onto the Seoul subway. Despite living in New York City and being familiar with the London Underground, Paris Metro, and a dozen other subway systems, the map of Seoul's rapid transit system was daunting. Laid out as a grid, the map showed sixteen lines in colors that were difficult to differentiate (a slew of teal, green, and blue shades predominated) and more than one hundred stations. Fortunately, I'd had the good sense to download a free transportation app that had been prominently advertised in every shred of tourist literature.

From the hotel, I input our destination, the Namsan Tower. It's the highest point in Seoul, and we thought it would give us an overview of the city. The app plotted the most efficient route, including where to change trains, how many stops there would be, and how long the trip would take. This was years before New York City created a similar app. We followed the directions to the closest subway station. The app even provided the time of the train we'd be likely to take, though because we were dawdling and looking at everything along the route, it had to update the schedule frequently.

The electronic ticket kiosk offered information in a dozen languages; buying a weekly ticket was a snap. I was surprised there was only one ticket vending machine since I'd read that the Seoul system is one of the most heavily used in the world. Then I saw locals swiping their phone across the entry barrier to gain access, something that has just begun in New York City a decade later.

Saturday was a good day to try the system. While busy, it wasn't as crowded as a typical weekday, when there were over seven million trips daily.

The map showed us where to board, though we didn't really need it. On every platform, train car, and throughout the station passageways, there were signs in Korean, English, and Chinese. We waited a few minutes seated on a comfortable bench in the spotless station. Electronic information signs outnumbered ads. The train tracks were protected by a floor-to-ceiling glass barrier so no one could fall into them or toss trash there. The station was well lit.

I was dazzled by the cleanliness, efficiency, and technology. The contrast between this modern system and New York City's antiquated one was beyond anything I'd seen or imagined.

Shortly before the train pulled into the station, an announcement about the time of arrival and destination was made in Korean and English. With a low whoosh, the train arrived, the glass doors opened, and passengers politely got off and on the subway car.

Even though the Seoul subway is very deep, the internet was always available as Korea has one of the fastest, most accessible internet systems in the world. I used my phone on the platform and on the train frequently to check maps and directions, and it never failed.

Arriving at the stop where we were to change trains, my phone vibrated and a map appeared. Judy and I followed the map to the next track, where we repeated the earlier boarding process seamlessly. At our final stop, we were directed to Exit 6, the one closest to our destination. As an added security measure, the station had a large, clear map prominently placed that showed the major buildings and landmarks in the area.

Once we got to the top of Namsan Tower, the view demonstrated what a large city Seoul is—buildings went as far as the horizon, broken only by parks and river. Downtown, most of the architecture was ultra-modern, with dazzling skyscrapers. A few older residential neighborhoods stood out, as did palaces remaining from hundreds of years before.

Gyeongbokgung Palace, situated in center city, looked so beautiful, even from a distance, that it had to be our next stop. Once we arrived, we saw multicolored buildings from the 1300s that were in such good condition they could have been built last year. Courtyards led from one structure to another, each painted red or green, with a sweeping curved roof, delicate columns, and symbols related to the royal family or function of the building.

Our fellow tourists were nearly all Korean. Though few spoke English, they made sure to point us in the direction of especially scenic views and then offered to take a photo of us in front of it. One woman handed us an umbrella to shade us from the sun. Another indicated where we could get a drink.

Walking through the vast complex, surrounded by Koreans taking in the grandeur, it was hard not to make comparisons to American tourists. By all measures, including politeness, dress, respectfulness, and even friendliness, the Koreans won hands down.

Back in center city, we stopped for a coffee in one of the many cafés. When I offered cash, the clerk seemed surprised. She took the bill and asked someone else how to handle the transaction. It was clear cash was a rarity. Everyone around us paid by swiping their phone. As the days passed, we hardly saw anyone use a credit card and never saw cash. In Seoul, paper money and coins were definitely passé.

Normally I have difficulty with buses in other countries; it can be hard to know which one to take and if it will get me to my destination. With our handy travel app, I felt confident as we stepped onto the sleek vehicle. Most buses in Seoul are electric, so they are quiet and environmentally friendly. The day was hot and humid and there was a lot of traffic. I thought about cities like Jakarta, New Delhi, Mexico City, and New York in the summer. By comparison, Seoul had startlingly clean air.

Riding at ground level gave us a better sense of the pulse of the sprawling city. Seoul has numerous outdoor video screens for news, information, and advertising. They are spread around instead of clustered, as in New York's Times Square or Tokyo's Ginza. They are a part of the overall look and feel of the city, rather than a tourist attraction. Modern sculptures were erected adjacent to ancient monuments. Silly figures decorated corporate office buildings. Throughout the city, disparate elements combined into an eclectic, cohesive whole. Koreans are very relaxed about this. Nothing seems forced or trendy or overly studied. It's stylish and fun.

At dinner that evening, Judy and I tried to put our finger on what makes Seoul so visually fascinating.

"They're willing to try almost anything," Judy said. "Things I couldn't imagine going together, they make fit."

"Even the lobby of our hotel has such kooky touches. Like the swing," I added. In the main lobby, three swings hung from the ceiling, and guests would frequently go for a ride on them while waiting. "There are so many unexpected things to look at and play with." She added that she felt freed from Japan's structured society.

We agreed that "playful" was the best way to describe the modern Korean aesthetic.

Dinner was at a BBQ restaurant in the hotel's neighborhood, Itaewon. The waitress helped us to select from the menu (no English, but photos). With the flip of a switch, she transformed our ordinary table into a small gas barbecue. Then came the food to be cooked—an overflowing platter of thinly sliced beef and vegetables. *This can't be for two people*, I thought. *She must think Americans are gluttons.* The only other time I'd seen this much meat served to two people was in Argentina, where they are known for consuming vast quantities. Looking around the room, this mound of food seemed to be average. She gave us a quick lesson on barbecuing, demonstrated how to dip the meat into the variety of marinades laid out— mild, sweet, spicy, and salty—and then left us to carry on.

Between cooking and eating the savory, lightly charred meat, I observed our fellow diners. The restaurant was packed with Korean families with small children, couples, and groups of young men and women. They laughed, talked, and ate with ease and unselfconsciousness. After coming from Japan where we'd only seen groups of men dining together after work, this was delightful to see.

Koreans are typically portrayed as driven, hard workers. That probably is true, but this other aspect of their collective personality is very appealing.

After dinner, tired, we channel surfed TV. Lots of news, soap operas, movies, cooking classes, and game shows—except for the language, it could have been American TV. The big surprise: at least three channels had baseball games. I knew the Japanese were crazy for baseball but had no idea Koreans shared their mania.

Over the next couple of days, we visited the Leeum Museum of Art and walked through neighborhoods, discovering a street where shop after shop sold traditional drums. At outdoor cafés, we people watched, seeing stylishly dressed women and men intermingled with teenage wannabe punks. We ate traditional Korean foods: *bibimbap*, a rice-based dish filled with grilled vegetables and a protein; *bulgogi*, a marinated grilled beef served with an array of pickled side dishes. There was also fresh fish and lots of fiery *kimchi* (fermented cabbage). The meals were delicious, and the look of the restaurants was as appetizing as the food. Even small, hole-in-the-wall places had been thoughtfully designed and served food on attractive dinnerware. My impressions were all very positive.

Then we headed to Icheon, a small village about an hour from Seoul, home to over three hundred studios and a museum dedicated exclusively to ceramics. For me, this was to be a highlight of my visit to South Korea. It's a place I'd dreamed of going to for years.

The view through the bus windows was less than entrancing. Seoul's population was growing, and with that growth had come urban sprawl. Almost half the country's population was within the greater metropolitan area. For the first half hour, we passed by apartment complex after apartment complex. Each block was comprised of a dozen or so identical concrete buildings tightly clustered together, each building around thirty stories tall, square, and dull. I wondered how residents ever see the light of day. Given the number of buildings under construction, the sprawl had not slowed down. This city expansion helped to explain why the Seoul subway system is so extensive and why they continue extending the lines.

Even after we had traveled past the outskirts of the metropolitan area, we came upon areas of these behemoth dwellings. I'm certain they are efficient, but they looked soul-numbing.

Icheon returned us to the beauty and grace of the country. The town became the center of traditional pottery beginning in the 14th century. There are stories about the ceramicists of the village being so esteemed that some were kidnapped by the Chinese and Japanese. It was the only way they felt they could learn the Koreans' advanced techniques for glazing and firing. We spent most of our day at the Haegang Ceramics Museum. The scope of work on display, both Korean and global, was staggering. Three floors of nothing but ceramics, from ancient Greek amphora and Korean Goryeo celadon to modern functional and sculptural ceramics. There were more shades of celadon than I imagined were possible.

I saw work that looked familiar. When I read the descriptions, I was thrilled that some were made by former instructors and classmates. It seemed astounding that I'd traveled to the other side of the globe, and people I knew well, like Ken Ferguson, Victor Babu, and Chris Gustin, were represented in the collection. Other works were by famed American and European ceramicists I knew only by reputation. And the work by people I was unfamiliar with, going back in history to the present day, from around the world, made me realize how little about ceramic history I knew.

Despite breaks for lunch, tea, and walking outside, the experience was overwhelming. Then we headed over to the cluster of potters' shops. When we visited, there were over seventy active studios producing a wide range of work, from delicate porcelain bowls and teapots to rugged stoneware planters. The proprietors spoke little English but were helpful and accommodating, wrapping our purchases securely for transport. We both came away with a lot of souvenirs.

The following day we headed to a very different kind of craft center—Seoul's silk market at Kwangjang. I was tagging along because the extent of my sewing capabilities is buttons and hems.

Following our ever-trusty GPS app, we entered a gigantic building, probably two city blocks long. I read later it is the oldest market in Seoul and has more than five thousand stalls. The size was nearly overwhelming. Walking up and down the aisles, we saw household goods, ordinary clothes, and a few silk shops. We stopped into one silk shop and left with gorgeous scarves, but no fabric, which Judy was looking for. The market seemed extraordinary only for its size. As we walked to the far end, we smelled, then saw, food vendors and stalls selling freshly prepared meals. The scents were tantalizing, but not what we'd come for. Could this really be the famed silk market? There were no signs in English and no one to ask. We stumbled about for a bit, almost ready to admit defeat, when we saw an elevator. On the second floor, we peeked out, and both gasped.

We entered into a magical visual feast. Displays of luscious, luminous fabrics in jewel tones went on as far as we could see.

"How are you going to decide which stall to shop from?" I asked Judy.

She shrugged, and her hands went up as if to say, "Beats me."

Most stalls featured hundreds of rolls of fabric with a few small, traditional outfits hanging from the rafters. I snapped photos as Judy strolled down the aisles, stopping occasionally to look at an especially lovely color or lustrous brocade pattern. She didn't buy anything; the choices were infinite.

The proprietor of one small stall beckoned Judy over. He didn't speak English, but he seemed eager to help, and Judy was so confused by all the choices she was happy to stay put. She pulled out her phone and showed him photos of her quilts. He looked impressed. She mimed having problems sewing this shiny, slippery fabric. With the assistance of pantomimes and drawings, the shopkeeper taught her tips about sewing silk.

While they were engaged, I looked around at nearby booths. In one that displayed a dozen finished children's outfits, two women, who I assumed were mother and grandmother, had a toddler in tow. They were selecting fabric for a traditional hanbok outfit for him. I know this because when they saw me watching, they beckoned me over. They flipped through a style book, discussing various options. The outfits consisted of shorts or long pants, a shirt, and a short fitted jacket, so there were a lot of decisions to be made. Every so often they would ask me for an opinion. I remained noncommittal, cheerfully approving everything with gestures and a broad smile. This happened to be an honest response—the combinations of bright-colored fabrics were uniformly striking. They couldn't have gone wrong, no matter what they picked.

Then I wandered through the aisles, carefully noting landmarks so I could find my way back. That was difficult, because so many of the shops looked similar. They were all a celebration of color and texture.

Meanwhile, Judy was selecting fabrics to buy. When I returned, she'd accumulated a tall pile of silk yardage. Both she and the proprietor had been having a wonderful time. He kept pulling out bits and pieces and asking if she wanted them. She hesitated; the fabric she'd selected would keep her occupied for years. Then he made it clear these fabric ends were a gift and that he would be offended if she didn't accept.

It took both of us to carry her haul. Using our handy app, we located the closest post office and shipped the fabrics home.

By the end of the week, I'd filled some of the gaps in my knowledge about Korean culture, but knew there was a lot more to learn. I wondered why so few people I knew had ever been to Korea. As someone we spoke with succinctly put it, "We don't get many tourists; people don't know about Korea." So, I will be an ambassador for the city and country—it is a wonderful place to visit. I hope to return there soon.

COOKING MY WAY AROUND THE GLOBE—
PART 2: SEOUL, SOUTH KOREA, 2012

I've been a fan of Korean food for many years. It has intense flavor and lots of variety, from barbecue to stews, and is always accompanied by a selection of side dishes. It's a cuisine that tempts me again and again. K-Town (Koreatown) in New York City is one of my go-to places for meals.

When we arrived in Seoul, one thing I most wanted to do was to take a cooking class to learn to prepare some of my favorite dishes—bulgogi (marinated barbecued meat), bibimbap (a rice dish), and *sundubu-jjigae* (tofu stew). The best way for me to learn is by doing; a recipe alone isn't enough to motivate me.

My friend Judy and I had a choice of several cooking programs. We decided on O'ngo Cooking School because the class included a great menu with hands-on cooking. Other classes had market tours, which I would have enjoyed, but instructors did most of the food preparation.

As with most things in Korea, the experience exceeded our expectations. The ultra-modern classroom had well-thought-out stations for a dozen students—stainless steel tables to allow for easy and thorough cleaning, cutting boards, stovetop burners, running water, professional knives, measuring utensils, bowls, and the ingredients for the first dish we would prepare, quick kimchi.

The students came from all over the globe. Though the class would be taught in English, it wasn't the first language for many people. I wondered how they'd follow an instructor speaking with a thick accent.

I needn't have worried. The instructor stood at the front of the room, with a large overhead well-lit mirror so we could see exactly what she was doing. She spoke into a mike, in perfect English, and introduced herself.

"I'm Insoon. First, I'll explain each dish. We're going to prepare a typical family dinner. I'll demonstrate the techniques used, then each of you will prepare the same dish."

Her breezy, friendly manner put everyone at ease. Her white chef's jacket lent an air of professionalism.

"If you have questions, please ask. This class is about you. I want you to see how easy and delicious Korean food is."

Sounded great to me.

"We're going to start with kimchi, a staple of Korean cuisine eaten at nearly every meal."

Insoon went on to say that while most kimchi is fermented for two to three days, there is also a version that can be eaten within thirty minutes of preparation. She jokingly called it "emergency" kimchi.

"It's as hot as standard kimchi but is pickled rather than fermented."

With precise chopping, she reduced a large napa cabbage into a neat pile of strips within a minute. My own efforts took a lot longer and looked much messier. But I didn't cut my fingers with the ultra-honed cleaver, so I decided it was a success. We then boiled a mix of water, salt, sugar, red pepper flakes, and vinegar and poured the brine over the cabbage. It sat while we moved onto our next dish, bulgogi.

Bulgogi also required good knife skills, this time with a thin slicing blade, again razor-sharp. The trick here was to start with beef that had been slightly frozen and to work quickly. Insoon demonstrated slicing against the grain to get super-thin slices. Classroom assistants handed out packages of frozen beef. To my surprise, I could do this with no problem.

To create the marinade, we mixed soy sauce, brown sugar, sesame oil, garlic, and minced ginger. The meat remained in a bowl soaking up those flavors while we prepared bean sprout salad, a traditional side dish.

This dish was a snap. We quickly blanched the mung bean sprouts in boiling water, rinsed them, and dried them off. The dressing for the salad was a simple combination of sesame oil, garlic, and soy sauce. We finished the salad with sesame seeds and finely chopped scallion. It looked fresh and appealing.

By now, the kitchen smelled wonderful, if somewhat garlicky. It got even better when we tossed the marinated beef into a super-hot skillet. The meat sizzled and smoked and cast an aroma I knew from every Korean restaurant I've ever eaten in. With a quick sear, the meat was ready to serve.

Insoon showed how to plate and garnish each of the foods. We carried the finished dishes into a dining area. The results were sublime. Accompanied by beer, we all felt a sense of accomplishment.

Now that I'd made it once, I could do it again at home. And I have.

TRAVELING IN PAIN:
ICELAND, 2015

Traveling used to be easy. I'd never had to consider the difficulty of mundane actions. But after experiencing severe back pain caused by bulging disks, arthritis, and pinched nerves, I began to think

carefully about travel. Every twist and turn has the potential for lasting pain. That pain is often a reminder of aging. It makes me even more determined to continue traveling, not knowing when I might be permanently grounded.

The announcement to prepare for landing woke me from a fitful sleep—in a few minutes, we'd touch down in Reykjavik. I was heading to Iceland in part because it is a relatively short flight from New York City.

After being on the plane for four and a half hours, my lower back screamed complaints—a constant dull ache punctuated by sharp stabs. I stretched my neck, then arms and legs, within the confines of the narrow coach seat. I hoped the orthopedic cushion, heating pad, and painkillers I'd packed would make the trip bearable. Closing my eyes, I prayed my back would cooperate for the next ten days. I was not ready for my world to shrink.

Outside the terminal, I met up with the small group I'd be traveling with. A few dozen miles out of Reykjavik, our minibus was almost the only vehicle on the narrow road. Within a couple of hours, our group was in remote terrain—it doesn't take many miles in Iceland to escape populated areas. We chanced upon tiny Icelandic horses jauntily prancing and running around a rough dirt track in the middle of nowhere. Clouds of geothermal steam poured from fissures in the earth, creating an almost impenetrable curtain blocking out snowcapped mountains. Then at the lodge, exhausted from travel, we ate a quick dinner and went to bed.

In the morning, we headed to the western coastline. At the shoreline lurked craggy outcroppings of stone, sculpted into stunning shapes by time and tides. Our guide, Uli, led us past a miniscule harbor where a half dozen weather-beaten fishing boats were docked to a narrow, well-worn path that skirted the edge of nearly vertical cliffs. I walked extra carefully, concerned about tripping and jarring my spine. Uli led us onto a narrow finger of land jutting into the sea. We huddled near the center, peering down into a pit descending to the ocean. Sea birds nested in crevices, their beady black eyes shining and alert for signs of danger. Stiff currents created a whooshing roar as water entered the pit and receded. Icy droplets made us flinch. I took a slew of photos, knowing I'd go home with too many pictures, none conveying the majesty in front of me.

I peeled off from the group, wanting to escape their chatter and leisurely amble down the path. I breathed in the frigid northern air and fixed the images in my memory. The surrounding snowcapped volcanoes glistened. Windows on a tiny building twinkled in the far distance, the only tangible evidence of humans.

I took a step, then froze. A knife had entered my spine. I willed myself not to scream. I couldn't move and didn't know what had happened. The blinding pain blocked out every trace of beauty.

No one was nearby. Looking down, I saw a small scuff mark in the dirt—I'd tripped on a large pebble, briefly lost my balance, and slid about three inches. That slight misstep had caused this searing pain. I willed myself to hobble forward. Near our van, I found a bench, lay down, and pulled one knee to my chest, stretching. Then I switched legs and repeated. By then, the group had caught up with me.

"Are you okay? What happened? You're white as a ghost!"

I explained I had stumbled.

"I've got painkillers—Tramadol, Vicodin, Percocet, if you want them."

More concern and advice followed. While comforting, none of it helped to diminish the pain. How could this have happened on the second day?

Hours later, two Aleve, more stretching, and a heating pad had dulled the pain. The knife had been extracted and was replaced by the constant dull achiness that follows a too-strenuous workout. I didn't go with the group to dinner because sitting in a chair, any chair, magnified the agony.

The hotel was ringed by hot tubs, fed from one of Iceland's many geothermal springs. I shivered my way into the chilly night, though at 9:00 p.m., the sun was still bright. At the tub, I gratefully sank into swirling hot water. Steam rose from my body and the surface of the water, creating a mini fog. Through the droplets, I caught glimpses of shimmering, snowy mountains.

An hour later my skin was red. I was light-headed and woozy, but felt better. Before ducking inside to escape the cold, I paused to take one more appreciative glance. At 10:00 p.m., it was still bright, not a single star visible, the sun not even close to the horizon.

The next day, when the group hiked up a steep trail to see an unusual geological formation, I stayed behind. Pat, a woman many years younger than I, also chose to forego the walk. I'd noticed she walked with ski poles and asked about them.

"I'm always afraid of falling; they help to give me confidence." Pat explained she'd been diagnosed with multiple sclerosis about ten years earlier.

"Why come on such a strenuous trip?" I asked.

"I don't do well in heat; my symptoms are less severe in the cold." Chuckling, she continued. "My husband and I have been to Antarctica, Alaska, the Canadian Rockies, and every other cold-weather tourist destination we could think of. Iceland was next on the list."

Pat, like me, had traveled since she was young and refused to give it up. She'd learned to do what she could, skip activities beyond her capabilities, but to keep moving no matter what and appreciate whatever was possible.

I listened to her story of diminishing capabilities with awe and fear. Awe at her bravery in joining such a rigorous trip and fear that my condition would worsen over time, making everything even more difficult. Pat's refusal to accept that she should stay at home, out of harm's way, made her a hero and role model to me.

As the trip progressed, pain became my constant companion. It sometimes limited what I was able or willing to do. Even when feeling okay, the fear of pain hung over me specter-like, reminding me that a minor mishap could curtail my activities even further. Despite my limitations, I feasted on the Icelandic landscape of plunging waterfalls, snowcapped volcanoes, quaint homes, geysers, fields of mud bubbling from geothermal activity, and clear skies that never seemed to go dark. I learned to graciously take a steadying hand when offered.

Tales of trolls and gremlins, feuds lasting centuries, and strategies for surviving harsh winters gave me insights into Icelandic culture. I dined on the freshest fish imaginable and tasted a smidgen of the very stinky *hakari* (putrefied shark, considered a delicacy). Migrating puffins put on a show, their tiny wings flapping furiously to keep their rotund, non-aerodynamic bodies aloft. Every evening I soaked in hot tubs.

One afternoon, while the group hiked on a snowy trail to see a waterfall, Pat and I stayed behind in a natural pool of warm, aquamarine water. While luxuriating, all thoughts of treacherous paths dissolved as we admired a field of intricate and somehow haunting lava formations rimming the water's edge. The view was framed by snowy volcanoes and a cloudless, cerulean sky.

For the remainder of the trip, I managed to avoid further accidents, though I spent a lot of energy on mindful walking. Yes, life had changed. I could no longer be the fearless traveler I'd once been, but I could also continue to travel. Pat had demonstrated that, despite the difficulties, it is possible to be adventurous.

Since then, I've made many trips all around the globe. I am careful and willing to put up with discomfort. I take whatever help is offered. I enjoy the food, scenery, and people. I've slowed down and go at a pace that is comfortable for me and don't feel compelled to see everything. When I need a break, I sit at a café and people watch. Doing that, I've met people and engaged in conversations that wouldn't have happened if I'd been speeding around seeing everything.

With careful planning and mindful traveling, the world remains open to me.

COOKING MY WAY AROUND THE GLOBE— PART 3: CARTAGENA, COLUMBIA, 2016

Every winter I try to go to a sunny, warm-weather destination to briefly escape winter. Colombia was a relatively short flight and Cartagena looked to be a fun place to visit for beaches, culture, and food.

After checking out the main attractions in Cartagena, my friends Maggie, Penny, Linda, and I were all interested in finding a cooking class. None of the tourist brochures or guidebooks offered any help, so we paid a visit to the local tourism office. After much searching and persistence, the tourism representative came up with one choice.

"It will be in English. I just spoke with the tour operator," the woman told us.

"What does the class include?" I asked.

"I think you go to a local market. And then you cook."

"Anything else?"

"That's really all I know."

"Do you have a brochure?" Maggie asked.

"Sorry, can't offer you anything else," the woman replied with a shrug. "You've found a well-kept secret. I never knew about this."

We jumped on it with only that scant information.

Early morning the next day, an affable man who introduced himself as Enrique picked us up at our hotel. "But call me Ricky," he said. He was a good-looking man, probably in his forties, with dark wavy hair and light bronze skin. The laugh lines around his eyes and mouth hinted at *La Buena Vida* (the good life). We piled into a well-worn Chevy van. Two young men from Toronto had been picked up before us. With six passengers, it was a tight fit in the van. Fortunately, our destination wasn't far from central city.

"Welcome!" Ricky boomed a greeting as he drove. "We're heading to the Mercado de Bazurto. It's a totally different Cartagena than Old City or the beach areas. This is where Cartagenians shop for food, household goods, clothing, and, well, almost anything. You're going to see the real Cartagena."

We crept through traffic, so he had plenty of time to point out sights, which in a suburban area were sparse and not very interesting.

"There's nowhere to park at the market, so my friend will come over to move the van while we're inside." Ricky urged us, "You'll need to get out quickly. People get really annoyed with cars that don't move."

As we approached the market, I understood what he'd been saying. It looked like marginally controlled chaos: cars and trucks loading and unloading, market workers pushing carts filled with crates, people toting laden shopping bags weaving between vehicles, street vendors doing business that edged its way from sidewalk into the street. Stray cats and dogs searched for dropped food or handouts.

Once we'd exited the van and wove our way through the street vendors, Ricky led us to the indoor market, a rabbit's warren of connecting rooms. Competing salsa rhythms came from every direction.

Fish vendors filled the first room. With peeling paint on the walls, rusted pipes, and wet, slimy floors, it was a far cry from sanitary. A fishy smell hit me with the force of a spray can aimed directly at my nose. Despite that, the fish cooling in buckets of ice or displayed on slabs of marble looked fresh, with shiny eyes. Ricky told us the snapper had been caught that morning. There was also flounder, tuna, parrot fish, and half a dozen other varieties. He chatted with several vendors, then started negotiating for the fish we'd be preparing. While the snapper was being wrapped, I asked the fishmonger if he'd mind me taking a photo. He was delighted and posed for me. His broad grin was erased, a solemn "businesslike" expression replacing it. The minute I put the camera down, the smile returned.

We made our way through several rooms of basic staples, enormous sacks of rice, beans, and grains. In a small anteroom were several booths with antique-looking grinders chugging away. The sellers poured dried corn into a funnel, and it extruded a thick paste at the bottom. We stopped there as Ricky explained this paste is used to make arepas, the Colombian corn cake we'd be preparing. He bought a plastic bag of the paste, plus a bag of dried corn. "You'll get to grind the corn yourself in a mortar and pestle. I want you to see how it is traditionally made and for you to taste the difference."

Our small group seemed to be the only tourists. We tried to be careful not to get in the way of the transactions taking place around us. I'd been to enough local markets around the globe that nothing about the market surprised or bothered me. The chaos, grubbiness, filthy, wet floors, and wandering animals contrasted with the crisp, colorful fruits and vegetables, bright-eyed fish, and most especially, the cheerful vendors. While this was a place of business, it was also very social. The buyers and sellers bantered and laughed while small children played under their watchful eyes.

We finished by buying coconuts, plantains, lemons, limes, and the herbs and spices for our meal. By this time, we were deep in the market, and it took a while to make our way out of the maze. I noticed Ricky took a roundabout route to avoid the meat section. Perhaps he thought that the blood and gore of freshly butchered pigs and cows would be too much for a group of North American tourists. Personally, I would have loved it. In markets throughout Asia and South America, I've been fascinated watching butchers at work. It seems a bit odd, but they seem to relish their profession. And I find the sight of a table filled with pigs' snouts or eyeballs both gruesome and utterly compelling.

Ricky hadn't said a word about where we would cook. Between people and our provisions, there wasn't a spare inch of space in the van. I peered around Linda, looking at the passing scenery, trying to figure out where we were headed and what kind of kitchen would fit all of us and the food.

After a brief ride through a residential neighborhood, Ricky turned into the driveway of a smallish, one-story house. "Welcome to my home!"

Oh, I thought. Maybe this wasn't a hands-on cooking class after all. But I figured our time in the market alone was worth the price we paid. We'd never have found or visited it on our own, and it had been captivating.

The front door opened and a middle-aged woman in a bright print dress appeared, holding a tray of shot glasses. Ricky introduced us to his wife, who murmured, "*Hola, buenos dias*." She nearly flew back into the house, and we didn't see her again.

"Take one, take one." Ricky held the tray, offering us each a glass. "This is guaro. It's Colombians' most popular drink."

When we each had a glass in our hands, Ricky raised his glass and said, "*Salud.*" We repeated him, then took a sip. I almost spit it out, but politeness forced me to swallow. It was like drinking moonshine aged for under a week, or maybe gasoline. Ricky let out a guffaw. "Sorry, sorry. But if I'd told you *aguardiente, guaro*, translates as 'fire water,' you wouldn't have tried it." The two Canadian guys seemed to have liked the guaro, and Ricky filled their glasses to the brim. The rest of us refused as politely as we could.

Still gasping, we headed into his home. The living room was bright and cheerful, with comfortable chairs and a large dining table. Landscapes, family photos, and a large cross decorated the cream walls. Three fans were strategically placed to move air through the room. At the far end was a kitchen that looked to be circa 1960, surrounded by a long L-shaped counter.

Ricky said we'd each be working on a different dish. Our meal would include fried fish, coconut rice, arepas, *patacones* (fried plantains), and *cocadas* (sweet coconut balls) for dessert. I was assigned to preparing the patacones.

Diego, Ricky's friend from the market, arrived. He'd be helping us prepare the meal. His English was limited, so Ricky explained what we should each do, and Diego demonstrated.

Along with Penny, my first assignment was to peel the plantains and slice them into thin disks. We sat at the kitchen counter, peeling and slicing. There was only one cooktop, so space was at a premium. Diego did most of the actual frying and grilling for all the dishes, the rest of us acting as prep cooks. He fried the plantains in batches, then laid them out on a cookie sheet covered in paper towels. After they cooled, he demonstrated placing one plantain slice between his hands and mashing it together so that the banana spread apart into a thin patty. Penny and I did it to the remaining slices. Then he fried them a second time until they were golden.

While we did that, two others farther down the counter were grinding dried corn for the arepas and shaping the prepared corn paste and the freshly made corn paste into patties. The third group grated coconut for the cocadas.

In a surprisingly short time, we prepared the full meal. As we sat down to eat, Ricky poured us each a large glass of a pale green liquid.

"This is *lulada*. It's made from lulo, a local fruit."

We were all a little nervous about trying it after his guaro surprise. Plus, the pitcher was filled with ice, something I avoid while traveling.

Ricky saw us all looking suspiciously at the drink. "No alcohol, no worries." He paused as he saw we were still reluctant to take a sip. "Oh, and the water has been purified. It's safe."

I took a tiny sip. It was a refreshing citrusy mix of sweet and tart.

As we started to eat, Ricky's daughters, who I guessed were about ten and twelve years old, came running and giggling into the living room. They were on their lunch break from school. After introducing them, he tried to get them to eat outside. They were having no part of it. They wanted to practice English and spend time with the foreigners. I guessed Ricky didn't do this very often, so tourists remained a novelty. None of us objected to having the girls join us. We moved our chairs so they could squeeze in between us. In Spanglish we managed a conversation. The girls were delighted, both from the experience and in getting their dad to allow them to stay.

While heavy on fried food and sweet from added sugar, the meal was delicious. The "tour" had been more about culture than cooking. I'd only learned to make fried plantains. But I wasn't disappointed. It isn't often that as a tourist you get to experience how ordinary people live. Given a choice of a fancy cooking school or this, I'd opt for the home version every time.

EATING WITH AMBIENCE:
UAE, 2017

I'd wanted to see Dubai and Abu Dhabi (states in the United Arab Emirates) for their architecture and innovative technology. The transition from undeveloped desert to the financial, tech, and cultural center of the Middle East happened quickly and with impressive results.

My friend Sue and I spent a week in the area, seeing the marvel of the cities rising from the sand. Almost 85 percent of the UAE population are expats. I learned about the area through the immigrant population who flooded there for work opportunities.

P hotos do not do justice to either Dubai or Abu Dhabi. Some of the architecture looks like it came straight from a sci-fi film. I'd see one corkscrew-like building and be wowed, only to be distracted by a zigzag building and one shaped like a sail. It felt like a movie set, Las Vegas, and total fantasy. New islands were created where none existed, and the desert has been transformed into arable land.

From the top of Burj Khalifa, the world's tallest building, one can see where the flashy city ends and dun-colored desert begins. I learned that most of what I saw didn't exist twenty years before.

Within ten years, it will look different. In twenty years, I doubt the desert will be visible even from the tower's great height; the distance to the city's edge grows greater every year as Dubai expands with lightning speed. This pace of development is like nothing I've ever seen, including in China, which astounded me with how fast buildings and bridges were being completed.

Desalinization and a steady supply of potable water started this transformation. Foreign workers have made the growth possible. Only 15 percent of Dubai's and Abu Dhabi's population are native born. I didn't meet a single one when I visited. The vast majority of workers in the hospitality and transportation industries, along with construction workers, retail employees, office workers, and healthcare providers, are foreign born.

I began asking people I met where they hailed from and why they'd come to Dubai or Abu Dhabi. Most were guest workers from India, Bangladesh, Pakistan, the Philippines, and other Middle Eastern countries. Some had become permanent residents; others were on three-year work visas. "I came to earn enough money to start a restaurant when I return home," a taxi driver from India told me.

"I can earn so much more money here. It is worth it to me to be away from my family," a hotel employee from the Philippines said. "My money will go to buy a house. At home, I couldn't do that. I see this as an investment."

"I'm studying to take the civil service test. When my contract is over, I hope to work as an accountant for the government. I have a degree in accounting, but I couldn't get a job at home in Bangladesh. Here there is a possibility." This was from a woman driver of a "pink" taxi. Pink taxis aren't literally pink, but taxis reserved for the exclusive use of women passengers and driven by women. These are necessary in a country where some women are very observant and conservative. When I asked our driver how long she planned to stay, she told me she had no intention of returning home.

Work contracts begin for a three-year period. The conditions of employment, as described to me, sounded like being an indentured servant. But the people I spoke with were enthusiastic about the opportunity afforded them. When a person signs a contract in their home country, the employer provides transportation to the UAE. The job often requires working very long hours, six days a week. Workers' housing is dormitory style, often with no cooking facilities. If the immigrant decides they don't like the job or living conditions, they can only escape the contract if they can afford to buy an airline ticket to leave. They can't switch jobs. One taxi driver told me he knew a few people who were homesick or miserable. "They are trapped." He then said the disgruntled were in the minority; most guest workers were achieving their goals.

Even in places where I expected to meet natives, like the Sheikh Mohammed Cultural Center or the Arabic Calligraphy Center, the staff were foreigners. The majority were Muslim and Middle Eastern and had lived in Dubai for decades but hadn't been born there. I had a lengthy conversation with a charming calligraphy instructor who told me he rarely comes into contact with anyone native born, even though he'd lived in Dubai for many years. He was also suffering from the impact of the rapid changes to his adopted home. He told me, "I go to a neighborhood I know well but haven't been to in a few months and I get lost. Everything changes so fast."

We stayed at a hotel in a residential neighborhood in Dubai. At the front desk, we asked for a recommendation for a nearby restaurant serving Middle Eastern food. Most cuisine in Dubai reflects the diversity of the population. We didn't know if we'd be able to easily find a Middle Eastern restaurant.

The front desk clerk directed us to a nearby street that he said had several excellent restaurants. Peering in the window of the first one we passed on the block, we decided it was not meant for us. The clientele was predominantly bearded men in traditional Muslim attire, flowing white robes, and headscarves. There wasn't a woman in sight.

A few doors down, we came upon a more promising establishment filled with men, women, and children. While we were the only non-locals in the restaurant, the staff greeted us warmly. Before we looked at the menu, they brought over a basket of warm pita bread and bowls of baba ghanoush and hummus. The menu had photos of food that made my mouth water. I assumed a food stylist had done an excellent job. When our meal arrived—lamb kabobs, fattoush salad, eggplant stew, baked halloumi cheese in a tomato sauce, and *machboo*, a rice dish with chicken and vegetables—everything looked just like the photos and tasted every bit as good as it looked. It was a mix of savory and tangy flavors, and different textures from creamy to chewy to crunchy. All around us, families talked, ate, and laughed. Some women wore full hijab, others dressed conservatively in long-sleeved dresses, and a few seemed contemporary in jeans and T-shirts. Everyone appeared at ease despite their differing attire.

The next afternoon, we headed to ultra-luxe Dubai, the Burj Al Arab hotel. It claimed to be the only seven-star hotel in the world. Sue had the foresight to make a reservation for a drink at the bar. Without a reservation, you can't get onto the property. I understood why. If uncontrolled, non-guests would overrun the hotel's public spaces. They'd be gawking (as we were) at the elegant decor, spectacular flower arrangements, and gift shop featuring insanely expensive items. It was the first time, and probably the only time, I will ever see a diamond-encrusted handgun.

Nothing conveys how upscale and beautiful this hotel is. We wandered around the property, set on a private island, then took the elevator to the top floor to the bar. I had the most expensive drinks of my life (minimum bar tab is $75 per person), and it was worth every dirham. I stuck with martinis, ordering the bar's signature cucumber martini, followed by one made with lichee, and another of passion fruit. They were served in an elegant glass, which, when filled with the jewel-toned liquid, was picture perfect. Sue drank red wine, which she said was some of the best she'd ever tasted. We got happily soused as we watched the sun set over the city and sea from our elegant aerie. Along with the drinks, the server brought over an elegant three-tiered serving dish filled with almonds, salted, spiced, and sugared. They didn't quite counterbalance the alcohol, and we were tipsy as we made our way to dinner at a much more downscale restaurant in a nearby mall.

The next evening, we sipped wine at the Emirates Palace hotel at its beachside bar, enjoying the gentle breeze and wonderful view. Then off by taxi to dinner at Pierchic, considered one of the best restaurants in Dubai. It was expensive, but like the Burj Al Arab hotel, worth it for the ambience. The restaurant juts out into the water via a long pier. Our table faced Burj Al Arab, and we watched as colored lights on the hotel transformed its appearance while we dined. Surprisingly, most items on the menu were Italian and more meat than fish. We did find a couple of fish entrées, and I ate a dinner of sea bass with tomato and vinegar. Sue ate Dover sole with eggplant, tomato, and olives. While delicious, I could have been eating in any good seafood restaurant on the globe. Nothing was unique about the preparation.

After dining at some of the most elegant and expensive restaurants in Dubai and Abu Dhabi, on our last night in the UAE, Sue and I headed off to the Al Mina fish market in Abu Dhabi for dinner. A friend of Sue's had recommended we go there for the experience and food. I assumed there would be restaurants serving what was available for sale in the market.

The market is huge, with over one hundred fishmongers displaying seafood that had been swimming a few hours earlier. It's noisy and a bit fishy-smelling but tempting and exotic. Arranged on beds of ice, the fish were as enticing as the displays in Harrods Food Hall in London. Though it was evening, the market was crowded, not with the restaurateurs and chefs who come early morning, but with taxi drivers and shift workers who come for the inexpensive and astoundingly fresh fish they can have cooked to order for dinner.

We watched as men in red overalls scaled, gutted, deboned, and fileted fish at cleaning stations scattered around the market. Buyers would bring their purchases over, and in minutes, they'd walk away with ready-to-cook fish.

Some varieties I recognized, like tuna, salmon, and sole. Others were exotic looking to Sue and me, and we wanted to find out what they were. Plus, we realized we had to choose the fish we wanted cooked and bring it to the restaurant. We found a young fish seller wearing a Brooklyn T-shirt who spoke English and was delighted to chat with us, especially when he found out we live in New York City.

"Have you been to New York?"

"I will go. My cousin lives there."

"Oh, where?"

"Brooklyn. He loves it. Invites me always."

"You should go. Great place." He nodded vigorously in agreement. Then I asked, "Where are you from?"

"India."

"Oh. Where in India?" Sue asked. India is one of her favorite places, and she's spent a lot of time there.

"Mumbai."

"What brought you here?" I asked.

"Money." With that, he pointed to the fish. He wanted to get down to business. I pointed to a striped, yellow fish. "What is that?"

"Hamra."

He looked at my uncomprehending face and shrugged. "Sorry, don't know the English name."

"Is it good?"

"All my fish is good." He laughed. "It's great!"

"Okay, okay. I get it. If you were going to pick one for dinner tonight, which one would you choose?"

He turned to his display and pondered for a minute, then asked, "Are you okay with bones?"

Sue said, "Sure."

I shook my head no. I'd swallowed a fish bone years before and had to go into surgery to have it removed, so I'm leery of bony fish.

"Okay. For you"—he pointed to Sue—"this one." He lifted what looked like a bigmouth bass with one hand and made a thumbs-up sign with the other. "*Samak*. Is delicious. Was swimming two hours ago."

Sue looked at the gigantic grayish fish with shining eyes and a gaping mouth and said, "All that for me?"

"Yes. When cleaned and cooked, will be smaller."

"How much?"

He mentioned a price that seemed a bargain.

Sue nodded yes.

"And for you"—he pointed to me—"no bones." He picked up one of the largest squids I'd ever seen, tentacles dangling from a long tubular body. Squid is one of my favorites, and I enthusiastically agreed. Again, the price was far less than I guessed it would be.

"Okay, now how do we get this cooked?" Sue asked.

He pointed to Mena Al Khaleej Fish Grilling, one of several restaurants that prepared the fish. "Bring it to them. They will take care of everything."

In the bare-bones restaurant, a variety of fish covered a sizable wood-fired grill. We handed over our parcels and were given a choice of preparations. We opted for olive oil and lemon. It was the only one we had any familiarity with, and the proprietor, who spoke no English, couldn't explain the other choices. Besides, simple preparation with olive oil and lemon is one of my favorites. The proprietor signaled we should come back in twenty minutes.

We staked out space on a paper-covered wooden table. Filled with men, there wasn't another woman in sight. They ate with gusto from enormous plates of fish and fried potatoes. The men initially looked at us with curiosity—we were an anomaly—but then ignored us.

Twenty minutes later, we collected our meals, so large they draped over the plates' edges. A sprinkle of salt, a squeeze of lemon, and we dug in. It was superb, the freshest fish ever.

That final meal sealed my enthusiasm for returning to the UAE. Great food, an evolving culture made richer by the mix of nationalities and ethnicities, and, of course, the futuristic architecture. I vowed to make a return visit to see the changes to Dubai and Abu Dhabi as well as to explore the other UAE member states: Sharjah, Ajman, Umm Al-Quwain, Fujairah, and Ras Al Khaimah.

GROUNDED:
NEW YORK CITY, 2020

I returned from London to New York City on March 16, 2020, the last day regular flights were permitted into the U.S. The original schedule was for me to fly several days later,

but Covid nixed that plan. Because several coughing passengers were on the flight, I voluntarily quarantined at home for two weeks, only going out to walk my dog.

New York City was the epicenter of the pandemic in the United States. The following few weeks were anxious and fraught with horrible news, rising cases, hospitalizations, and deaths. Staying home seemed prudent, though I anticipated my grounding would only last for a few weeks or months.

As we all discovered, the pandemic dragged on and on. As each month of isolation passed, I grew increasingly despondent. With creativity and force of will, I managed to find ways to re-create some of the joy I experience when traveling.

After six months of staying close to home, I became more than a little antsy. I hadn't spent that much time in one place since childhood. I also couldn't remember the last time I'd slept in my own bed for such an extended period. But knowing three people who'd died from Covid and several others who'd been hospitalized or extremely ill, I was not about to take any risks. Walks in neighborhood parks didn't feel safe because armies of cyclists and joggers who didn't wear masks breathed heavily and passed close by. Public transportation was out of the question. It also felt unsafe.

Because I live alone, it became very important to me to stay connected with friends and family in any way possible. Every Wednesday, I arranged for my extended family, scattered across the country, to talk on Zoom. On Fridays, a group of friends did the same. Those calls and volunteer activities, also on Zoom, became my tenuous lifeline to the world.

My first excursion in mid-May was like a jailbreak. I retrieved my car from the garage, wiped every inch of the interior with Clorox wipes, then drove to Westchester to visit a friend. The highway was the emptiest I'd ever seen it. Sitting six feet apart on her deck, we gabbed and soaked up the sun. That little taste of freedom left me renewed and ready to return to my cell.

That led to visits with other friends and family, always outdoors, wearing masks and six feet apart. It was great to escape the city, but going to suburban homes didn't satisfy my growing wanderlust. What to do? I pondered that question, looking at it from every angle. Then it hit me. Explore New York City and the surrounding area's hidden corners. Though I am a native New Yorker, there were parts of the city I hadn't ever been to or hadn't visited in years. My car could safely transport me to neighborhoods and parks in other boroughs or in the counties surrounding the city.

That first adventure in June—a Sunday morning drive through Manhattan—shocked me. The random route led me south, stopping occasionally to walk and take photos. Typically, Sunday mornings are quiet in the city. During the early days of the pandemic, Manhattan went beyond quiet. Most neighborhoods were eerily desolate. On Fifth Avenue, there were almost no people or cars, and many store-fronts were boarded up. How could this have happened to my city? I felt like an extra in a postapocalyptic sci-fi movie.

Farther south, several large areas had been cordoned off for police cars. An exception to the emptiness was the lively Hudson River Park in Lower Manhattan. That area was filled with people, kids, dogs, kites, joggers, and walkers. It seemed like a smidgen of normalcy.

I took more solo drives around Manhattan, exploring parks and neighborhoods. None of my friends were as willing as I to take a risk and stayed as close to home as they could. Their concern was understandable, and as I'd often traveled by myself, I was okay with going alone.

After a few weeks, I ventured into Brooklyn. I used to know Greenpoint well, a neighborhood on the Brooklyn/Queens border, because the factory my father owned was located there. A couple of years earlier, my brother Roy and I explored a bit of the area. At that time, it was beginning to be gentrified, but it still retained much of its identity as a working-class Polish American area. When I drove there in 2020 to clear my head, it instead made my head spin. Greenpoint had been transforming swiftly, with numerous construction projects, most along the waterfront where there are clear views of Manhattan. The industrial area still existed but was isolated. The dullness of the factories had been transformed by street art. Sides of buildings were used as canvases, depicting car-toon figures, larger-than-life realistic portraits of local people and celebrities, sea creatures including a twenty-foot-long octopus, dogs and cats, and abstract designs.

That set me off on a new quest: to see sections of the city known to be magnets for street artists. Bushwick, also in Brooklyn, had a reputation as a gritty but trendy area to live in. It is also home to the Bushwick Collective, a multi-block area of street art. The brainchild behind the Collective is Joseph Ficalora. When he was twelve, his father was killed on the street for his gold chain. Joseph channeled his anger and loss into art. He transformed the neighborhood into a gallery. He learned to wrangle city permits to allow local buildings to be covered with murals—and graffiti. Now, a jumble of street art, light industry, restaurants, and homes meld together in true New York City fashion.

The artwork in Bushwick exceeded what I'd seen in Greenpoint. Professional artists had covered block after block with eye-popping murals. There were portraits, fantastical creatures like a forty-foot-high tiger on the prowl, political commentary, a pack of cards featuring images of local people as kings, queens, jacks, and jokers, and more. I spent hours wandering around, admiring, and photographing the artwork, and barely saw another person. I spoke with no one, and though the experience equaled any I'd had on travels to foreign lands, the absence of people made it a bit surreal. Exploration is about discovery and surprise, and also the ability to share my reflections. I capitalized on Facebook, posting about every excursion in the hopes of getting reactions from others.

After Bushwick, I became captivated by street art and visited locations in Astoria, Queens; Manhattan's Lower East Side; Harlem and East Harlem; Newark, New Jersey; and other areas in pursuit of it. Each area featured different artists and had a unique personality. Some locations featured mainly cartoons, others political, self-referential, abstract, or hyper-realistic paintings. If museums and galleries remained shuttered, I could still see wonderful art.

Another quest became a visit to all the city's gardens. Usually, I'm a regular at the New York Botanical Garden in the Bronx, but that stayed closed for many months into the pandemic. So, I sought out others.

When I was first introduced to the Central Park Conservancy Garden many years ago, my friend referred to it as the secret garden. It's really not much of a secret. But it is a serene, enchanting, formal garden. Located off Fifth Avenue near 105th Street, it's entered through the Vanderbilt Gate, which at one time was an entrance to the Vanderbilt mansion. The mansion is long gone, but it was easy to imagine upper-crust New York socialites from a century ago strolling in formal wear through the immaculate, pristine greenery. But even in this lovely setting, there were constant reminders that the pandemic raged on. Located across the street from Mt. Sinai hospital, the peace was frequently interrupted by ambulance sirens. Each time I heard one, I sighed and wondered when this would be over, and life might return to something resembling normal. I rightly feared it would be a long time.

Until I started my quest to explore my surrounding area, I'd never heard of Gantry Plaza State Park. An internet search for New York City parks led me to it. Located in Long Island City, a short hop from Manhattan by car, subway, or ferry, it has lengthy walking paths with outstanding views of the United Nations, Chrysler Building, 59th Street Bridge, and the East River. The park is named for the restored gantries—industrial structures used to load and unload rail cars and barges—that prominently occupy the center of the park. Built in 1925, these gantries played a crucial role in freight transportation to and from Brooklyn, Queens, and Long Island.

The park curves around the shoreline and is beautifully land-scaped with walkable piers jutting into the river. With Manhattan as a backdrop, there is beach volleyball, a playground, a café (closed during the pandemic), lots of inventive seating and landscaping. Loads of people were out enjoying the day, exercising, playing, and admiring the views. The transformation from run-down industrial site to beautiful, well-used park made me love New York City even more. My walk became a respite from the continual sound of ambulance sirens and the monotony of Zoom meetings from inside my apartment.

That visit to Gantry got me obsessed with viewing Manhattan from as many angles as possible. Google searches led me to previously unvisited parks in Queens, Brooklyn, Roosevelt Island, and New Jersey. Each new perspective increased my appreciation for the density, beauty, and dynamic life of the city, even during the strangeness of the pandemic.

Those excursions also helped me to understand why I am so addicted to travel. Deep within me burns an insatiable hunger to see and try new things. When I board a plane to somewhere I've never been to before, I am guaranteed that all my senses will be engaged with new sensations. It's impossible to know exactly what will happen, who I'll strike up a conversation with, what I'll learn, what trouble I'll get into. My adventures in my local area only partially fulfilled the deliciousness of travel but were better than staying at home.

As the pandemic continued, I began to wonder if I'd run out of parks to explore. When I read on the Parks & Recreation Department website that New York City has more than seventeen hundred parks and playgrounds across the five boroughs, I knew I needn't worry.

Hudson River Park, which didn't exist until twenty years ago, transformed four miles of decaying piers and parking lots along the

West Side of Manhattan hugging the Hudson River into a beautiful, heavily used area. I'd explored the southern end many times and now hoped to walk the entire distance. Though I started early on a Sunday morning, people filled the park, so many I became nervous about the density. I wore my mask, used a lot of hand sanitizer, and cut my walk short. Someone I knew had recently been admitted to the intensive care unit with Covid. So much for seeing all the city parks. It was time to venture out of the city.

On July 5, I drove the farthest I'd gone since returning from London on March 16. I didn't go far. The Rockefeller Preserve is in Tarrytown, New York, about thirty miles from Manhattan, but a world away. I used to walk there regularly when I lived in Westchester and know the trails well. In 1983, the Rockefeller family gave nearly eighteen hundred acres of land to the state. Paths had been laid out for the family to go on carriage rides, and broad trails hug the Pocantico River. I saw more greenery in two hours than I'd seen since the previous summer. I breathed in the silence and fresh air with great relief. During the walk, I met only a few other people. It felt safe, if somewhat lonely.

Several weeks later, I drove through the Holland Tunnel to New Jersey for views of Lower Manhattan's skyline, Ellis Island, and the Statue of Liberty (from behind). Over the years, I've taken several children to the Liberty Science Center, located within Liberty State Park, and loved the sight of the city from across the Hudson River. But I'd never really spent time on the paths that skirt the waterfront. The views are expansive and striking. Near the old ferry terminal is a striking monument to September 11, titled "Empty Sky." The walls frame the site of the Twin Towers. It reminded me how resilient New York and New Yorkers are. If we could hang on, we'd get through this.

By late July 2020, I was getting desperate to escape the city, which was in the midst of a heat wave. When the low temperature is eighty degrees and humidity is high, the air heavy and sticky, staying in air-conditioned comfort is a wise choice. But the cool air didn't do anything to improve my mood. Some people experience homesickness when they are away from home. I was sick of home. I longed for a change of scenery. Escapism on my mind, I started a post-pandemic wish list—places I'd never visited and would travel to when Covid finally faded away. Malta, Madagascar, Norway, Botswana, Qatar, and Denmark headed the list, which filled several pages.

Since I couldn't actually go to any of those places, my mind revisited trips I'd taken to far-flung parts of the world. In my memories, I saw deserts across the globe with swooping dunes, mountain ranges that appeared to go on forever, and ocean shorelines where the next landmass was thousands of miles away. Golden fields of sunflowers and rapeseed shimmered in gentle breezes. I thought about cloudless sunrises and intense flaming sunsets. Recalling places filled with humanity was even more fulfilling. I had cheered with a crowd at a cricket match in London and stood in the midst of what was now unthinkable—a swarm of people at a Mardi Gras parade in New Orleans, arms outstretched to snag trinkets tossed from floats. I relived arriving in Sydney, Australia, the day the Olympic Committee announced they'd been awarded the 2000 Games. The Aussies near the ferry terminal turned it into a huge party, drinking, dancing, and kissing everyone in sight. I was stuck in my locked-down area, but after a lifetime of globe-trotting, I lessened the loss by reminiscing about places and experiences I've loved.

In August 2020, as the pandemic stretched on, a few things

returned to slightly more normal. I got a haircut, and no longer appeared to be wearing a fright wig. The CDC rescinded the advice to allow packages to "air" for several days before opening them. Paper towels and toilet paper became available. But so many "normal" things remained absent: hugs, walking outside sans mask, eating inside a restaurant, live performances, and travel.

The New York Botanical Garden is high on my list of happy places; walking through the lush grounds, seeing artfully designed beds of gorgeous flowers and breathtaking landscapes, always cheers me. In August, the garden reopened with ticketed, scheduled times to limit the number of visitors. The day tickets became available, I snagged one. I arrived there the first morning as the gardens opened. It was glorious. I made reservations to go almost every week. Being outdoors, walking in the garden, felt safe for many of my friends. It was a relief to have company.

After visiting Snug Harbor in Staten Island, Wave Hill in the Bronx, Lasdon and Untermyer Parks in Westchester, and slews of other gardens, I began to exhaust the well-known gardens in the area. I set myself a challenge to visit all the Audubon Society sanctuaries in the area—there are many. Less than ten miles from my former home in Ossining, I had passed by the entrance to the Pruyn Sanctuary hundreds of times, but never entered it. When I visited during the pandemic, my car was the only one in the lot. I wandered for over an hour through the butterfly garden and on trails deep in the woods. Apart from a few bug bites, it was a perfect walk.

I felt exceedingly fortunate to have a car. Escaping to open places and exploring helped to keep me sane. Had I been limited to areas I could get to by public transportation, I fear I would have gone mad, especially since museums, stores, galleries, theaters, restaurants, and other places I might have gone to remained closed. As the pandemic stretched on, the ache from the loss of travel became more acute.

I traveled farther north to visit the Storm King Art Center. I've been a frequent visitor there since the late 1960s when I taught crafts at a camp a few miles away. Then it allowed me to unwind from campers' endless demands. Later it became a place for me to soak up peace and beauty. The center owns over twenty-five hundred acres. Many have been landscaped to display a collection of monumental sculptures. The term "landscaping" doesn't do justice to what the curators have created. The land, trees, and grasses form larger sculptures designed to enhance the beauty of the collection.

On another journey north, I visited Magazzino, an Italian art museum in Cold Spring that opened in 2017. It had just reopened its doors with timed reservations, mask requirements, and strict social distancing measures. While I wasn't overly impressed with most of the exhibition, being in a museum felt like one step closer to normalcy. The airy space had enormous windows that provided natural light and bound the indoors with the outdoors. While I didn't speak with anyone, I loved watching people as they observed and puzzled out what they were seeing. My excursion goals began to change. I needed to see not only wonderful sights but also see, and if possible interact with, people. Observing and talking with people from other cultures is a joy that's difficult to replicate except by traveling. Learning about their lives and how they think has helped me to shape my opinions and behaviors.

On rainy days, I sorted through old photos. One stormy day, I searched through journals and photos of New Zealand from a trip in 1998. Each picture conjured up vivid memories. I remembered the lush ferns and endless waterfalls but had forgotten that we'd seen dozens of rainbows. I revisited Milford Sound, Pancake Rocks, and Abel Tasman Park. And saw a lot of sheep.

On another flight of memories, I toured Barcelona in January 1985. My hotel had been right on the route for a Twelfth Night parade. From the miniscule balcony, I had a perfect view of the crowd and floats, including the three kings bearing gifts and a truck filled with coal for those who had misbehaved. High in the Andes Mountains in Venezuela, I arrived at a hotel in the town of Merida just as a wedding was getting underway. The parents of the bride invited me to attend, and I became an honored guest. In Bolivia, I arrived on the day the local Madonna left her niche in the cathedral and was carried around the main square. Behind this solemn procession came Mardi Gras–like dancers shimmying in glittery costumes and dancing their way in spike heels around the cobblestoned streets. The tiny town was filled with people from miles around, dressed in their brightest finery, who sang and danced and drank in the streets.

These had all been unplanned, unexpected, and lots of fun. In my new reality of sleeping in the same bed every night and seeing the same walls every day, I missed travel's element of serendipity. Life seemed too ordered, too circumscribed, too dull, no matter how many day trips I took.

Typically, by October, I would have traveled a dozen times or more. With Covid, that pattern was incinerated. Semi-desperate to go somewhere, to wake up in a new location, two friends and I rented a house on the North Fork of Long Island for a few days. Wineries dotted the landscape. Farm stands brimming with seasonal produce were in abundance.

The house we rented was situated mere feet from Long Island Sound; the views of the expansive, dramatic sky were mesmerizing.

Within a single hour, we witnessed a drenching downpour, bright sun, and every permutation between. Throughout the day, I marveled at the speed of changing light, the intensity of blue, and varied cloud patterns. Sunset brought more captivating visuals, as did the star-filled night.

Traveling farther east to Orient Point, we admired views of the sound and bay, visited a lavender farm, discovered an antique fire truck, and a Greek restaurant with food that reminded me of Crete. Each day ended with a glass of wine and a riveting sunset.

Back in Manhattan, near my apartment, the vegetation remained mostly green in mid-October. But at the northern tip of the island, a few miles away, autumn was emerging. Fort Tryon Park became a favorite haunt. There were fewer people than at Riverside Park or Central Park, flower-filled gardens, views of the Hudson River, and easy parking. Vivid orange, gold, and red were beginning to appear. Autumnal flowers blazed with color. As if to emphasize the season, squirrels were super-abundant. A few paused from nut gathering to pose.

Each October, there seems to be a single day that is the epitome of autumn. The air is cool and crisp, skies are blue, and trees have reached their apex of color. I wait for that perfect day, dropping whatever I'm doing to be outside and absorb its infinite beauty. Some years, that perfect day escapes me. But when I do catch it, I am cheered beyond what might be expected, and that feeling lasts for days. In 2020, as Covid raged on and winter approached, I became nearly desperate for that autumn perfection. I wanted to find a way to bottle the feeling and slowly sip from it. As with everything else that year, that day never came.

November arrived with its shorter days and gray skies, a foreshadowing of a gloomy winter ahead. I dreaded the coming season.

Every winter, I travel somewhere bright, warm, and most importantly, sunny. As I soak up the sun, it resets my equilibrium. But the pandemic erased that possibility. Instead, I used a full-spectrum light box and vitamin D to chase away my seasonal affective disorder (SAD). My apartment was filled with plants. I developed lists of projects, books to read, and bought art supplies to keep me occupied. I knew none of that would erase my coming lethargy and depression.

I travel because I like to shake up my routine. A college professor taught me years ago that experimentation with different ways of doing things and breaking routines is exercise for the brain. It makes people more alert, healthier, and helps stave off Alzheimer's disease. I figure reading a map and navigating a new city, deciphering a menu in another language, and seeing new plants and animals helps to keep my brain young. And it's a lot more entertaining than trying to write or brush my teeth with my left hand. The pandemic had forced me into stale routines that left me despondent.

While my routines during Covid became monotonous, the political atmosphere was tense. Watching the news was difficult. I began to figuratively bury my head in the sand.

The day before the U.S. presidential election, I needed to escape. Though only one hour by car from New York City, I'd never traveled to Sandy Hook, New Jersey, the narrow island that juts north into New York Harbor. I wanted to turn my face to the sun and look out far into the Atlantic Ocean. The ocean beach stretches for miles, pristine and empty. On the bay side, relentless tides sculpted pools and dunes. I focused on those images and avoided the news.

Time slowed down as November plodded along. Gray rainy days, more illnesses and deaths kept me indoors. Editing old photos and internet searches helped to pass the time. As Thanksgiving approached, the CDC and local health officials were pleading with people to avoid in-person get-togethers. With one regular member of our annual gathering in the hospital with Covid and family members unable to fly in, we decided to postpone our celebration. We had no idea when it might be rescheduled.

Prior to 2020, I could count on one hand the number of Thanksgivings I hadn't shared with family. When I was a child, there were so many of us, a kiddie table was needed to accommodate the crowd. As the older generation passed away, my generation took over. This was the first Thanksgiving I'd ever spent alone. I tried to reassure myself by repeating I was healthy, had a lovely home, and wasn't worrying about money, as so many people were. Still, I was miserable.

Time crawled, but December arrived on schedule. One of the pandemic's consequences, for me, was a diminished awareness of the holiday season. Instead of a festive and frenzied atmosphere, the city felt desolate. There were mini-reminders, hearing Christmas songs while in the grocery store and the Christmas tree sellers in my neighborhood. But for the most part, the city just felt sad.

Every year, elaborate holiday decorations abound in New York City. They usually attract people from around the globe. No holiday season is complete without a stroll down Fifth Avenue, culminating in a peek at the Rockefeller Center tree. Each year, I typically headed to the area in the early morning to avoid the swarms of visitors.

Walking down Fifth Avenue on December 19, the sidewalks were eerily quiet. I had a 2:00 p.m. appointment across from Rockefeller Center. Any other year, I would have dreaded going there midafternoon, so close to Christmas. Hordes of tourists come to see the massive Christmas tree, skating rink, and decorations, making the sidewalks nearly impassable. This visit felt worse—there was almost no one. The decorations and massive tree were up with no one to appreciate their cheeriness. As I approached the tree, a guard said, "You're not supposed to get this close, but . . ." and waved his arm at the nonexistent crowd. I gained a new appreciation for the festive throngs. I missed them.

My one truly upbeat outing was to Brooklyn. I'd seen holiday displays around the U.S. and abroad but had never gone to see the lights in Dyker Heights. It's a neighborhood well known for over-the-top decorations. Visitors come from around the city and country, and tours roam the area. In 2020, it was perfect—outside, free, and joyous. The crowds of pedestrians and cars were dense. I drove through, stopping frequently. Traffic backed up, but no one cared. I'd stop, hop out, take a few pictures, jump back in until the next "WOW" house, which was never far. I gave thanks to all the homeowners who participated. They brought much joy to a city sorely in need of it.

It's been a while since I've gone all out on New Year's Eve. It's something that age either steals or cures you of, depending on your point of view. When I was much younger, it was a big deal. Being at a large, boisterous party seemed essential for ringing in the new year. The older I got, the less I cared. A quiet dinner with friends and a bottle of good wine satisfied me. I ended 2020 drinking a glass of wine on my own. I never made it to midnight.

The start of a new year brought me hope, at least symbolically. The vaccine was about to be approved. I saw it as the beginning of the pandemic's end.

January crept along. Winter in New York City tends to be gray. When I ventured outside, it was like *The Wizard of Oz* in reverse. I'd leave my color-saturated apartment into a monotone world devoid of green.

During this period of travel deprivation and isolation, I came across my travel schedule from January/February 1992. During that time, I was ferociously traveling for both business and pleasure. I took six separate business trips, three overseas, and was away from home for a total of five weeks. My journal from those months is one continuous moan about exhaustion and wanting to sleep in my own bed. In 2021, all I wanted was to sleep in another bed, preferably one very far away.

The January issue of *Condé Nast Traveler* included a list of the fifty most beautiful cities in the world. I've visited thirty-eight on the list and live in one of them. Many on the list were unsurprising: Paris, Cape Town, Rio de Janeiro, St. Petersburg. But the list missed some that I believe are worthy—Oaxaca, Kuala Lumpur, Fes, and Dubai, among others. I gathered new must-see places to add to my already long list. Bergen, Norway; Doha, Qatar; and Valletta, Malta were on my list, but inched a few spots higher. Daydreaming about travel became an obsession.

I spent hours on the internet searching for unusual places. Inspired by a photo of an astounding bridge in Da Nang, Vietnam, I googled "weird bridges." That unearthed a gold mine of wacky, gorgeous, and gravity-defying bridges around the globe. Fujian and Changsha in China, and Da Nang, Vietnam, moved onto my list of post-Covid destinations so I could see their dragon and golden hand bridges.

February 2021 in the city brought about one snowstorm after another. During a storm that lasted for two solid days, the most appealing activity was to hibernate. I'd never done so little in my life. Everyone had gotten tired of snow, even kids. With online learning, they didn't even get a day off.

After a year of seeing empty or sparse shelves in the paper goods aisle, the tide turned by March 2021. Shelves were well stocked with every major brand. Covid rates in the city dropped as more people, including me, got the vaccine. Almost everyone remained masked and careful. The days slowly got longer. I noticed each of those extra minutes and was grateful. Then, toward the end of the month, I saw three robins outside my building. After a year of bad and worse Covid news and a long winter, that was heartening. I was hungry for any signs of hope.

Airlines were almost giving away tickets; prices were low, and there were no fees to make a change. I made my first flight reservation in over a year. Visiting a friend and relatives in Colorado in May would be my first trip. I looked forward to packing a bag, driving to the airport, boarding, and that first glorious moment when the plane lifts off. I intended to spend every moment looking out the window and reveling in the joy of flying.

On March 15, I received my second Covid shot. March 16 marked one year of Covid lockdown. It had been a very long year, and the pandemic raged on. Still, I felt safer and more willing to take risks traveling. I flew to Raleigh to visit a cousin.

Back in New York, a discount coupon and controlled occupancy made going to the top of One World Observatory irresistible. I'd been planning to visit since it opened in downtown Manhattan in 2015. It was worth the wait. A deep blue cloudless sky made it the ideal day for viewing New York City from above. With 360-degrees views, every few steps brought another breathtaking panorama. I loved the mix of long-established landmarks, like the Statue of Liberty and Brooklyn Bridge, and the new, often-startling architecture, like Hudson Yards and 56 Leonard. I was entranced at seeing my city as a tourist might—with awe at the beauty of New York.

A RAY OF HOPE:
NEW YORK CITY AND BEYOND, 2021-2022

Spring came with the 5:37 a.m. sunrise on March 20. The forecast was for a warm day, with calm skies and bright sun. I had never so eagerly anticipated a change in seasons. This equinox offered more promise of a new beginning. Fully vaccinated, my confidence grew. I could once again venture into the world. Having travel plans to look forward to made me happy. Knowing I could go somewhere or meet someone on a whim made me even happier. I had survived a dark winter.

During "normal" times, living near Lincoln Center means being in the middle of a feast of great cultural offerings. The dearth of that during Covid was a great loss. But in April, as more people were vaccinated, the city began to reemerge. Live performances began popping up in the neighborhood. Signs near Lincoln Center Plaza promised "Restart Stages," which were empty shops converted into "musical storefronts." Passing by one, I was treated to a quartet playing Bach in a vacant restaurant with the music broadcast onto the street. On my return, musicians played Vivaldi. Live music and springtime—hope was in the air.

In April, I also took my first of several road trips. As soon as my friend Sue and I knew when we'd both be fully vaccinated, we made plans to escape the city. We drove, mostly on rural routes, to Pennsylvania. Spring was bursting out everywhere. In Hawley, we stumbled upon the Dorflinger Glass Works Museum. In its heyday at the end of the 1800s, it had been one of the largest fine glass producers in the U.S. Prohibition caused its demise; you don't need decanters or wineglasses if you're not drinking. The docent was delighted we'd shown up. We were the first, and possibly the only, visitors of the day. He gave us a thorough tour and told us great stories. Randomly discovering an unexpected, unusual gem was joyful. Not that I needed reminding, but for me, coming upon quirky places is one of the best parts of travel.

Over the next few months, museums opened, and I visited as many as possible. I found new exhibits, like Citrovia, a lemon-themed art installation in a construction zone; Banksy: Genius or Vandal; Maya Lin's Ghost Forest; and Showstoppers!, a display of Broadway costumes.

I took more road trips. Sue and I headed to the Finger Lakes region of New York State. On the first morning, driving north, I saw a tiny sign along the highway that said, "Pez Museum." I couldn't resist pulling off to see it. It was a hoot with more Pez paraphernalia than I ever imagined was possible.

Next stop was Cooperstown, mecca for baseball fanatics. Main Street is studded with shops selling every imaginable item of baseball paraphernalia, from shlock to serious collector items at astronomical prices. The big draw in town is the Baseball Hall of Fame. While I'm not much of a fan, walking through the exhibits, I was struck by how baseball is part of the American zeitgeist. I recognized most of the players, concepts, teams, and overall history. My father and brothers were passionate Brooklyn Dodgers fans. Once the team moved to Los Angeles, they switched allegiance to the Yankees. Mickey Mantle was a hero in my home.

Driving northwest, we arrived in the Finger Lakes region, home to dozens of wineries. Our first stop was Lakewood Vineyards. We were the earliest arrivals that day and were greeted by Tammy. After pouring us tastes of luscious wine, she took our area map and sketched out a full day's itinerary.

Tammy's marked-up map in hand, we drove on rural roads to Keuka Lake, enjoying the thickly wooded landscape. We stopped at three vineyards—Chateau Domaine Laseur, Weis Vineyards, and Rooster Hill Vineyards. To ensure we could drive safely, we sampled only a couple of wines at each.

Apart from the wineries, Tammy told us about the Spotted Duck, a creamery serving a flight of ice cream. "It has to be your final stop of the day," she'd told us. The flight included twelve flavors, including basic vanilla, butterscotch brownie, candied coconut, cinnamon stick, extreme chocolate, blueberry streusel, and more. Sue and I decided a flight of ice cream was a brilliant idea, and we considered ways to introduce it in New York City.

We spent a full day at the Corning Glass Museum and another day exploring Seneca Falls, the birthplace of the women's rights movement.

On a solo trip in interior New England, as I sped down the highway on my way to Northampton, Massachusetts, I saw a small sign for a "Bridge of Flowers." At the next exit, I got off and followed additional signs to Shelburne Falls. It was a twelve-mile detour, but when you have no set plans, that's not an issue. When I'd done a Google search for potential places to visit on my trip, the Bridge of Flowers hadn't been listed. It should have been at the top of the list.

It was gorgeous. Transformed from an abandoned trolley bridge, it is now a densely packed garden with views of the Deerfield River and town. The standouts in the display were throngs of dahlias in a potpourri of colors, sizes, and shapes against a backdrop of flowing water, a quaint New England town, and lush landscape.

A third trip with my friend Sue took us along the New England coast. I was making up for lost time by exploring as often as I could. We stayed at old favorites like Mystic Seaport (Connecticut) and Newport (Rhode Island). Visiting Salem (Massachusetts) in October turned out to be a mistake. The town was overflowing with tourists. Downtown Salem was awash in witchy tackiness and silliness. Parking was a nightmare. Every exhibit, store, and eatery had a queue of visiting witches and warlocks (as well as ordinary folk like us).

Just as I began to think about broadening my explorations, the highly contagious Covid variant Omicron emerged. People around me became ill, even those who'd been vaccinated. Winter was again approaching. Would this never end? Would it ever be possible to travel internationally?

Winter's gray months passed, and time again slowed down. Each day required an effort to get motivated. I took more domestic road trips, but I acutely missed international travel. After spending most of my life exploring, I longed to go somewhere completely new to me. But Covid's tenacity and capricious ability to mutate, and the lack of vaccines in developing countries, meant international travel would be curtailed for the foreseeable future.

After a booster, my bravery returned. In May 2022, more than two years after I returned from my final overseas trip pre-Covid, I flew to France. It had been the longest period I'd spent in the U.S. since I was seventeen years old.

Traveling through France gave me a new appreciation for details.

Curving streets, with ancient doors and shutters, charmed me—they're so different from New York City. Tiny details caught my attention—doorknockers and handles, signs, rooflines, and windows. Several towns I hadn't visited before—Lyon, Beaune, and Arles—went onto my "must-return-to" list. In Paris, I spent time in familiar places: the Tuileries, Musee d'Orsay, and L'Atelier des Lumières. Then I sought out places that were new to me, such as the Louis Vuitton Foundation, Parc de La Villette, and the Paris canals. And, of course, I ate fabulous food as only the French can prepare it—croissants, coq au vin, steak frites, tarts, clafoutis, and too many more to list.

When I returned from the trip, friends and acquaintances remarked on how good I looked. I wasn't surprised. I had reunited with the love of my life.

AFTERWORD

While Covid was raging, I created a bucket list of destinations. The problem is that it grows longer each time I hear a podcast or read about an exotic, beautiful, or quirky place. If I manage to travel until I reach one hundred years old, I still won't have crossed everywhere off my list.

Covid isn't quite over as I write this, but it is no longer the impediment to travel that it had been. I've been taking advantage of that and scheduling as many trips as possible. My goal has been to take at least one trip a month.

Since September 2022, I've returned to London, the last place I visited pre-Covid, been to Italy twice, and shopped at the Christmas markets in Vienna, Salzburg, Munich, and Zurich. In the U.S., I've finally gotten to see the fabulous Crystal Bridges Art Museum in Arkansas, spent a long weekend with family at Disney World, revisited New Mexico, Colorado, Raleigh, Baltimore, and Washington, D.C. I'm booking tickets for South America and Asia.

Some friends think I'm overdoing it, or just plain nuts. My dog isn't very happy. But my mania for travel can't be contained. I hope it never is.

My other hope is that these stories have inspired you to take your own journeys, near or far. The world is filled with extraordinary people, quirky places, and curious cuisine. Go out and explore them.

To see photos from the journeys described, as well as pictures from my other travels, please visit my website:

www.karengershowitz.com

You can also find me at:

https://www.facebook.com/karengershowitzauthor/

https://www.instagram.com/karengershowitz/
and @karengershowitz

https://twitter.com/KarenGershowitz/ and @karengershowitz

https://www.linkedin.com/in/karen-gershowitz/

https://www.youtube.com/channel/UCaPItU6rOKfJiW9jRxA_-TYQ

ACKNOWLEDGMENTS

My mother, Mary Lotker Gershowitz, encouraged me to keep a travel journal for each trip I took. She was my first and most important influence on developing a love of travel. Thank you, Mom, for the encouragement and for instilling in me endless curiosity.

There are two huge groups of people who need to be thanked: travel companions who helped to make trips more enjoyable and members of my writing community who read through endless material.

Travel companions on the journeys described in this book include Michael Taylor, Martin Fager, Judy Plows, Sue Shapiro, Diane Mitchell, Maggie Anderson, Linda Leonard, Jeff D'Angelo, Susie Frank, Penny Manning, and Lisa Ernst. Since many of these trips were taken solo, thanks are due to the numerous people who have been kind and generous when I've been roaming the world on my own.

Writing community members who encouraged me and helped to improve the quality of this book include Kathy Brubaker Davies, Liz Burk, Theresa Campion, Jane Cassidy, Cynthia Ehrenkrantz, Jack Eppler, Matthew Hahn, Carol Hymowitz, Phyllis Melhado, Dominique Padurano, Coree Spencer, and Elizabeth Tingley.

A very special thanks to my editor, Laura Petrecca, whose thoughtful suggestions greatly improved the quality of this book.

Thanks, too, to the team at She Writes Press for all of their help, especially Lauren Wise and Brooke Warner.

If I've forgotten anyone, many apologies. A complete list of people to thank could be a whole book.

ABOUT THE AUTHOR

Karen Gershowitz has been traveling solo since age seventeen, when she flew to Europe and didn't return to the US for three years. In her career as a marketing strategist and researcher, she traveled the world conducting thousands of meetings, focus groups and interviews. When traveling for pleasure, those same skills helped her to draw out people's stories. She learned about their lives, as well as local customs and fashions and what makes them laugh. Her first book of travel stories, *Travel Mania*, explores the confluence of travel and life events and how travel has changed her beliefs and life direction. *Wanderlust* continues those stories, addressing issues readers have asked to hear more about—memorable food, people, and places she experienced in her travels. She hopes these stories tickle the travel bug in readers and set them off on their own adventures. Karen lives in New York City.

SELECTED TITLES FROM SHE WRITES PRESS

She Writes Press is an independent publishing company founded to serve women writers everywhere. Visit us at www.shewritespress.com.

Travel Mania: Stories of Wanderlust by Karen Gershowitz. $16.95, 978-1-64742-126-7. After flying to Europe at seventeen, Karen Gershowitz became addicted to travel and adventure—and went on to visit more than ninety countries. In these engaging stories, she reflects on the amazing ways in which travel has changed her life.

Notes from the Bottom of the World by Suzanne Adam. $16.95, 978-1-63152-415-8. In this heartfelt collection of sixty-three personal essays, Adam considers how her American past and move to Chile have shaped her life and enriched her worldview, and explores with insight questions on aging, women's roles, spiritual life, friendship, love, and writers who inspire.

Searching for Family and Traditions at the French Table, Book One by Carole Bumpus. $16.95, 978-1-63152-896-5. Part culinary memoir and part travelogue, this compilation of intimate interviews, conversations, stories, and traditional family recipes (*cuisine pauvre*) in the kitchens of French families, gathered by Carole Bumpus as she traveled throughout France's countryside, is about people savoring the life they have been given.

A September to Remember: Searching for Culinary Pleasures at the Italian Table, Book Three by Carole Bumpus. $16.95, 978-1-63152-727-2. Join Carole Bumpus and her husband in Book Three of the Savoring the Olde Ways series as they take you on their first culinary trek through Italy—Lombardy, Tuscany, Compania, Apulia, Lazio, and more—a trip of unforgettable characters, sumptuous traditional foods, and sublime beauty.

Bowing to Elephants: Tales of a Travel Junkie by Mag Dimond. $16.95, 978-1-63152-596-4. Mag Dimond, an unloved girl from San Francisco, becomes a travel junkie to avoid the fate of her narcissistic, alcoholic mother—but everywhere she goes, she's haunted by memories of her mother's neglect, and by a hunger to find out who she is, until she finds peace and her authentic self in the refuge of Buddhist practice.